The Astronomer and the Witch

Ulinka Rublack is Professor at the University of Cambridge and has published widely on early modern European history as well as approaches to history. She edited the Oxford *Concise Companion to History* (2011), and, most recently, the *Oxford Handbook of the Protestant Reformation* (2016). Her monographs include *Reformation Europe* (2005), *The Crimes of Women in Early Modern Germany* (1999), and *Dressing Up: Cultural Identity in Renaissance Europe* (2010), which won the Roland H. Bainton Prize.

Praise for *The Astronomer and the Witch*

'In this enthralling book, Ulinka Rublack reconstructs the struggle over Katharina Kepler's fate. We enter a small-town world of rivalries, friendships, deference, power, and vulnerability, a world in which religious faith, scientific knowledge, and folk belief are dangerously intertwined. Vividly drawn and subtly observed, *The Astronomer and the Witch* opens a window onto the inner life of a past that is strange and remote, but also unsettlingly familiar.'

Christopher Clark

'. . . an enthralling and many-sided book . . . at once a vivid introduction to a fascinating and cultural world; a profound analysis of a witch trial . . . and a deep study of one of the greatest scientists who ever lived.'

Professor Anthony Grafton, Princeton University

'Rublack tells [this] story with a novelist's panache. Even if you know what happened, it's a compelling book. She sketches the vivid details that make the time, place, and characters come to life . . . unmissable.'

Mark Greener, *Fortean Times*

'Ulinka Rublack's book about Katharina Kepler, and her sons extraordinary defence of her, is fine-grained microhistory, but it's also revealing of the larger ideas that framed their world . . . Superstition and science, rather than being successive stages in the ascent of reason, co-existed so closely and dynamically that the definition of neither is reliable. *The Astronomer and the Witch* illustrates this complexity, and its transitions, with agility and sensitivity.'

Malcolm Gaskill, *London Review of Books*

'This book takes you right to the heart of life in the seventeenth century, with all its sense of intellectual possibility, its dreams, and its fears. Rublack tells a shocking story . . . In gripping prose, Rublack presents a whole new account of scientific thinking and its relationship to natural knowledge at the dawn of a new era. The most compelling book I have read for a long time.'

Professor Lyndal Roper, University of Oxford

'[An] important new book . . . [which] offers an extended meditation on family relationships, and in particular that indelible but intangible bond between a mother and her son.'

Jan Machielsen, *Times Literary Supplement*

'[A] superb study . . . The author wanted her book to provide a 'better understanding of individuals, but also of families, a community, and an age'. It succeeds triumphantly.'

Jonathan Wright, *Catholic Herald*

THE
ASTRONOMER
& THE WITCH

JOHANNES KEPLER'S
FIGHT FOR HIS MOTHER

ULINKA RUBLACK

OXFORD
UNIVERSITY PRESS

OXFORD
UNIVERSITY PRESS

Great Clarendon Street, Oxford, OX2 6DP,
United Kingdom

Oxford University Press is a department of the University of Oxford.
It furthers the University's objective of excellence in research, scholarship,
and education by publishing worldwide. Oxford is a registered trade mark of
Oxford University Press in the UK and in certain other countries

© Ulinka Rublack 2015

The moral rights of the author have been asserted

First Edition published in 2015
First published in paperback 2017

Published in the United States of America by Oxford University Press
198 Madison Avenue, New York, NY 10016, United States of America

British Library Cataloguing in Publication Data
Data available

Library of Congress Cataloging in Publication Data
Data available

ISBN 978–0–19–873677–6 (Hbk.)
ISBN 978–0–19–873678–3 (Pbk.)

Printed in Great Britain by
CPI Group (UK) Ltd, Croydon, CR0 4YY

For Francisco

Table of Contents

Timeline of Key Dates in Johannes Kepler's Life and Major Publications, 1571–1620

1571 Johannes Kepler born on 27 December in Weil der Stadt; his parents are Heinrich Kepler and Katharina Kepler, née Guldenmund

The Kepler family moves to nearby Leonberg, in the Lutheran territory of Württemberg **1575**

1578 Johannes Kepler enters the local Latin school

The family moves to Ellmendingen in Baden **1579**

1583 Johannes Kepler returns to Leonberg and passes a scholarship exam in Stuttgart

Johannes enters the elite **1584**
boarding school in Adelberg

                  1586 He changes to the elite
                                  boarding school in
                                  Maulbronn

Johannes inscribes himself at **1589**
Tübingen University

                  1590 His father Heinrich dies

He receives his first degree **1591**
and remains in Tübingen to
study theology

GRAZ

                  1594 Johannes Kepler starts
                                  teaching mathematics at
                                  the Protestant school
                                  for aristocratic sons

Kepler publishes his first **1596**
book, *Mysterium
cosmographicum* ('The
Secret of the Universe')

                  1597 He marries the Lutheran
                                  Barbara Müller

Johannes and Barbara are **1598–1600**
forced to leave Graz in
October 1600

PRAGUE

| | 1600 | Johannes Kepler collaborates with Tycho Brahe |

Publishes *Apologia Tychonis contra Ursum* — 1601

| | 1601 | Tycho dies, and Rudolph II appoints Kepler as imperial mathematician |

birth of his daughter Susanna — 1602

| | 1604 | Publishes his treatise on optics |

Publication of *De Stella Nova* (On the New Star) — 1606

| | 1607 | birth of his son Ludwig |

Johannes Kepler travels to Württemberg; publishes the 'New Astronomy', *Astronomia Nova*; and a treatise on astrology, *Tertius interveniens* — 1609

| | 1610 | He responds to Galileo's discoveries in his *Dissertatio cum nuncio sidereo* |

Barbara Müller dies; publishes *Dioptrice* — 1611

| | 1612 | Rudolph II dies |

LINZ

1612 Johannes Kepler has to leave
Prague with his children
because of the Counter-
Reformation and finds a new
position as mathematician
for the Inner Austrian
Estates in Linz

He marries his second wife, **1613**
Susanna Reuttinger

1615 Katharina Kepler is accused
of witchcraft

Johannes Kepler travels to **1617**
Württemberg to help his
mother

1617–19 *Ephemerides Novae*

Beginning of the Thirty Years **1618**
War; Kepler begins to publish
his textbook *Epitome
Astronomiae Copernicanae*

1619 Publishes his major work
'Harmony of the World',
Harmonices Mundi

Johannes Kepler travels **1620**
to Württemberg to defend
his mother

Note on Dates

⎯⎯⎯⎯⎯⎯⎯⎯⎯⎯⎯⎯

The Gregorian Calendar was introduced into German Catholic lands in 1582 following Pope Gregory VIII's bull *Inter gravissimas*; this had the immediate effect of cutting out ten days and further days were eliminated according to an exact timetable for future years. However, most Protestant territories, including Württemberg, continued to follow the Julian calendar. Hence there was a discrepancy of more than ten days between Protestant and Catholic areas.

List of Illustrations

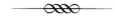

List of Abbreviations

Caspar and von Dyck, *Kepler in seinen Briefen* Max Caspar, Walther von Dyck, eds, *Johannes Kepler in seinen Briefen*, Munich: Oldenburg 1930, 2 vols.

Frisch, *Opera* Christian Frisch, ed., *Joannis Kepleri Astronomi Opera Omnia*, Frankfurt/Erlangen 1858–71.

HStASt Hauptstaatsarchiv Stuttgart

KGW Johannes Kepler, *Gesammelte Werke*, ed. by the Deutsche Forschungsgemeinschaft and the Bavarian Academy of Science, Munich: Beck, 1937–

Pfeilsticker, *Dienerbuch* Walther Pfeilsticker, *Neues württembergisches Dienerbuch*, Stuttgart J. G. Cotta 1957–74.

StAL Stadtarchiv Leonberg

UAT Universitätsarchiv Tübingen

WLB Württembergische Landesbibliothek

Maps

Boundary of the Holy Roman Empire

Boundaries between empires, kingdoms, etc, outside the Holy Roman Empire

Approximate boundaries of some territories within the Holy Roman Empire

* Places in which Kepler lived or stayed during his life

DENMARK

HOLSTE

Lü

EAST FRIESLAND

Ha

HOLLAND

Lüne

Bremen

BRUNSWICK

North Sea

ENGLAND

Amsterdam

The Hague

HOLLAND

ZEELAND

Breda

Bergen-op-Zoom

Osnabrück

Hannov

Hildes

Münster

Halbe

WESTPHALIA

Göttin

Calais

Dunkirk

Antwerp

FLANDERS

Brussels

Maestricht

Jülich

SPANISH

BRABANT

Liège

Cologne

HESSE

E

NETHERLANDS

Aachen

NASSAU

THURINGIA

Frankfurt-on-the-Main

Würzbur

FRANCON

Seine

Oise

Luxembourg

Mosel

Rhine

Worms

Mannheim

Mergentheim

RHENISH PALATINATE

Heidelberg

Rothenbur

Paris

Marne

Verdun

Metz

Zweibrücken

Speyer

Wimpfen

Nure

Güglingen

Heilbronn

Nancy

Strasbourg

Ellmendingen

Leonberg

Ellwangen

Nö

Pforzheim

Stuttgart

Weil der Stadt

Göppingen

WÜRTTEMBERG

Rösswälden

Doná

LORRAINE

Tübingen

Ulm

Aug

Rottweil

SWABIA

Hohentwiel

Überlingen

Kempten

FRANCHE

Rhine

Lindau

Basel

L. Constance

Bregenz

FRANCE

Besançon

COMTÉ

Bern

SWISS CONFEDERATION

Chur

LES GRISONS

Rhine

L. Geneva

Val Telline

L. Como

SAVOY

MILAN

Po

MAN

Turin

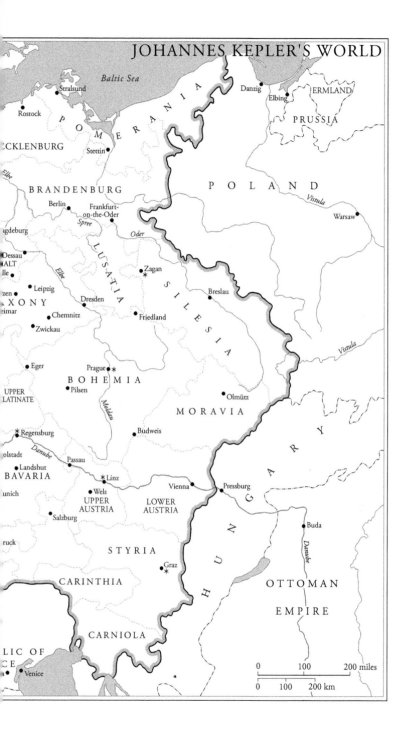

JOHANNES KEPLER'S WORLD

Baltic Sea

Stralsund
Rostock

POMERANIA

Danzig
Elbing
ERMLAND

PRUSSIA

CKLENBURG

Stettin

BRANDENBURG

POLAND

Berlin
Frankfurt-
on-the-Oder
Spree

Vistula

Warsaw

gdeburg

Oder

Elbe

Dessau
ALT
le

LUSATIA

Zagan

Leipzig

zen

Dresden

Breslau

SILESIA

Vistula

XONY
eimar

Chemnitz

Friedland

Zwickau

Eger

Prague

Pilsen

BOHEMIA

Olmütz

UPPER
LATINATE

Moldau

MORAVIA

Regensburg

Budweis

Danube

olstadt

Passau

Landshut

BAVARIA

Linz

Vienna

Pressburg

HUNGARY

unich

Wels

UPPER
AUSTRIA

LOWER
AUSTRIA

Buda

Salzburg

ruck

STYRIA

Graz

Danube

CARINTHIA

OTTOMAN

EMPIRE

CARNIOLA

LIC OF
CE

| 0 | 100 | 200 miles |
| 0 | 100 | 200 km |

Venice

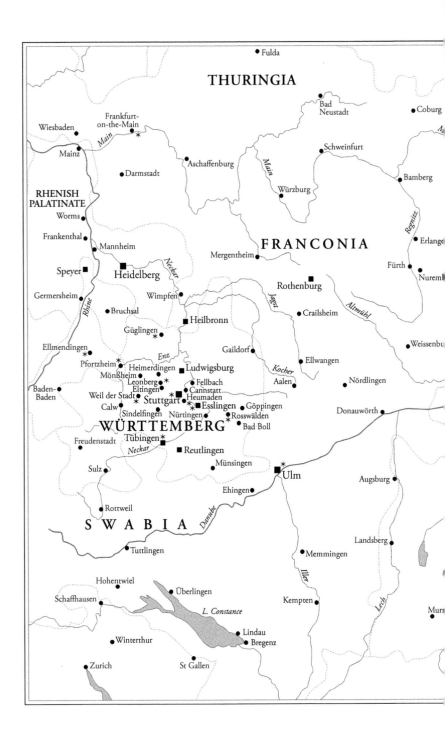

THURINGIA

• Fulda

Bad
Neustadt

• Coburg

Wiesbaden •

Frankfurt-
on-the-Main
✳

Schweinfurt

Mainz •

• Darmstadt

Aschaffenburg •

Main

• Bamberg

RHENISH
PALATINATE

Würzburg •

FRANCONIA

Worms •

Frankenthal •

Mannheim •

Mergentheim •

• Erlange

Speyer ▪

Heidelberg

Neckar

Fürth •

Nurem

Germersheim •

Wimpfen •

Rothenburg ▪

• Bruchsal

Rhine

Crailsheim •

Jagst

Altmühl

Ellmendingen
✳

Güglingen
✳

Heilbronn ▪

Gaildorf •

• Weissenbu

Pforzheim ✳

Enz

Heimerdingen ▪ Ludwigsburg

Kocher

Ellwangen •

Mönßheim •
Leonberg •✳
Eltingen ✳
Weil der Stadt ✳ Stuttgart •✳
Calw ✳ ✳Heumaden
Sindelfingen

Fellbach •
▪ Cannstatt

Aalen •

Nördlingen •

Baden-
Baden •

✳▪ Esslingen • Göppingen

Nürtingen •
•Rosswälden
✳ • Bad Boll

Donauwörth •

WÜRTTEMBERG

Freudenstadt •

Tübingen ✳

Neckar

▪ Reutlingen

Sulz •

Münsingen •

Ulm

✳

Augsburg •

Ehingen •

Rottweil •

S W A B I A

Danube

Landsberg •

Tuttlingen •

Memmingen •

Iller

Hohentwiel
•

Überlingen •

Kempten •

Lech

Schaffhausen •

L. Constance

Mur

Winterthur •

Lindau •
• Bregenz

Zurich •

St Gallen •

KATHARINA KEPLER'S WORLD

Prologue

⊸⊸⊸

This book is about the world of Johannes Kepler (1571–1630), one of the most famous astronomers who ever lived. Kepler defended Copernicus's sun-centred universe, discovered that planets move in ellipses, and defined the three laws of planetary motion. In honour of these achievements, a planet, NASA mission, and planet-hunting spacecraft are named after him. New York has its Kepler Avenue, Rome its via Giovanni Keplero, and Paris the rue Kepler. Kepler's astonishingly wide-ranging work has been edited in twenty-five tall volumes, which include breakthrough research on optics and mathematics as well as writings on astrology and religion. A Philip Glass opera takes audiences across the globe into the mindset of a man struggling to reconcile faith and reason. Novels explore his life; yet one of its most fascinating features still requires adequate exploration and recasts our sense of the astronomer and his time.

* * *

29 December 1615 found Kepler with his family in the Upper Austrian town of Linz. He had just turned forty-four and was preparing for New Year celebrations, by far the most important date for sending greetings and gifts to patrons and friends. Suddenly, a messenger knocked on the door to deliver a letter which had been sent three months earlier. As Kepler recognized his sister's handwriting, the

esteemed mathematician of the great Habsburg emperors quickly unfolded the worn paper. The news could hardly have been worse. His aged mother had been accused of witchcraft and she had immediately taken those calling her a witch to court for slander. Yet the governor in the German duchy of Württemberg himself was involved in the accusation, and the faction against Katharina Kepler was strong. All this had taken place back in August. Johannes Kepler was outraged that his siblings had not informed him at once and suspected there was more to tell (Figure 1).

Twenty-four witnesses in the small town of Leonberg would eventually testify, including the local schoolmaster, who had been her renowned son's schoolfriend. He complained that the illiterate widow had constantly pestered him to read out letters Johannes had sent to her from Prague (where the mathematician then served Emperor Rudolph II). She had also magically appeared through closed doors demanding that he should write a letter to Johannes for her. One day, Katharina had allegedly stopped the schoolmaster in the street, although he had been on his way to church. The old woman begged: 'You have done so much for me, and I have a very good wine in my cellar. Do come and have some.' He had only sipped the drink, but instantly noticed that his thighs began to hurt. Soon the pain spread so much that he needed to walk with two sticks. Eventually, he was paralysed.

The proceedings that led to a criminal trial against Katharina involved Johannes Kepler at the height of his career and lasted six years. In the pioneering work he prepared for publication during the same period, his *Harmony of the World*, Kepler confidently presented himself as ideal reader of the universe. He claimed that God had waited 6,000 years for an 'apt contemplator' who thoroughly understood his divine building-plans. Just a year after the publication of the *Harmony*, in the early hours of 7 August 1620, Katharina was woken by her daughter. The ducal governor and his men were coming to take her; she should hide quickly. When found, the

The text around the portrait reads:

IOHANNES KEPLERUS ASTRONOMUS S. CÆS. MAIEST. ET ORDD: AUSTRIÆ MATHEMATICUS.

Ecce Mathematicum KEPLERUM Cæsaris olim
Eximium, facies cuius in ære micat.

m m 4

Figure 1 Johannes Kepler, portrait, in Jean Jacques Boissard, *Bibliotheca Chalcographica*, 1650–54, after a 1620 engraving by Jacob von Heyden. © Cambridge University Library

seventy-three-year-old woman was lying naked under her bed-covers in a big chest. Katharina was taken to prison on the duke's order.

The imperial mathematician formally took over his mother's legal defence that same year. No other public intellectual figure would ever involve himself in a similar role. Kepler put his whole existence in Linz on hold, stored up his books, papers, and instruments in boxes, moved his family to southern Germany and spent nearly a year trying to get his mother out of prison. Even close friends did not expect Katharina would escape the stake.[1]

* * *

Their pessimism was justified. Katharina Kepler was accused at a time when witches were wildly feared and intensely persecuted. Statistics are notoriously difficult to compile, but even the most reliable estimates remain shocking. About 73,000 men and women were tried for witchcraft and 40,000–50,000 executed in Europe between 1500 and 1700. Some 22,000–25,000 were executed within the boundaries of present-day Germany between 1560 and the end of the persecution. Seventy-five per cent of those accused in Germany were female. In 1631, the Jesuit Friedrich Spee, an early critic of the persecutions, wrote anonymously: 'There are thought to be more witches in Germany than elsewhere, bonfires are burning everywhere.'[2]

A widow, who was illiterate, but not poor, and had lived in her Lutheran community for many years, Katharina Kepler became one of the thousands of German-speaking women who had to face a trial at the end of their lives. She vehemently denied that she had brewed poisonous drinks to make friends and neighbours mortally ill. Like others caught in the spiral of communal blame, the Keplers found themselves suddenly drawn into a family drama to save their mother.

Johannes Kepler was under no illusion about the precariousness of his own position as the accusation against his mother began to unfold. Many of his ideas were at odds with central currents of the age, which was one of bitter religious oppositions. Protestants were split into two dominant groups: those who followed the teachings of the German reformer Martin Luther, and others who developed the Frenchman John Calvin's ideas. They could detest each other as violently as they could hate Catholics and defined doctrines which everyone born into their church needed to adhere to rigorously. Katharina had brought up Johannes as a Lutheran. Yet as a teenager he had begun to struggle with one of the faith's most challenging ideas—that Christ was omnipresent and truly present when believers received bread and wine in the ritual of communion. As an adult, he refused to sign the Lutheran tenet of faith—the 1577 Formula of Concord—on these grounds. Kepler thus appeared to many a supporter of Calvinists. Most Christians today happily ignore such doctrinal issues, but theologians in Württemberg, Kepler's home territory, told him not to overstep the boundaries of his profession and to keep away from religious speculation. Tübingen University, his alma mater, never offered him a position due to his perceived dissent.

After the death of Emperor Rudolph II in January 1612 Kepler's professional options kept narrowing. Rudolph had created an exceptionally heterodox and tolerant sphere of intellectual enquiry at his court. The new Holy Roman Emperor, Matthias, confirmed Kepler's post, so that he would be able to continue calculating orbits from observation. At the same time, Matthias pursued the militant enforcement of Catholicism in the Habsburg lands. This made it impossible for Kepler to live in Prague as a Protestant.

Thanks to the patronage of some local noblemen, Kepler taught, from 1612, at a tiny school in the Lutheran enclave of Linz, the Upper Austrian provincial capital, and reluctantly set about travelling to mountains and villages to make a map of the region for an additional post as 'district mathematician'. He remained highly recognized internationally and was even offered a position at the University of Bologna in 1616. But how could he accept? Kepler knew all too well that Italian scholars developing the Copernican idea that the earth circled around the sun were under suspicion by the Roman Church, which was keen to expose further 'heresies' before the Inquisition. Giordano Bruno, the heterodox Dominican mathematician (who horrified Kepler as an advocate of cosmic infinity and chaos), had been burnt in Rome in 1600. Galileo Galilei, whose ideas Kepler had supported in print, would be forced by the Holy Office in February 1616 to declare that he abandoned the 'opinion that the sun stands still at the centre of the world and the earth moves, and henceforth not to hold, teach, or defend it in any way whatever'. Kepler's own work would soon be censored by the Roman index for claiming not only that the earth moved around the sun, but also that the earth possessed a soul and thus was alive.[3]

In January 1616, Kepler wrote to the magistrates in the Württemberg town of Leonberg about Katharina as 'his beloved, aged mother', increasingly 'bereft of comfort' in age. He confessed his fear that she might be misled into making intemperate remarks that would lead to her being tortured by half-learned judges and even to her death. There were vexed reflections on the connections between his own fate and his mother's:

> the report seems to suggest that I, too, was accused of forbidden arts, so that this impudent opposition party, blown up by I don't know what kind of drinking rites, have, so to speak, blown me and my 15 years of imperial service over a house, and want to take all of my mother's heart.[4]

Even at the time, these were peculiar expressions to use. They reveal the depths of Kepler's anxiety that the case might blow away all of his achievements and completely demoralize Katharina. He would ask for permission to travel to Württemberg and fight for his mother's rights with his own life and property. Next, he would rally all his friends, patrons, and people whose favours he had gained to his cause, until justice was done.

INTRODUCTION

———⊗⊗⊗———

*T*he Astronomer and the Witch enters a haunted world in which almost everyone believed in the existence of witches and the devil (Figure 2). Since the mid-1970s, studies of witchcraft have attempted to explain the mental climate of societies which faced extraordinary challenges during the height of the persecution, from 1580 to 1650. Climatic changes led to some years of repeated harvest failures when extremely cold periods of winter and spring were followed by cold and wet summers. Kepler predicted one of these harsh winters for 1595 and later confirmed that Austrian herdsmen had returned home with frozen noses which fell to pieces as they wiped them. Their cold limbs started to putrify, and eventually they died.[1] Hailstorms could be so ferocious that they destroyed not just crops and cattle but church steeples and other buildings. The population growth over the sixteenth century made resources scarcer and employment harder to get. Prices rose, hunger spread, plague and illness struck.

Anyone could be drawn into witchcraft. It was this horrific idea which, in some areas, began to corrupt social trust. Harm might spread through touch, as well as gifts that were commonly exchanged: an apple, a cake, or a drink. Witches could be neighbours, family and

Figure 2 Albrecht Dürer's early depiction of an ageing witch riding backwards on a goat, making bad weather, is a small engraving from *c*.1500, 11.4 × 7.1 cm.
© Trustees of the British Museum

friends, or domestic employees, transported to the Sabbath for a mass-gathering with the devils to celebrate a reverse mass. Sixteenth-century images and sensationalist writing familiarized this scary figure of the demonic witch as an old, envious hag with her broomstick, keen to attack fertility and madly dance at the Sabbath.[2]

* * *

Detailed research allows us to track how the persecution intensified. A tiny Lutheran county next to Württemberg recorded the first large spate of over sixty executions for witchcraft between 1562 and 1564.[3] Greatly alarmed, a doctor called Johann Weyer argued that witches were deluded, often depressed women in need of proper medical treatment. Their pact with the devil (which he thought was real) was based on force and fear, rather than among equal parties. It could not be subject to secular punishment. Weyer's concerns were largely ignored as Germany, alongside other parts of Europe, plunged into a prolonged period of harvest failures between 1569 and 1575.[4]

The persecution exploded between 1580 and 1599. Hundreds of people were accused in the Catholic bishopric of Trier. This was a large region in which all but two harvests were destroyed. Victims included a significant number of men as well as women and were from a broad social spectrum. The local suffragan to the archbishop, Peter Binsfeld, became the first cleric since Heinrich Krämer, the author of the notorious *Witches' Hammer* in 1486, to provide an up-to-date practical handbook advising how to structure interrogations through leading questions about the Sabbath. In Binsfeld's view, a single denunciation by anyone found guilty justified torturing any suspects they had mentioned. This procedure led to mass trials.[5]

At the same time, Jean Bodin, a contemporary French political thinker, vigorously argued against Weyer claiming that witches were a dangerous sect organized by male masters of sorcery. Burning witches appeared to Bodin as politics in action to save the land.[6]

Witches now also began to be fiercely prosecuted in the duchy of Lorraine. Communal accusations led to up to 300 witchcraft trials in every decade between 1580 and 1630. A staggering 80 per cent of these ended in a death sentence. One general prosecutor argued that his case-material amounted to proofs 'beyond doubt' that women and men could effectively harm others through diabolical practices.[7]

Twenty years after these mass executions had begun, an erudite Jesuit called Martin Del Rio presented one of the most influential demono-logical treatises. His *Investigations into Magic* (1600) was not just unusually comprehensive but included terrifying anecdotes. One of them skilfully recounted how a doctor's ten-month-old daughter had nearly died because someone kept placing 'instruments of malefice' such as bones and coriander seeds in her cot. While the man twice called for an exorcist, his wife suspected that because their darling daughter was 'very attractive, the cause lay in the envy or the venomous magical hatred of some old woman'. Rio provided a vivid sense of Sabbath meetings and followed Binsfeld and Bodin in reminding lenient judges that God had ordained them to root out the evil army of witches.[8]

Not everyone in Europe or Germany agreed with such militant views. In Bavaria, rising prosecution figures from the 1590s onwards led to decades of bitter debates about whether it was necessary and just to execute witches and round up those they denounced. Many accused women courageously revoked their testimony (which was usually extracted through torture). Some protested that God himself would fight those 'wanting to turn them into witches'. There was much uncertainty about whether witches could really harm, change shape, and fly on broomsticks, or were merely deluded.[9]

Leading theologians in Lutheran Württemberg followed a coher-ent view: Katharina and Johannes Kepler heard all through their lives that hailstorms, earthquakes, lightning, frosts, floods, and famine were part of God's terrifying providential punishment rather than caused by witches. Christians needed to contemplate heavenly signs by reflecting on their own sins and showing repentance. Immediately after a devastating storm had struck vines and crops in May 1613, the Tübingen divine Johann Georg Sigwart exhorted people that if they repented their sins, a stern, fatherly God would eventually extend his grace, just as sunshine followed rain. Why, Sigwart asked, did God, as overall 'director' of the universe, allow witches? He was simply outwitted by the devil, that 'quick expert on nature', who was able to foretell when God was about to punish people. The devil then ordered his excitable band of witches to mix their potions and salves. This tricked these deluded women into imagining that it was their own diabolic means that could cause natural catastrophes.[10]

Although Lutheran pastors believed that witches still deserved to be executed for their malicious *intentions* (rather than causing actual harm) they tended to caution that God himself would reliably separate wheat and tares at the Last Judgement. Tübingen professors of law agreed. As a result of this cautious approach, Württemberg secular courts interrogated or prosecuted only 600 women and men on charges of witchcraft from 1560 to 1750 and executed around 197 victims; figures which are significant, but small in comparison to the 3,200 witches executed in the other 350 territories that made up south-west Germany between 1561 and 1670.[11]

* * *

Many of these executions were brought on by a fourth large wave of trials in Germany, during ten years of price rises between 1607 and 1617, the series of persecutions which would engulf the Keplers too. Most dramatically during this decade, two executioners in the tiny Catholic German territory of Ellwangen were permanently employed specifically to severely torture and burn hundreds of witches. Ellwangen was less than 100 kilometres from where Katharina Kepler lived. Almost 300 women and men were executed as witches between 1611 and 1612. Male and female family members

Figure 3 This statue of a pensive woman with well-defined shoulders, veined skin, sagging breasts and folds of skin in the abdominal area conveys how a fascination with naturalism and beauty informed an exploration of the ageing maternal body, 15.9 cm, south German, 1520–25, carved pear-wood, partly pigmented. © Victoria and Albert Museum

were hunted down on the assumption that this could be a hereditary crime.[12] These mass killings showed that rumours, denunciations, and torture easily spiralled out of control. Yet even in Württemberg, which was generally cautious, some accusations could seem too pressing to be ignored.

* * *

As one reconstructs Katharina Kepler's case in detail, life in a Lutheran duchy and one of its small towns unfolds as if under a magnifying glass. The Kepler case belongs to Germany's best-preserved witchcraft trials. Because of her famous son's involvement, two big bundles of records have been preserved intact in the state archive ever since they were discovered in 1820. In addition, the community in which Katharina lived is exceptionally well documented. We can therefore trace her world and its beliefs with unusual precision. This involves understanding what mattered to everyone at the time: how common people made a living, fed themselves, raised their children, what they aspired to, how they solved conflicts, created ideas about the supernatural, or how they made medicine. No one here suffered an inexplicable collective 'mania' or inhabited a 'Freudian Disneyland', as one commentator claims. Neither is there any evidence that local judges 'couldn't understand Kepler's science' and, in turn, as the single available book on the subject in the English language suggests, 'supplemented their prejudices with church dogmas, both Lutheran and Catholic, to argue against his mother'. Such arguments are a historical invention.[13] Rich archival sources, including further witchcraft trials, open up a panorama of early modern life before our eyes, including one of its most haunting dramas. It is possible for a historian to ask how Katharina herself made choices and experienced her family and community, rather than merely relying on other people's judgements of her, even those of her famous son. Most modern accounts cast

Katharina Kepler either in the role of a heroic victim or a villain. Some even imply that she *was* witch-like. I hope that readers will feel doubtful of any such verdicts by the time they finish this book, but will understand which elements in the records lay behind them.

* * *

Discovering Katharina's life and trial means recasting our sense of Johannes Kepler himself. It is reductive to see Kepler as a champion of rational thinking that mechanized the universe. In fact, our neat distinctions between the rational and irrational, religion and magic, obscure how knowledge about humans and nature mattered to him and many of his contemporaries. This in turn explains connections between some of his ideas and those of his mother.

What happened to a living tree or stars, they both believed, might register in your body; for micro- and macrocosm, human nature, the world of plants, and the universe were interlinked. Above all, the world was always God's creation, and Kepler was inspired by his belief that nature, and even human instinct, could reveal traces of God as its maker. The astronomer thus adored snowflakes for the regularity and stability of hexagonal cells of which they were made, and even wrote about children he saw blowing soap bubbles into nearly perfect spheres. He likened the earth to a woman in labour, who gave birth to perfectly geometrical crystal shapes, which humans to their astonishment could mine. God had not just devised a functional clockwork universe, but a wonderfully clever and entertaining world to marvel at. He had given all humans the instinct to mimetically reproduce some of its regular features with pleasure. Dance steps and compositions replicated patterns derived from geometry and had only been discovered by humans because they were created in God's image. Musical octaves even touched 'ignorant' folk.[14] People of whatever social station, gender, and age thus had it in themselves to comprehend and participate in the vital principles of God's universe. All humans, Kepler wrote, were 'tiny specks of dust' who carried God's image inside them and continued the work of divine creation.[15]

Kepler in turn championed a set of ideas in which the agency of demons or opponents of Christendom got short shrift. Just like his mother, and whatever hardship he faced, nothing compelled him to think of his life overtly in relation to Satan or witches (which some people believed raged rampantly in a decaying world). Rather, he believed that the world was in a perpetual process of creation and renewal which allowed it to move towards beauty and perfection.[16] Satan remained a far more abstract agent of 'dissonance'. Kepler left no doubt that he himself was above all interested in identifying natural causes, or what made humans evil, rather than immediately explaining everything through the agency of God or the devil.[17]

Fired by his fascination with cosmic constellations, Kepler, in 1606, published his treatise *De Stella Nova*. It reflected on a recent supernova, which he regarded as a new star. The star's significance lay in the fact that it had appeared close to the conjunction of Mars, Jupiter, and Saturn in the sign of Sagittarius. Kepler enthusiastically presented the age he lived in as positively influenced by this very special planetary conjunction. The universe beyond the Moon and planets was mutable. Unlike automatic clocks, which he admired for their enactment of regularity but criticized for their inability to reflect change, God's world could thus be dynamic, surprising, illuminating, and varied, if people kept on positively responding to the possibilities of their time.

Kepler's treatise was based on the premise that the earth itself is a living organism, and that many of its reactions could serve as comparison to what happened in the heavens. He believed in spontaneous creation on earth, so that some plants or animals, for instance, could self-generate as transmuted and more superior forms, from bogs and other putrid matter rather than emerging through seeds or eggs. The perspiration of trees turned into caterpillars with artful bodyshapes, that of women (who were humorally believed to be more wet) into different types of fleas, excesses of waters into new sea monsters, of the earth into 'extraordinary flutters of butterflies'. The new star, he explained, similarly meant that the heavens had purged themselves of decayed stuff. It had not existed before it appeared, but was produced by physical causes. All creation was so rich in its changing manifestations that it stimulated any living spirit to similarly constantly grow, enrich itself, and move on through greater knowledge.[18]

This unsual combination of ideas from studies of nature and motion enabled Kepler's breakthrough conception of irregular regularity—so that a regular orbit still allowed for the irregular movement of planets. He was ready to challenge ideas about cosmology. 'You say that my oval does away with the uniformity of motion,' Kepler defiantly wrote in 1607 in response to the traditional argument that the circle was more perfect than the ellipse and devoid of magnetic power, only to exclaim: 'Well then!'[19]

Kepler's remarkable belief in dynamic progress and intellectual flexibility was bound up with the notion that cosmic change had already stimulated humans to positively change. *On the New Star* set out an extraordinary list of interconnected Renaissance achievements to celebrate. These revealed the same processes of divinely inspired transmutations of old, expiring forms into new ones. Men came together more easily for collaboration, Kepler wrote, while medieval barbarism had been superseded by modern public order through laws and firm government. Military technology and strategy had advanced. The European oceanic expansion had exploited advances in navigation to increase prosperity, trade, and Christian faith. Universities and teaching had expanded and deepened education, as scholars had replaced monks, resulting in a better understanding of ancient knowledge. Kepler's list went on. The astonishing range, subtlety, and development of the mechanical arts, such as navigation, architecture, or engineering, and continuing improvements in printing demonstrated the extraordinary speed of knowledge: 'every year...the number of writings published in every field is greater than all those produced in the past thousand years'. Through human inventions and books, Kepler summed up excitedly: 'there has today been created a new theology and a new jurisprudence; the Paracelsians have created medicine anew and the Copernicans have created astronomy anew'. He affirmed: '*I really believe that at last the world is alive, indeed seething*, and that the stimuli of these remarkable conjunctions did not act in vain.' The new star, and humans who knew how to respond to it, were changing the world.[20]

For Kepler, a new philosophy therefore provided a deeper understanding of the earth in relation to the cosmos—and was to benefit humans in fresh and exciting ways. *New* was one of Kepler's catchwords. In contrast to many of his contemporaries, Kepler made it part of his mission as a scholar to avoid fearmongering about the immanence of the world's collapse and Last Judgement. Instead, Kepler presented a coherent, detailed account of cultural and political progress which made it possible to see the world in extremely uplifting terms. In 1604, he wrote that his optical research results were as important as 'discovering a new sea' which could be navigated for the benefit of mankind.[21] Such research led to better instruments and responded to political challenges. European progress in navigation led to greater interconnected trade in the Baltic, which benefited the population through lower prices of grain.[22] Through gradual scientific progress, rooted in rational methods and empirical observation as much as in profound belief, a more accurate account of the world, and better policies and societies could be achieved.[23]

This positive outlook was a world apart from the fatalist writings of contemporaries such as the Lutheran pastor Daniel Schaller, for instance, who from 1595 onwards repeatedly argued that everything was in decline, that the earth had physically aged, the light had become darker, the earth was less fertile, there were fewer fish, stones and iron were less solid, and that the final point of ruin had to be close.[24] Even Johann Arndt, a Lutheran best-selling author greatly interested in natural philosophy, saw the 'evil of man' growing ever greater and the world doomed as a foul, muddy prison about to be destroyed in the Last Judgement. Protestant apocalyptic ideas endorsed what Martin Luther had already revealed: the papacy was a biblically foretold 'Antichrist', the devil's terrifying ally. He brought about the end of the world.

Kepler leads us into a world in which this doom-laden Lutheran theology, with its pessimism about human qualities, existed alongside a forward-looking mentality cultivated by men like him, by energetic Protestant rulers and their wives at several German courts, who drew on plural spiritual traditions, as well as through busy initiatives in major Imperial Cities towards innovation and reform. Many princely courts were active in their broad support of learning for the benefit of society. As a young mathematician, Kepler experienced the Lutheran Württemberg court as an intellectual space as much as an experimental, practical, and ambitious one, in which Sibylle von Anhalt built up expertise in herbal medicine and her husband, Duke Frederick, sponsored alchemical research for medical purposes and invested in a spa. Such practical learning connected them to ideas of positive regeneration by taking the products of the earth—minerals, plants, water, geothermic heat—to improve life on earth. This was an extraordinary mental leap from the lingering medieval idea of temporal existence as self-inflicted misery after the Fall. Kepler's ideas thus need to be seen in relation to a far broader spectrum of people, including many women, who were fascinated by knowledge about mechanics and nature. He did not live in a sealed-off world of male 'laboratory science'. This

paret. Nam hæc impuritas ætheri commixta, diei noctem infert, nocti diem.

1. Interdum enim obsidet solem materia fulginosa, obtundens Soli radios; ut anno cædis Cæsaris penè toto; sic anno Chr 1547. cum quatriduo toto sanguineus solis vultus apparuit, non in uno solum loco, sed per totam Europam.

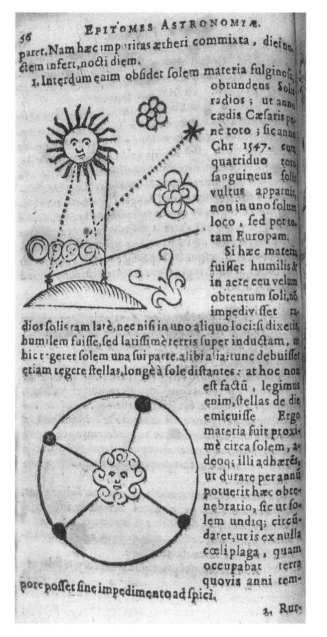

Si hæc materia fuisset humilis & in aere ceu velum obtentum soli, non impedivisset radios solis tam latè, nec nisi in uno aliquo loci: si dixeris, humilem fuisse, sed latissimè terris super inductam, ut hic tegeret solem una sui parte, alibi alia: tunc debuisset etiam tegere stellas, longè à sole distantes: at hoc non est factû, legimus enim, stellas de die emicuisse Ergo materia fuit proximè circa solem, adeoq; illi adhærès, ut durare per annû potuerit hæc obtenebratio, sic ut solem undiq; circûdaret, ut is ex nulla cœli plaga, quam occupabat terra quovis anni tempore posset sine impedimento adspici.

2. Rur-

Figure 4 Johannes Kepler, woodcut from his textbook *Epitome*, made by his friend Wilhelm Schickard, which projects the alive dynamism of the universe. Modern editions of Kepler's works obscure decorative elements in the interest of 'science'. © By permission of the Master and Fellows of St John's College, Cambridge

eventually allowed him to understand how Katharina approached healing and to write in her defence that she had gathered valid medical experience based on Christian beliefs.

Exciting, ambitious, and creative, Württemberg men in Kepler's circle promoted entirely new ways to think and do things. Kepler closely cooperated with a young Lutheran pastor, Wilhelm Schickard, who would eventually become a professor of astronomy in Tübingen. As well as mastering languages ranging from Hebrew to Ethiopian, Schickard supplied Kepler with the most innovative designs imaginable of celestial phenomena. Their friend Johann Valentin Andreae, another Lutheran pastor, published one of the first utopian visions on urban living and implemented social reforms in one of the duchy's towns. Christoph Besold completed the trio of friends. A professor of law at the staunchly Lutheran University of Tübingen, he ranked among the most influential political scientists of his time and ordered for his enormous library the latest books on the widest possible range of subjects in modern Spanish, French, and Italian. This allowed him to translate writings by the heterodox, imprisoned Italian philosopher Campanella, whom Kepler was interested in as well.[25]

There is thus no intellectual mileage in making Kepler appear modern in any easily recognizable way. Even so, he can help us to foreground the progressive, dynamic trends in his society, which have often been sidelined in order to depict a rigid country thoroughly hemmed in by religious ideals and state control. Kepler fought to get his writings into print, and sometimes even bought his own paper in order to do so. Still, there he was, selling at the Frankfurt book fair and lucky not to live in Italy, where his books could only be purchased from selected booksellers who kept his work 'under their desks' for well-known clients. Kepler was not allowed to teach at the University of Tübingen, but could count on cooperating with several of its professors. He fought bitterly for his family's honour, and was able to navigate brilliantly a legal system that allowed for his mother's defence. Württemberg politics revolved around the estates' constant claim that humans had been created in God's image, so as to insist on legal justice. Kepler had been brought up with this ideal and made it the foundation of his own philosophy.

Highlighting these possibilities in Germany's public sphere, education, and law provides a much needed sense of the dynamic in its institutions and debates, which explain how this society could eventually reform itself.[26] By 1700, few Germans faced prosecution for witchcraft. A landmark fight for justice had been won. Kepler never published his defence, but it presents a pioneering attempt to dissect the prosecution's case through legal objections.

How did he accomplish such a feat? Kepler's daily professional life was not confined to an elevated realm that cut him off from the challenges of dealing with an accusation for witchcraft. His success was marked by his robust ability to confront enmity and disputes by sticking to a powerful line of argument, while meticulously attending to detailed point-by-point refutations. He brought these skills to work, ferociously, in his mother's defence. There was no solid argument, he claimed, and the procedure that tried to turn allegations into reliable evidence was wrong. The constant need to counter his own competitors had prepared him to meet and master the biggest challenge of his entire career.

* * *

Johannes Kepler, in sum, will be our guide to what it could be like to forge debates about evidence and justice north of the Alps in the age of Galileo. Yet, above all, this is a book about a son and siblings whose widowed mother became targeted as a witch. This allows us to rediscover Germany's witch trials as a story about families. At the height of the persecution, everyone seemed at risk. As late as 1687, one accusation traced a man's lineage back to two female relatives executed in 1619.[27] There would be rumours about suspects for many years, and this already put families under tremendous strain. If it came to a trial, sons, husbands, and sons-in-law could play a crucial role in impugning the alleged witch or in defending her life. It would be reassuring if we could say that the children closed ranks against Katharina's accusers. In fact, each sibling reacted differently to their mother's plight and the strain of the proceedings against her. In *Harmony*, published in 1619 before Johannes began defending his mother, even he suddenly alleged that his mother upset 'her town' and was 'the author of her own lamentable misfortune'. His youngest brother, Christoph, became more and more ambivalent about his commitment to Katharina as the accusations against her progressed to a trial. A local craftsman on the make, he was determined not to let this case ruin his life and, eventually, he withdrew from the defence. Relatives responded not only with compassion and love, but also uncertainty, fear, repudiation, and guilt, and could be overwhelmed by a sense of shame. They were involved not just as rational beings, but through their fantasies and dreams, as children of an alleged witch, and as siblings who took different sides in the drama that unfolded. Katharina Kepler, as well as her famous son, thus emerge as the kind of person we all are: part of a family that depends on us, hates or loves us, abandons or supports us. Their trial takes us to the heart of what it means to be kin: to live (emotionally and symbolically) each other's lives and die each other's deaths.[28] This is the untold story of witchcraft and the family in all its harrowing detail.

I

KATHARINA'S LIFE

⸺⸺∞⸺⸺

Katharina Kepler lived in sixteenth-century Württemberg, the largest principality in south-western Germany, in the heart of Central Europe. To the west lay the Black Forest mountain range and France; to the east and south-east the Swabian Jura rose just above the waters of Lake Constance on the border with Austria and worked its way inland. Executioners banishing offenders from the duchy shouted at them to pack themselves off beyond the Rhine, which ran along its western border, or the Danube, which lay towards the south and east. Württemberg had its own long navigable river, the Neckar, which ran virtually through the middle of the territory, running past the major towns: first Ludwigsburg, then Canstatt, in the vicinity of Stuttgart, the capital of the duchy with about 9,000 inhabitants, and finally Tübingen, with its well-known university, founded in 1477.

Marked by its vineyards, fertile orchards, forests, and fields, the duchy was a busy region of burghers and peasants in a dense network of small towns and villages. Although the nobility had no formal political rights, local representatives were elected to meet the duke in Stuttgart at territorial diets, or parliaments, to decide on government

Figure 5 Württemberg harvesting work, detail of woodcut in Johann Bauhin *De aquis medicatis nova methodus*, 1612. © By permission of the Master and Fellows of St John's College, Cambridge

debt, major wars, and taxation. All citizens were constitutionally assured fair criminal trials. In return for such privileges, every village household owed the duke labour services, paid one-tenth of the grain harvest, taxes in cash, and ground rent on much of the land. In 1534, Württemberg had introduced Lutheranism, and henceforth remained one of the bigger pieces in the complicated jigsaw of political and religious allegiances which made up Germany. Pastors read out a growing number of state laws about sex, gambling, dancing, and drinking after their Sunday sermons. These measures were to increase tax revenues, ducal power, and Lutheran faith to morally fortify the country and protect it from Catholic armies and God's wrath.[1]

* * *

Katharina Kepler was born into this world of religious divides and concern about order either in 1547, as she herself thought, or in 1550, as her father believed.[2] People often remembered the year they were born through past dramatic events, and this anchored individual lives in challenges which touched the land at large. Katharina's father recalled that he had been 'born in the year of the great hail', and Katharina told Johannes that she had been born three days before 'Martini' in the year of the Schmalkaldic War, when Spanish troops fighting for Catholicism had occupied the well-defended neighbouring town.

Her home was the village of Eltingen, 17 kilometres west of Stuttgart. Katharina's parents were peasants and also ran an inn called the Sun. Her father, Melchior Guldenmann, who was later described as a 'pious and honourable' man, acted as mayor for nearly twenty years, from 1567 to 1585, which meant that he kept all the village's account books for the duke—noting income from common land, the forest, flocks of sheep, and fines—as well as organizing community assemblies and settling disputes.

The village possessed a large, elegant church, built in 1487, just across from the Guldenmanns' home. Its Lutheran pastors would preach to their congregation about the struggle between God and Satan, in which an almighty God would finally triumph over evil. Animals, plants, human bodies, and souls all testified to His creation. Yet humans had succumbed to sin and needed to repent all their wrongdoings daily through prayer and by cultivating their faith. God guided them like a father through providential punishment, especially bad weather, famine, or war. He might also punish them individually—through illness and grief—to spur them on to a godly life. Spiritual comfort remained a trial.[3]

Eltingen had no school, but every morning, for as long as she could remember, Katharina put on a skirt over her long linen shirt and went out to help at the inn and in the fields. Children were expected to earn their full board from around the age of twelve, and were thought to be mature when they reached fourteen, by the time of their admission to the Eucharist. No archival evidence indicates that Katharina left her village, or that her mother died early, as some historians suggest.[4] As an Eltingen teenage girl she would have known how to clean, feed and herd animals, cut grass and grapes, make hay and fire, hoe, sow and harvest, trim vines, prepare food, separate grain from the chaff, dry peas, gather the right herbs, cook, bake, sew, spin, knit, mend and wash things, clean the house, as well as deal with money, customers, and servants. These were some of the skills she needed for her future life as a tireless wife. If she disobeyed, she was likely to be beaten, as leniency was thought to corrupt children.

Like any young Lutheran woman, Katharina knew that she needed to build up her own family if she wanted to create a secure and respected existence. Convents had closed down, and single women were frowned upon. Her duties as wife would be to suffer the pain of childbirth, oversee the household, work alongside her husband, and have regular sex to make sure he resisted illicit temptations. A marriage match was determined by wealth, health, and geography for most people in this period, but also by affection and attraction. A father's consent had to be obtained, and parents would expect to remain involved with their daughters after they married, not least to be cared for in old age. Luther had expected all young people to get married young in order to avoid sin; in reality, for those below the upper classes serious courtships took place once a woman had matured beyond her teens.

Katharina was in her early twenties when she met a young man named Heinrich Kepler. His father, Sebald, was a merchant in Weil der Stadt, a nearby Imperial City, and had just been elected mayor. This made him an authority in the wider region and he had already been included in one of Germany's political summits. Heinrich's grandfather, too, had been on the town council and appointed mayor. Proud of their ancestors, who were said to include a warrior who had distinguished himself in imperial service, the Keplers applied for the continued use of a coat of arms, which Emperor Maximilian II granted them in 1564. The arms consisted of an 'angel with yellow hair, dressed in red', who placed its hands on a shield. Above the angel swirled a red and golden ornament with a golden crown out of which 'a yellow pointed high hat rose, on its tip a bushel of black heron's feathers', with small yellow decorations.[5] The Keplers would have used it to claim prestige wherever they could.

By spring 1571, Katharina Guldenmann had walked the well-trodden path westwards from her village to marry into this distinguished family. She moved in with Heinrich's parents, into a compact, half-timbered house on Weil's market square, where Heinrich helped in his father's business selling linen and cotton, candles, and locks.[6] On 27 December that same year, Katharina gave birth to a weak and small baby, at 1.30 in the morning of a day which saw the frosty weather pass away and snow turn into rain. The parents, while fearing for the child's life, named their premature boy Johannes, after St John the Evangelist, the saint commemorated on that day.[7] Two years later, Katharina bore another son. He was christened Heinrich, after his father.

For most young wives, weddings were followed by pregnancies at regular intervals, with the consequent long periods of lactation, as well as a daily life of close cooperation with a new husband and in-laws at work. Württembergers gave their male and female offspring equal amounts when they married and so children often inherited money or, more commonly, strips of pastures, vineyards and fields, as well as tools and livestock. Wives therefore spent much of their days on land they jointly owned and from which they maintained their family. They rarely took a break from working, even making hay and other heavy tasks during their childbearing years. Moreover, although single women were legally excluded from apprenticeships and therefore from most professional careers, women married to craftsmen were expected to work alongside their husbands, learning on the job, as well as helping to market goods and looking after debts owed to the couple. Wives, in other words, were co-workers. And as their labour came at no cost, it was much in demand, while there were also opportunities for wives to develop new skills.[8]

However, instead of laying solid foundations for his family life, Heinrich soon became restless. Aged twenty-seven, he left to enlist as a soldier for the Catholic Spanish to fight Calvinist rebels in Flanders who were trying to liberate their lands from Habsburg rule. It was not unusual for a Lutheran during these years to fight against Calvinists, but it is likely that religious convictions were of minor importance for Heinrich's decision. He would have been lured by the risks and attractions of an unconventional life and exceptional pay. Large troops were increasingly raised for long periods of paid service in the Netherlands to cut down on the costs of recruiting, moving and equipping them.[9] Hence the excitement of receiving a salary loomed larger even than the experience of distant travelling in most mercenaries' lives. A man named Burkhard Stickel from Stuttgart, for instance, who came from a well-off family like Heinrich's, fought in Flanders and moved on to Italy, Corfu, and then North Africa to help build the fortress in the port city of Goletta, which would be quickly lost to the Turks. In 1570, aged twenty-nine, he recorded how his fellow soldiers haggled with the tough Spanish governor, the Duke of Alba, in the Netherlands to be paid for thirty-four months of service: 'three months they gave us in cloth, velvet or silk, the rest in money'.[10]

Katharina did not want Heinrich to abandon her. In 1575, after one year of his absence, she left her small children with a friend and went all the way to Flanders to bring her husband back home. Her determination was plain. Maybe she asked Heinrich why he had left her to do all the work on their land and in the company of her unwelcoming in-laws. It was also well known that unmarried women accompanied troops and that illicit sex was common among the soldiery. Whatever their conversation, Heinrich returned to Weil with Katharina, but then left again to fight, returning once more to his father's house the following autumn. Johannes, meanwhile, had survived the smallpox, but was left with scars and permanently impaired eyesight.

Finally, in 1575, Heinrich seemed prepared to buy a house and settle down. The couple took their boys and moved from Weil to the nearby town of Leonberg, purchasing three hectares of fields and 1.7 hectares of meadow land (twice the size of a football field). Two years later, for the sizeable fee of 100 florins, they purchased their status as citizens—which meant that they could use communal resources and Heinrich could vote for local representatives.[11]

* * *

It is easy to see why Katharina and Heinrich might have considered Leonberg an appealing place in which to bring up their family. It was

Figure 6 A reconstruction of Leonberg during the late sixteenth and seventeenth centuries. © Stadtarchiv Leonberg, Zeichnung Erich Nawratil

close to where both of them had grown up and only 13 kilometres away from Stuttgart. Leonberg was Lutheran, with 1,000 inhabitants, and was safely situated on a mountain plateau. The walled town was accessible only from the eastern side and surrounded by a ditch 30 metres wide and 10 metres high (Figure 6). By the time the Keplers arrived, Leonberg's old castle had been turned into a new residence for the dukes of Württemberg who hunted in the district's rich forests. Communal buildings were given a new look in a late arrival of Renaissance styles. The Gothic town church received an attractive turret and was soon completely renovated from the inside. In 1566, a Tübingen stonemason crafted a trim knight bearing ducal and civic coats of arms for the well on the sloping, triangular market square in the centre of town. In 1580, the town-hall was enlarged and streets and alleys were paved.

Many artisans worked in their houses just off the market square and brought the town to life with a bustle of movement, sounds, and smells. Occasionally, male and female offenders stood with heavy irons locked around their necks before the executioner whipped them across the square and out of the upper town gate.[12] Around the time of the grape harvest in September, Italian and Dutch traders, puppet-makers, spice sellers, belt-, hat-, and bag-makers, as well as other craftsmen sold their wares at an annual fair.[13] Pigs were slaughtered in the market in the winter. A weekly market on Wednesdays attracted local sellers as well as men who trailed the region to advertise the latest medicinal cures and sell their healing stones. Men annually swore their Christian oath of loyalty to dukes on the square. Women met each other every day at the well to fetch water (Figure 7).

Figure 7 Leonberg market square with the town hall to the right (*c.*1480) and the well, embellished in 1566; Katharina was later interrogated on the second floor of the town hall. © Photograph: Christoph Rublack

The Keplers' house stood at the upper end of the market place. Wealthy people lived here, in large multi-storeyed buildings, close to the town hall. Three neighbouring families had been granted coats of arms by the Holy Roman Emperor. This was where Heinrich evidently felt he belonged socially, next to the men who sat in court and council, earning their living as merchants and traders, and, like their wives, frequently serving as godparents for the rich and poor, some for over fifty children. However, Heinrich Kepler never built up his own business, nor would he ever wear the long, dark, fur-trimmed woollen gown of the town magistrates.

The neighbouring Schertlins, Besserers, and Drehers, by contrast, stood out for their substantial wealth built on their businesses as merchants and lenders. The Besserers' address was No. 1 Market Square, and their cellar stored 15,000 litres of wine for sale.[14] Men from these families served on Leonberg's council and court for generations. The Korn family became very wealthy too, as they supplied the office of civic scribe, which was at the heart of the duchy's administrative structure. Paid by the number of pages they filled, the Korns created a formidable set of local records including property sales, inventories, marriage contracts, wills, court records, tax assessments, lists of mortgages, and city council records as well as meticulous registers. Apart from spilling ink and filling books, they also traded wine. Jacob Korn, who would write down and copy parts of the Kepler case, even added a tower with a spiral staircase and painted decorations to the front of his large house and commissioned a new sandstone frame for its portal. Borrowed from castle buildings, such architectural details stood out as a triumph of sophistication among Leonberg's sturdy timber and brick constructions, with their large iron locks and worn timber stairs.[15]

Lutheran pastors told their congregations that a virtuous life pleased God more than marble, but also that those at the top of society held greater responsibilities and were justified in signalling their status through a certain amount of display.[16] In return for a fee to charitable foundations, wealthy families thus began paying large sums for elegant funerary monuments in the town church to avoid being buried in the cemetery outside the lower gate. Jeremias Schwartz, a local stonemason, crafted monuments from wood or simple stones, but often painted them black to imitate marble, and to set off gilded inscriptions recording reassurances about the Resurrection. When Sebastian Dreher died aged sixty-three, the family placed an epitaph in the centre of the church wall with the cheerful inscription 'May God on his great day award him with a happy resurrection through the merit of Christ', as well as an image of the deceased wearing fashionable breeches and a top-hat (Figure 8).[17]

Artisans made up around 40 per cent of all Leonberg households, and among them were nine tailors, eight weavers, seven carpenters, and six bakers. In addition to their relatively poorly remunerated crafts, they owned fields and livestock, or kept inns, sold other goods, or found casual employment in the castle. Most Leonbergers lived primarily from tending their animals and cultivating oats, spelt, barley, a little rye and wheat as well as wine on slopes unsuitable for cereal cultivation. All their bread and cakes would have tasted unlike any today. Dough from spelt rose quickly and made light-grey bread and cakes which were nutty in taste, easy to digest, and had more protein than wheat. In addition to spelt, people mostly ate porridge made from water and oats, which slowly released its carbohydrates and sustained them for their many hours of manual work. Small dumplings might be added to broths and soups. Apart from bread and grain, they also ate eggs, a little butter and cheese, honey and jam. There would be some meat from hares and wildfowl (which they were allowed to hunt), imported calves, pigs during winter, and fish from local rivers. As for vegetables and fruit, Leonbergers ate cabbages, onions, peas, beans, mushrooms, beet, salad, apples, plums, pears, berries, and nuts they found or cultivated in small

Figure 8 Jeremias Schwartz, Epitaph for Leonberg's wealthy citizen Sebastian Dreher, who died aged sixty-three; note the tooth-pick as jewellery. The paint has faded away. © Stadtarchiv Leonberg, Photograph Karin Mueller, Leonberg

gardens. Much of this food was seasonal in supply, while spelt and oats were staples throughout the year and pulses as well as some fruit were dried. After the harvest, grain was carted in loads of 170 hectolitres per village to the ducal court to pay the tithe, while the rest would be carefully stored in barns to avoid damp and mould.[18]

Salt was expensive, and though people might have cooked with herbs, they liked to use small quantities of lard as the key ingredient to create a rich, fatty taste for what were usually frugal meals. People could nonetheless speak with enjoyment about food, appreciating dried apple slices eaten with local wine, or eating bread dipped in milk for lunch in the fields during harvest time. Women owned specialized equipment for baking small cakes, which they gave to each other as gifts, particularly during late February when everyone celebrated carnival with unruly parties, masks, and great noise. Throughout the year, simple meals were frequently shared with relatives or friends, such as soups, 'cabbage and bread', or, more fancily, 'egg-cakes', that is, an omelette washed down with Württemberg's ubiquitous light, fruity wines.

Württemberg wine already enjoyed high esteem. It was marketed in the Danubian region and dispatched as a diplomatic gift to the Habsburg imperial court in Vienna. Its best grape varieties were cultivated on steep terraced slopes north of Stuttgart and along the smaller rivers Rems and Murr, to be trodden by foot or squashed down by wooden blocks before being pressed and poured into barrels to age. Everyone preferred light, low-quality wine to impure water.

This diet, moreover, was perfectly adjusted to a fragile, tightly regulated ecology which supported only a limited rise in population but skilfully avoided famine. Some 60 per cent of all Leonberg households owned animals, mostly cows for milk. Cows required constant care, had personal names, could be appreciated for their beauty, and lived very much as part of the household, in a stable that was often part of the ground floor rather than a separate

building. In winter, the saddler Stahl kept his cows on matting of
dead branches to create additional warmth, and Katharina would
carry in straw by hand rather than by cart from her storage barn
outside town for her animals.[19] Each cow gave five to six litres of
milk a day when fed on pastures, but during winter turned gaunt
and dry.[20] They were only slaughtered for meat as a last resort, as an
independent supply of milk sustained nutrition levels so much
better than a feast on beef, which was difficult to preserve. This
was why milk could be spoken of as food to be 'eaten' rather than
drunk, and milk soup was a common dish. Calves were treasured,
and any illness of livestock was taken as seriously as human sickness. Women often received a cow as dowry—and they were worth
four times as much as a pig.[21] Calves and cows stood at the centre
of what people most worried about in connection with their
own lives.

How many cows and sheep might be owned by one family
meanwhile was carefully monitored by the magistrate to avoid
over-grazed meadows. Fields were left fallow at regular intervals for
the soil to recover. If too many animals were fed on one field, they
would get weak and ill, and not provide enough milk, meat, or
manure. Manure was the key to preventing soil depletion. Without
enough dung, there was no grain. Grazing animals were not allowed
to graze in forests either, because they would feed on young saplings
and endanger the woodland, which was all-important for heating,
cooking, washing, crafting, and construction. Only pigs, which were
mostly fed on waste and required little care but provided crucial
surplus nutrition for winter months, as well as that delicious lard,
were sent into the forests in autumn to feast on fallen acorns—
although people, too, knocked down acorns with long poles and
brought them back into town, as their tannin prevented disease in
pigs.[22] People knew about all these delicate environmental balances.
Their aim was to sustain many small producers, rather than to enable

a few men to exhaust local land. The dukes, meanwhile, were happy to tax as many households as possible.

* * *

Life in Leonberg thus meant keeping to strict rules and rhythms. Early in the morning, most people would feed their cows, clear the stable, and drive animals to the communal herd. By 1582, there were 225 cows and 550 sheep, which provided wool and were milked for seven weeks in summer, between St John's Day and St Laurence's Day.[23] Many chicken and cockerels, goats, pigs, some dogs, a few horses, geese, and cattle added their sounds to the vigorous mooing and bleating in town—in 1623, a total of 213 pigs were counted. Every Friday, women would mix flour with water, knead the dough, let it rest, rise, and finally bake their loaves of bread. Leonberg would feel and smell different that day, but this meant that women usually missed the sermon, for church was on Wednesdays, Fridays, and twice on Sunday, when the town's gates were closed to ensure that adults and children sat in their pews. On Ash Wednesday, local lads customarily presented the ducal governor with a cake and, afterwards, celebrated with the twenty litres of wine he handed them in return. Dances, church-wakes, and wedding feasts provided entertainment. Every Pentecost, the community planted birches in pots outside the Gothic church to celebrate life's renewal in spring. Taking communion ritualized spiritual renewal. The parish celebrated the Eucharist at regular intervals ten to twelve times a year, and everyone considered honourable would attend at least several times to confess and forgive others for their sins. Leonbergers registered and reported all those who did not take communion at least once a year. Such individuals were considered dangerous, as they had not called on God's help and grace to transform anger into love.

Strong walls completely surrounded the town to make it safe against destruction from outside. Able-bodied male citizens had to own a weapon and at least a cuirass, armour for their front torso, to make up a civic defence. By 1589, 155 citizens were registered. Gates were controlled by keepers and nobody was allowed to be out on the streets after nine o'clock in the evening during summer, or after eight o'clock during winter months, so much so that in 1600 a barber surgeon complained that when people from the district urgently called for him during the night even he was not allowed to leave through the gates.[24] There was little chance to escape the guards who patrolled Leonberg's streets after dark singing the hours. By the eleventh hour their loud chant beckoned:

> And who now still sits playing cards, or sweats over work,
> I am telling for the very last time,
> Go to bed now and sleep well!

A local journeyman drinking wine with foreign friends once cheekily shouted 'Yes!' in response, and was sternly rebuked. Similarly, in 1620, a shoemaker for carrying wood into his house during the winter between the hours of nine and ten, or the fur-maker's brother-in-law for gambling too late, as well as Ludwig Weißscheidel for playing the drums.[25] In addition to watchmen, forty-nine further communal offices needed to be filled to oversee local affairs each year, ranging from those who supervised the quality of craft products to lowly herdsmen. These citizens were reappointed every year with an oath to execute their office reliably, and most of them were married men. The only office for a woman was that of midwife, and fourteen local mothers annually chose or confirmed her position.

Literacy rates significantly rose during this period. Leonberg's school fee was lowered in 1541 and paid from the alms chest for the poor. Two decades later, schooling was recommended for every child and Württemberg's provisions for schooling became the most ambitious in the German lands. From 1580, Leonberg girls were taught reading and

writing to gain knowledge about Lutheran beliefs and thus be prepared
for Holy Communion, which formally marked a transition into adult
life around the age of fourteen. Education in general focused on
religion, and Leonberg's school was situated right next to the church.

Gifted boys were encouraged to go beyond this basic education by
attending Latin schools and getting scholarships for boarding schools
housed in former monasteries to prepare them for university. Every two
years, on average, one Leonberg boy would study at university, mostly at
the Lutheran university of Tübingen, and receive a gift of wine or
money from the magistrate upon completing his degree. At least thirteen sons of Leonberg day-labourers and lowly craftsmen would achieve
university degrees by 1611, though almost always in theology, rather
than in the more expensive legal studies. A man called Bastian Dietlin,
for instance, only owned half a house and parts of a vineyard when he
died, yet both of his sons had studied supported by ducal scholarships.
The two students who would matriculate in Tübingen just before and
after Johannes Kepler were sons of a Leonberg rope-maker and tailor.[26]

Although the lives of many Leonberg inhabitants focused on the
town, there was access to ideas from outside. After all the harvesting
had been done, in November people travelled to sell their wares at
larger town fairs, such as the Pforzheim fair to the west of Leonberg.
Girls went into service and boys into apprenticeships in other towns.
Married men might be asked to attend a ducal bird-shooting in
Stuttgart. Men and women took to the baths for medical cures,
including some poorer people on charitable support. Broadsheets
circulated and their worrisome news about cannibals in far-away
Livonia or sensational crime elsewhere enlivened sermons. Itinerant
peddlers also sold prints, and there was a book-stall at the annual
autumn fair. Stuttgart had book-sellers. In 1573, the civic scribe's
widow lent 'many books' to one of her widowed friends. A plasterer
owned Sebastian Münster's *Cosmography*, which described Europe,
Asia, and Africa and included many detailed engravings of cities.

Broadsheets further stimulated such interests and shaped local talk. Hans Knauß, who sat on the local council from 1591 to 1603, left seventeen books when he died, among them cosmographical writings. Jacob Harnisch, a forest administrator, even bequeathed twenty-four books to his family, mostly by popular classical writers, such as Cicero, Ovid, and Aesop.

* * *

Faced with such a well-defined communal life within Leonberg's walls, a man like Heinrich Kepler evidently dreamt of escape, perhaps in emulation of his ancestors who were lauded for their bravery. In 1583, Duke Ludwig secretly requested his governor to list those who had illegally left the wider district to become soldiers and was presented with a list of twenty-four names, five of them from Leonberg, including Heinrich Kepler. Most of these men were very poor and were trying to make money fast. They were men like the gate-keeper Hans Bub, who left in 1586 and never returned. His wife and children received a weekly half florin of alms to survive. Another of these men was wealthy, had fought at the battle of Pavia, and then settled back into a local office. Heinrich stood out from this list. Of middling wealth, he would fight again and again until he died.

Several times, Katharina would realize she was pregnant after Heinrich had left. Johannes was six years old when a baby brother died soon after birth, while his father was absent. Württemberg women suffered particularly high infant mortality at this time. Despite much medical effort to protect mother and child, for every 1,000 babies they carried through the long months of pregnancy, at least 250 died at or close to childbirth. Women's hard physical labour and malnutrition took their toll. Husbands would almost invariably stay at home during the time of the birth, and afterwards relieve women of work for a rest period of fourteen days, called 'lying-in'. Mothers spent this resting time propped up on a day-bed in the main chamber, looked after by a lying-in maid, or relatives and a host of visiting female friends. It was one of the rare times they felt treated generously and thus strengthened to fight the evil spirits believed to attack women after childbirth.

Katharina would have had to be up on her feet again every time Heinrich was far away and have the baby carried to its baptism within days of the birth without its own father being present. Johannes Kepler would later be astonished how much trouble it took to look after his own wife. 'For what a business, what an activity', the astronomer incredulously penned to a friend, 'does it not make to invite fifteen or sixteen women to visit my wife, who lies in childbed, to receive them hospitably, to see them out!' He would never have seen his father make any effort of this kind.[27]

Yet, as we have seen, Heinrich kept coming back to the family. Upon his return in autumn 1579, he was disfigured, wounded by an explosion of gunpowder. Soon after, the bailiff punished him for disorderly behaviour. Next, the Keplers had to sell their house. During the same year, Heinrich attended a shooting match in the duchy, won the trophy flag, due to his superior martial skills, presented it to the duke and received a reward in return.[28] Nevertheless, the Keplers now moved away from Leonberg's market square. They decided to buy a village inn, also called the 'Sun', just like the inn Katharina had grown up in.

* * *

Wer nichts wird wird Wirt—'Someone who is not going to become anything becomes an innkeeper'. This is how an old German saying harshly characterized innkeeping as a profession. Being an innkeeper was not tied to an apprenticeship or studies, but was something that men like Heinrich Kepler could try their luck at. It was one occupation in which women were very active, as it was not regulated by guilds. Inns played an important role in public life, and many contracts were settled on their sturdy pine or oak tables, followed by drinks. People exchanged news, played cards, discussed all matters of life, and met travellers. Innkeepers were at the centre of things. And, as Katharina knew from her own family, they might well achieve some wealth and respect. This was her first attempt at running a business with Heinrich, in addition to farming their land and other hard peasant labour, which Johannes Kepler later recalled being forced to help with for two years around the age of ten. His mother would have cooked, served, cleaned, sourced food and wine, and collected debts, most likely with the help of servants. Yet Heinrich and Katharina had no connections to the village, which lay just outside Württemberg's boundaries. It would have been hard to gain respect, not least because even the slightest difference in dialect distinguished outsiders from true locals. After four years, Heinrich ran into trouble.

Many German inns were called 'Sun', long before the sun was thought to be at the centre of the universe. Like so many others, this culture celebrated the sun. Solar monstrances—receptacles of gold to expose the consecrated host, or relics adorned with brilliant suns— were a familiar spectacle for Catholics. Renaissance humanists celebrated the sun as God's visible representative. Alchemists felt sure that the Philosopher's Stone originated from father gold (the sun) and mother silver (the moon) as celestial parents. Kepler wrote, 'Nobody doubts that the sun is more beautiful than the earth.' His work showed that it was also superior.[29] Moreover the sun and the moon were turned into powerful metaphors when writers compared men in humoral terms to the dry, powerful, superior sun and women to the cold, moist, murkier moon. In 1578, one of the many advice books on marriage imagined that their properties perfectly complemented each other:

> He is the Sun, she is the Moon,
> She is the night, he the day's might,

> And what the sun burns by day,
> Is cooled at night by the power of the moon:
> In this way, too, the wild is calmed.[30]

But marriage was known to be a fragile state. Everyone in this society knew couples who seemed hardened like stones through years of quarrelling and, in the extreme, abuse. Lutherans allowed few couples to divorce and their marriage courts notoriously protected violent husbands. After the Reformation, marriage was hailed as the very foundation of society—a microcosm of the state, of order, work, concern for each other, and Christian education. Unhappy spouses had little choice but to run away or bear the vicissitudes of life.

*　*　*

One of the most unpredictable elements in mid-life was prolonged fertility. Early in 1584, just as their first daughter, Margaretha, was about to be born, Heinrich and Katharina managed to return to Leonberg after their interlude as innkeepers and bought a house between the communal laundry house, where women did their washing, and the lower civic gate. Three years later, Katharina gave birth to a son, Christoph. Entering their forties, the Keplers thus suddenly found themselves parents of two small children again. In 1584 and 1587, the bailiff punished Heinrich for being involved in minor quarrelling.[31] By 1582, Johannes had left the family. He finished Latin school in Leonberg and then attended Württemberg's most competitive boarding schools for the gifted, in the former monastery of Adelberg. Later he moved on to Maulbronn, where a boy unable to take the constant praise of Johannes's talents teased him about his father. Johannes tried to avenge himself, only to be beaten up in turn.[32]

Johannes longed to be proud of his name. Yet when writing his father's brief biography he noted that in 1589, aged forty-two,

Heinrich Kepler suffered an accident, took his anger out on Katharina, and once more ran away. People speculated that he served as a military commander. Some later claimed that Heinrich had died near Augsburg; but the family never heard from him again. That same year, Johannes gained one of five ducal scholarships for Tübingen's *Stift*-college, inscribing his name in the university's books on 5 October: 'Joannes Keppler Leomontanus'—from Leonberg.[33] Katharina's father pawned a meadow to support his talented grandchild's expenses, and Johannes claimed that his annual six florins of scholarship money were just enough to pay a cobbler, mediocre tailor, and washerwoman. A theology degree at this time cost parents 200 florins. Despite Johannes's scholarship, Kepler's family could not afford legal studies, which the rich Dreher family's sons pursued, nor could they finance a doctorate. As a result, Johannes had no prospect of marrying into ducal office-holding elites. He was destined to become a Lutheran pastor. Other students might be egged on by fathers with a flood of letters promising extra *Gulden*, gold rings, and Italian journeys for doing well, but Kepler had to fend for himself, demonstrate constant diligence, and behave immaculately.[34]

Katharina bore her last son after Heinrich had left her that final time. This was to be the third baby she had had without her husband being at home, and the third to die almost immediately. She cared for Margaretha and little Christoph. After 1595, she took her widowed, very elderly and soon immobile father to live with her at home—Melchior Guldenmann, who believed he had been born in 1514. She now cared for him and once again worked the land without the help of a husband or grown-up children. She was used to relying on herself, as her first two children had never given her much help at any stage. Johannes had never been physically strong, and already as a teenager had spent his leisure time memorizing the longest psalms, working through Greek grammar, writing comedies, and indulging in his love of unusual words, rather than working in the fields. He even asked his parents to explain to him particular views when they instructed him in religion according to the Lutheran Augsburg Confession. In sharp contrast to Johannes's scholarly success and pre-mature life of the mind, his brother Heinrich had been fruitlessly apprenticed, first as cloth-cutter and then as a baker, before, at sixteen, following his father's footsteps by joining an army.

Katharina inherited a house, fields, and meadows from her husband. Five hectares of land had been registered for the Keplers in a 1575 tax-book, which placed them among the Leonbergers of middling wealth. Katharina bought a quarter part of a new house in 1595, for which Johannes let her use his paternal inheritance. In 1600, some months before his death, Katharina's father made his will. He expressed his gratitude for five years of total care in ways which went far beyond routine requirements. She would have had to lift her old father, and to make sure he stayed clean, fed, and warm enough. He movingly recorded his daughter's 'complete love and loyalty and steady, hard-working care' for him, and left her money.[35]

Two years earlier, in 1598, Katharina had moved her family from her cramped lodgings to a small wine-grower's house, in the streets leading back towards the church, which she had bought for the sizeable sum of 330 florins. Next to her was a barn and, on the other side, Bartlin Eberlin's house, a craftsman she appointed as her legal guardian. She had achieved more comfortable circumstances, but was still short of help to work her land, or organize a plough-team, bring in the harvest, and make hay. Sebald, her wealthy father-in-law, would leave her remaining family no inheritance whatsoever (Figure 9).[36]

Yet there would be plenty of good news. Johannes had not become a Württemberg pastor, but in 1594, just before finishing his degree, he moved on to a teaching post as mathematician in the Austrian town of Graz. Katharina and his grandfathers, Johannes explained to the Tübingen divinity professors, had always wanted him to serve and honour God as minister. As 'unlearned

Figure 9 Leonberg house of the type Katharina Kepler would have lived in with her elderly father and children. © Photograph: Ulinka Rublack

people' they trusted the professors' decision to send him to Graz, especially if he could still study the Bible, theological writing, and get some practical training from a clergyman. No such training emerged, but in 1596 Johannes published his first book and corresponded with Galileo, deeply excited about the possibility of forming a scholarly community to publicly defend Copernican views. One year later, aged twenty-seven, he married a well-off young widow. By 1600, his reputation was such that he worked in a team with the Dane Tycho Brahe, to succeed him in 1601 as Emperor Rudolph II's imperial mathematician in Prague, earning an annual salary of 500 florins. In 1602, Katharina proudly travelled to visit him as soon as he was installed in his new post.

Katharina's life in this new century improved. As her younger children became strong, healthy teenagers, they provided reliable help for their maturing mother. Christoph was apprenticed to learn a luxury craft that was increasingly in demand—the making of pewter-ware—and aged eighteen he became a wandering journeyman. He crossed the whole of Germany, heading towards the north, as his famous older brother had asked him to. By the time he reached Königsberg, ill and exhausted, in November 1607, he delivered a letter from Johannes and his recent pamphlet *On the New Star* to Papius, his brother's former schoolmaster at Graz.[37]

After his safe return, Christoph settled down as Leonberg's only master pewterer. Soon, the Kepler family had further milestones to celebrate. Margaretha, who had grown up to be an attractive girl with no shortage of suitors, married in 1608, aged twenty-four and still a virgin. Katharina had evaluated eligible young men, once by walking to Tübingen to see a very distant, interested relative in 1606, which deeply alarmed Margaretha, causing the young woman to write to her brother. Johannes in turn asked his former professor Mästlin to inform him about this man's 'position, reputation, spirit and mind'.[38] In the end, Margaretha settled for Georg Binder, a man acceptable to her and known to her mother. The son-in-law's father was a reputable pastor not too far away, who belonged to Württemberg's honourable families, and Georg had come to Leonberg as a local teacher. Now, aged twenty-eight, he had been elected to his first position as pastor in Heumaden, a village close to Stuttgart, with its small, pretty Gothic church and a vicarage ready to move into. Katharina could expect this marriage to remain honourable and reliable. She had wanted her oldest son to be a pastor; now she had, at least, a daughter installed in the office of a pastor's wife. Margaretha would enjoy a better life than she had done.[39]

Entering her sixties, and despite the fact that she was widowed and had no daughter living with her any more to write and read for her, Katharina thus for the first time in many years might have felt that life seemed relatively settled for her and her three successful children. Between 10 and 15 per cent of households were typically headed by women in Württemberg communities. It was far more unusual for them to find a husband to remarry than for any male widower to find a younger wife. Even so, on the whole such women managed to support themselves well through agricultural work, selling hay, and providing credit at the statutory 5 per cent interest, as Katharina did. Others ran mills and practised a whole range of crafts that they were allowed to continue after their husbands' deaths, including healing.

Much of what they did went unrecorded. Thus we only know about one sixty-two-year-old Württemberg widow who supported her nine children by continuing her husband's tanning business because in 1662 the courts reprimanded her for tanning a rotten wolf-skin. Widows also rented out animals, such as cows, to those who could not afford to buy one, sold lard and hay, produced wool and spun, were laundresses, cared for orphans, or could be shop- and innkeepers. They created many opportunities, despite being excluded from guilds and from political representation in communal decision-making bodies. There is thus no reason to infer from the mere fact that a woman was an elderly widow that she would have lacked a purpose in life or was desperately poor. In the tax register of 1614, Katharina's name is entered alongside thirty-six Leonberg widows who proudly paid taxes as citizens in their own right, among a total of 286 tax-paying citizens.[40]

Katharina's children were now independent, but her youngest son could help her work the land, and in addition she could also rely on her daughter nearby. She had no parents or parents-in-law to take care of and was financially secure. And she was still alive—her only brother, Hans, who was three years older, had died as a well-off peasant in Eltingen, her home village, in 1602. Katharina had lived in the same house she herself had bought since 1598, while with Heinrich she had frequently moved house. Above all, Katharina might well have felt that she had left behind a life of endless worrying about whether her husband would return and what his stay might entail. Even Heinrich the Younger, her trouble-making son, had found a position through Johannes's connection in Prague. In the years before being accused of witchcraft, there would have been little for Katharina to worry about and much to be proud of.

2

A LUTHERAN COURT

———— ⬗ ————

I n the first decade of the seventeenth century, another woman who
had been exposed to denigration and abandonment in her marriage
brought change to Leonberg's settled ways. In 1608, the recently
widowed duchess Sibylle of Württemberg chose to move from Stuttgart to a permanent residence in Leonberg's small castle. Unusually for
a royal marriage, she and her husband Frederick, the future duke of
Württemberg, had married for love when she had been seventeen.
Then, in quick succession, she had given birth to fifteen children, ten
of whom survived to adulthood. Almost as soon as Frederick took over
government in 1593, he signalled that Sibylle was no longer attractive
to him by engaging in a string of affairs. He was still, however, deeply
jealous of her, as well as punitive, and at times preferred hastily written
notes to their fraught encounters. She constantly devised tactics to
manage him emotionally. An energetic woman in her forties, Sibylle
clearly expected a new phase in her life to begin in Leonberg, rather
than that she should merely withdraw into passivity.[1]

* * *

Leonberg was closely connected to the legacy of Frederick's and
Sibylle's reign. Frederick had been a ruler with great ambitions,

loyal favourites, and little patience with local representatives. By
1599, the estates, which represented communities in political assemblies with the duke, eloquently protested against legal injustice, by
claiming that torture had been used outside formal trials and that a
poacher had even been hung without trial. Not only did such
instances violate the constitutional rights of citizens, they also failed
to respect that 'every human' was created as 'a likeness of God', as
stated in the Bible. Frederick briskly retorted that such prattle was of
no concern to him and that he would treat those acting against him
in whatever manner he pleased.[2]

The duke's passions were grand architecture as well as economic
and technological innovations (Figure 10). He wished the duchy's
economy to grow through improvements in infrastructure, fortifications, milling, water supply, mining and metal production, wine, silk
and linen production, as well as the cultivation of new varieties of
fruit trees, animal breeding, and bee keeping. The estates' caution
about setting up large-scale textile production in collaboration with a
merchant trading company led a furious Frederick to remark that
they equalled woodworms in intelligence.[3]

Determined to turn the Württemberg court into a sophisticated
place and a German power to reckon with, the well-travelled, stout-
bodied duke put great effort into diplomatic relations with other
Protestant nations. He also put pressure on his estates to provide funds
for a standing army ready to defend the country against Catholics.[4]

Frederick built up the court's magnificence with more determination than any previous duke. Soon, expenses for his abundant
festivities mounted. In 1599, Frederick used his exceptional collection of Latin American feather-cloaks, skirts, and shields to stage an
enormous parade which closely imitated Theodore de Bry's engravings of Americans. The duke himself was dressed up as fertile Lady
America, who had come to visit her oldest sister Europe and made
Württemberg her key destination. Guests were looked after by

Figure 10 View of the interior of the Ducal Pleasure-House in Stuttgart, a pioneering large, light German Renaissance building to receive international guests, with hunting scenes on the ceiling, female personifications of fame and wisdom in upper corners and maps on the sides. Etching 1619, 37.4 × 51.4 cm. © Trustees of the British Museum

Moorish, Turkish, and Indian servants, and entertained by a court dwarf named 'Simple', as well as acrobats and the English director of music, John Price. Dancing took place in an enormous newly built casino with a ceiling depicting the heavenly constellations and a double outdoor staircase opening out onto carefully designed gardens in a classical style. The Stuttgart 'pleasure'-house and gardens were land-marks of German Renaissance-style building. Pyrotechnicians and engineers collaborated to construct sensational fireworks, one showing the burning of a monastery and members of the Jesuit order.[5]

Sibylle shared in the excitement of all these events and projects, especially Frederick's interest in alchemy and medicine. All over

Europe, there was a deep fascination with chemical properties and visually exciting reactions. Emperor Rudolph II and other patrons could become so closely involved in experiments to draw out a metal's *spiritus* that the elements' violent explosions singed beards or eyebrows.[6] This was the age of the prince practitioner. The Protestant Maurice of Hesse (1572–1632) left five volumes of personal correspondence on alchemical–medical subjects alone. Maurice was widely praised in England for his multilingual abilities and musical accomplishments. In addition, he possessed unrivalled bone-setting skills and a readiness to experiment, as well as the ability to read, confer, and write about the body and nature. In this way, many rulers around 1600 became Baconian men—they were open to progressive learning through practice, discovery, prolonged studies, and scientific teams in order to spearhead harmony and progress in their realms.[7]

Alchemy was not only the quest to turn base metal into gold, but was linked to a whole set of beneficial activities of a practical chemical kind, for example: the improvement of health, brewing beer, making sugar, refining salts, dyes, leather, glass, and gunpowder manufacturing.[8] Alchemical operations in Württemberg soon began to take place on a grand, professional scale. In 1597, one Stuttgart alchemist ordered 468 kilogrammes of saltpetre, 842 kilogrammes of lead, 935 kilogrammes of white copper, and 468 kilogrammes of mountain antimony (a shiny grey metalloid), all to be delivered to the Old Pleasure-House next to the castle. With its light rooms, hot ovens, distillation equipment, note-books, clocks and pens, this bustling place functioned as a state-of-the art laboratory for many years.[9]

In 1603, James I's diplomat Lord Spenser presented Frederick with the English Order of the Garter. It was a badge of international distinction and much treasured by the duke. Erhart Cellius, the Tübingen professor of poetry, oratory, and history, and one of

Johannes Kepler's teachers, marked the occasion with a poem on Frederick's merits. The poet particularly stressed the extraordinary medical benefits of alchemical discoveries made under Frederick's patronage. The right herbs could produce water capable of reinvigorating a half-dead man; salts and powders could also be made alchemically to purge the body of everything that could make it ill. Even earth, wood, stone, and iron could be burnt into 'subtle oils' which sustained people's health through the use of divinely created natural matter until God commanded their death. Alchemy, in short, was praised as a magnificent art to facilitate a more enjoyable life. It was full of wonders, provided there were furnaces and generous patrons to pay for them.[10]

By the time Frederick died in 1608, the Old Pleasure-House accommodated a team of twenty-one people operating fourteen portable copper furnaces and four ovens. Here they worked out the composition of matter to understand the secrets of the universe, or 'universal medicine'.[11] In addition, Frederick supported smaller laboratories elsewhere in the duchy.[12] Whilst such pursuits had potential for fraud, or failure, they were surrounded by a great sense of excitement and possibility. The lure of secret knowledge generated contact between learned people and rulers across Europe.[13]

Alchemical ideas were first cultivated in medieval monasteries and by this time were frequently developed by Lutheran clerics. Thus, Frederick's court preacher Lukas Osiander and his son Johannes were provided with space in the ducal laboratory in 1595. Such ideas included the notion that an intellectual elite might rediscover mystical thought and secret 'stores of knowledge' in God's creation in order to transform society.[14] An interest in what could be termed 'occult' could be firmly part of a Christian universe, believed to be animated by supernatural power, and the possibilities of material as well as spiritual transformations through scientific inquiry. Age-old knowledge mixed with new forms of hands-on practical work, and expertise in both realms, was claimed to be vital. Osiander the Younger thus vouched that his fellow alchemist Conrad Schuler, whom Frederick showered with properties, was 'altogether an idiot' when it came to practical work, while Schuler's assistant was skilled in the laboratory but 'knew nothing of theory'.[15] Schuler himself piously affirmed that he solely intended to aid the 'disciples of the universal medicine who would help the poor and needy' through the help of God, who himself would determine the outcome of any experiment.[16]

Despite such rivalries, working with and observing chemical experiements for many contemporaries appeared to be part of an actively lived, dynamic faith which went beyond bible reading.[17] It promised to keep Protestant courts involved with practical, useful, pious, and forward-looking concerns rather than immoral pursuits. For Germans, this primarily meant refraining from the sin of *Saufen*: excessive drinking.

* * *

A further aspect of this increasing spiritualization of nature which caught on in Württemberg lead to considerable excitement about the benefits of two sulphurous baths and a water source which had been discovered on the southern edges of the territory, in Boll (Figures 11, 12, and 13). It was while digging for salt that miners had found these waters, which even today have excellent mineral properties. Immediately, Frederick ordered his architect, Heinrich Schickhardt, to design a bathhouse and park, and sent his physician, Johann Bauhin, to examine and write about the water's properties and effects. Barrels of these sulphurous waters were sent to immobile patients. Bauhin's extensive text about the 'Württemberg wonder-bath' went through seven Latin and three German editions. The book highlighted the most marvellously shaped fossils unearthed during digging. Labourers had brought the author fossils of snails and shells, which he thought of as the 'earth's intestines'. Such objects fascinated contemporaries because they were seen as the 'great, diverse and

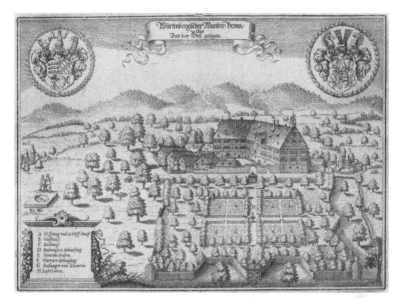

Figure 11 The Württemberg Wonder-Bath in Bad Boll, *c*.1644, with details of the spa and pleasure-garden. © Stuttgart, Württembergische Landesbibliothek

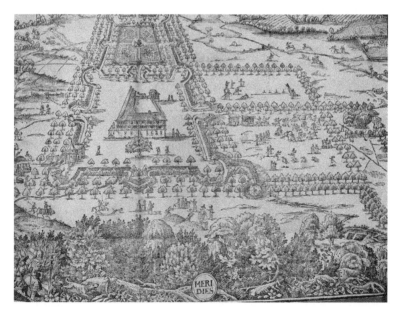

Figure 12 The earliest known depiction of the spa and Frederick's garden in Boll. It represents entertainments on the right and workmen as well as male and female spectators involved in digging for fossils in the centre front. From Johann Bauhin, *De aquis medicatis nova methodus*, 1612. © By permission of the Master and Fellows of St John's College, Cambridge

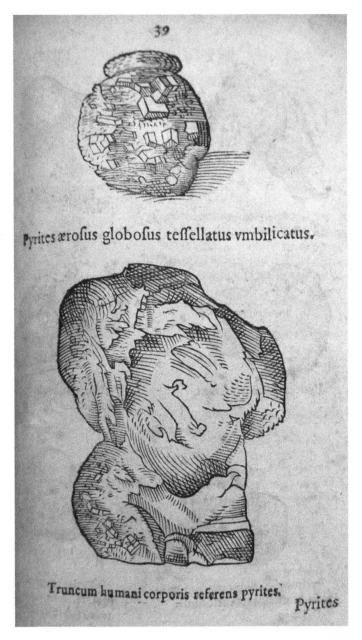

39

Pyrites ærosus globosus tessellatus vmbilicatus.

Truncum humani corporis referens pyrites.

Pyrites

Figure 13 Fossils dug up at Boll. For Kepler and other contemporaries such fossils documented God's playful test designs of shapes in nature. From Johann Bauhin, *De aquis medicatis nova methodus*, 1612. © By permission of the Master and Fellows of St John's College, Cambridge

wonderful' store of God's artistry captured in stone. Fossils and healing waters were further proof of God's miraculous creation for the benefit of mankind. All these benefits could be revealed if only a man like Frederick spearheaded innovation alongside learned, ingenious men of practical ability (Figure 14). Soon, gardeners planted tobacco plants as well as potatoes shipped from the Americas, while Duke Frederick's name was etched in a display of evergreen box (*Buxus*) around a large sundial.

This was a remarkable public works project by the standards of the time. The duke annually awarded six deserving Württembergers and six poor women or men from outside the duchy a stay at the spa, where they had to behave in orderly, pious ways. He allowed Catholics to take the cure, too. Bauhin's books detailed how many people from all over the duchy had been cured of a whole range of illnesses during their stay. By 1607, a book advertised the duke's own journey to these waters with several of his knights and officers, including a description of each of their maladies. In this, particular strands of Lutheranism developed their understanding of the sacred with great optimism. They discovered how God had created 'sources of relief from the illnesses inflicted upon human beings for sin'. Temporal life could get better.[18]

These ideas make it difficult to maintain the argument that small German Protestant courts cultivated a unifying atmosphere of despair.[19] In 1601, Frederick even named a town he had created 'Joy-town': Freudenstadt. Situated on the edge of the Black Forest, it had a perfect geometrical layout, in the centre of which stood an enormous market square surrounded by arcaded town-houses and an elegant church. Here was manifest transformation.

* * *

This exhilarating combination of learning, piety, and empiricism attracted many educated women, who were excluded from

Scarabei genus.

Poſſet ad Bupreſten referri, qui Ger. Golð⸗
keffer dictus : magis tamen mutabili colore,
pro varia ad lumen obuerſione. Captus 24.
Sept. 1596, in Kirchen / viuebat adhuc in charta Ianuarij
15. anni 1397.

Cantharis guttata, quæ aſellorum inſtar atta⸗
ctu conglobatur.

Scarabeus paruus nonnihil compreſſus, alis
rubris punctis nigris ita affabre variato, vt fa⸗
ciem humanam quodámodo æmuletur. Qui⸗
buſdam Gallicè *Gelines de noſtre Dame,* id eſt, Diuæ Virgi⸗
nis gallinæ. In vrbe Kirchen obſeruatus menſe Octobri.

Scarabei genus oblongum, anguſtum fuſcum figura 4,
eſt penè nigrum.

Scarabeus, Germ. Roßfeffer / paruus
appictus forte iunior vt putat pictor,
Lonicerus l. 2, pingit.

Scarabeum Maialem vulgò dictum
Meyenkeffer vidi cũ pararentur foſſ
baln. adm. menſis Octobris ſeptima.

Meylánder & Schmaltzkeffer Scarabei nigri, lógi, par⸗
te poſteriore craſſa, nigra, ſimiles aliquatenus Roßkeffer.
Dicunt pinguedinem expeti, vtilem ad vulnera : vidi
menſ Septembri in Eichelberg.

Páuo aquaticus, inſectum ex grandiorum muſcarum ge⸗
nere, pulchrum, quaternis alis magnis, corpore oblongo,
teſſelato colorum emblemate variegato, aquas obuoli⸗
tans. Auguſto menſe vidi.

Inſectum

Figure 14 An interest in the observation of nature and its divinely created variety now
extended to insects—this book charts what type of beetles were spotted in Württemberg, when and where. From Johann Bauhin, *De aquis medicatis nova methodus,* 1612.
© By permission of the Master and Fellows of St John's College, Cambridge

universities. Sibylle used her reign to develop her medical and botanical expertise. This fulfilled her role as Lutheran mother to her country, a *Landesmutter*. Like other princesses, she enthusiastically experimented with purifying materials as well as inventing new drugs by distilling substances.[20] She was closely involved with the ducal pharmacy, which was headed by a woman and included a regular position for a ducal 'herb-man or -maid' to dig out roots and collect plants at the most beneficial times, a post occupied by one Elisabeth Bernheuser from 1601 to 1608.[21] This was skilled labour that required astrological knowledge and the ability to get out of bed even earlier than the usual rising time at five o'clock, or, with a lie in, by six in the morning. Sibylle's voluminous compendium, with hundreds of precise medical recipes from her sister-in-law Eleonore, included instructions for painkillers such as:

> *How to dig the root for heavy pain*
> *One has to dig it out in March or April, towards the end of the month, on a*
> *day when sun and moon are in the sign of Aries and it has to be dug out in*
> *the morning before sunrise, many dig it out during the dogs' days, when the*
> *sun rises in Leo and the moon recedes.*[22]

Medicine was composed, usually, of at least ten ingredients. A *heart-water*, for instance, was a compound of rosemary, fresh may flowers, marjoram, lavender, wreath-sage, sour thistle, white ginger, carnations, red laurel berries, oak mistletoe, and shredded deer-horn, from an animal caught between 'two ladies' days' (*Frauentage*). Even hunting could thus be undertaken in pursuit of optimizing medicine. Conrad Gesner's famous animal book advised that wolf excrement infused in white wine and then drunk or tied to an arm helped against stomach ache.[23] For medicine preparation, mixtures of different ingredients were distilled several times and then left to rest. Anything done in a rush was considered unreliable. Eleonore's tome of medical knowledge included many recipes which other reputable women and men had supplied and also included favourite local creations, such as 'duke John Frederick's Aqua vitae for the feet'. All this gathered and developed experience from using these cures day-to-day, which lent such medical practices authority. In 1600, Eleonore had become the first woman to print such a recipe collection.[24]

* * *

Experiments with liquids and growing things, sourcing, mixing, and trying all sorts of substances were supported by a culture of careful observation, collecting, and comparison, in which many men and women across society participated. Leading thinkers endorsed experience of the 'singular things of nature' (that is, experiments and observation) rather than generalized, abstract knowledge. Medical chemistry gained particular prominence through followers of the sixteenth-century medical reformer Paracelsus. Some learned men now sought out butchers and fishmongers, perfumers, jewellers, or dyers in order to benefit from their knowledge. Objects formed of baked medicinal clay—*terra sigillata*—produced in Europe and the Orient were used for healing. All this involved a hands-on and sensate engagement with a diversity of natural substances, some of which might freely be mixed with human bodily products, such as urine. A key sixteenth-century botanist such as Conrad Gessner was already happy not only to smell but to eat the leaves of New World plants to test their effect.[25]

Women and men across society kept exchanging information about herbal benefits. Many of these ideas restored ancient knowledge, or enriched old ideas with insights through newly found natural substances from across the globe. Printed herbals were produced, most notably by the Tübingen professor Leonhart Fuchs, which made it easy to identify plants because each one was represented in a large, naturalistic woodcut illustrating roots, leaves, and flowers. Fuchs, who gained admiration for his handsome looks and clear voice, encouraged the 'common man' to grow specimens of God's noble creation for the benefit of mankind in their gardens and added an index of disease names to help readers in finding remedies.[26] Botany and medical education were part of a whole Protestant programme of lay education and innovation as a celebration of nature's diversity and delights. Fuchs was happy to include certain plants on purely aesthetic grounds, and was excited about versatile healing plants such as aloe from India and Arabia, which was now 'frequently planted in Germany but has never fully matured and flowered' (Figure 15).

Increased travel across Europe and exchanges with other continents continued to foster excitement about mineral, animal, and vegetative worlds elsewhere. New World commerce shaped European learning. Carolus Clusius (1525–1606), Europe's foremost botanist, was perfectly positioned in the Netherlands. He corresponded extensively with several women in different countries and languages, promised to pass on 'rarities' such as roses and carnations, and accompanied at least one letter to an aristocratic pen-friend with big baskets filled with bulbs, seeds, and roots.[27] High-born ladies were riveted by gardening and the challenges of constructing hothouses. The new plants with their unknown colours, smells, and other properties infused their lives with an exhilarating sense of change and advancing knowledge.[28] The grandest of these gardens, the Hortus Palatinus, was begun in 1614 on a steep hillside in Heidelberg by the Calvinist prince Frederick V for his English wife, Elizabeth Stuart. It was designed by Salomon de Caus, the French Huguenot engineer, who had tutored Elizabeth in drawing and was keen to share with the princess his 1615 work *Les raisons des forces mouvantes* on 'delightful', mechanically clever, water- and air-driven musical automata and other garden features. This was the height of natural and artistic harmony.

The Lutheran pastor Johann Arndt, whose *Six Books of True Christianity* were published between 1605 and 1610, agreed that

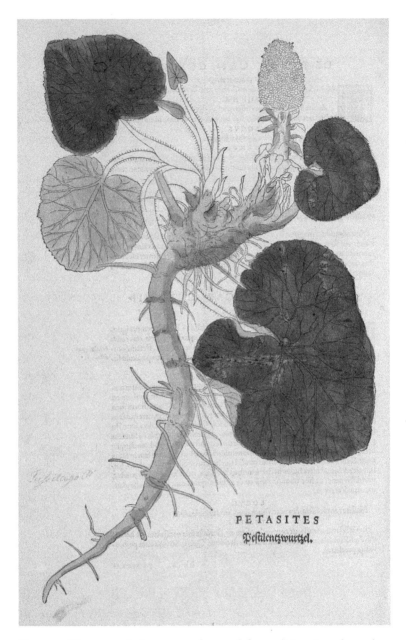

Figure 15 The roots of plants were often used for medicines in early modern Europe. This is Petasites (Butter-bur), as described by Leonhart Fuchs in his *De historia stirpium*, 1542. Its thick, long, white root had an overpowering smell and was bitter. Fuchs wrote that 'by experience' it strongly induced perspiration when reduced to a powder and taken with wine; thus it helped wonderfully against pestilential fevers. Woodcut 32 × 20.5 cm. © Cambridge University Library, Sel.2.81

natural philosophers needed to ask about 'correspondences and harmonies' between the heavens, earth, and seas, and argued that all creatures were bearers of a divine message. Weeds and common flowers were medicines because they bore the 'living handwriting and signature of God' and thus were spiritual guides to 'God's love, benevolence and omnipotence'.[29] Philipp Hainhofer, the internationally famous Augsburg art-dealer, was among those who professed not to be able to 'get enough' of reading Arndt's alert for an active Christianity rooted in an admiration of all creation, which praised mountains as God's 'treasure-troves' or seas as his 'larder'. This spiritualized Hainhofer's own flourishing trade with rare antlers, 'chymically' or 'gallantly' made objects, including precious stones or walrus teeth which, he promised clients, were of such medical strength and complexity that they resembled 'half a pharmacy'.[30]

These passions spread to fashion. This was expressed memorably in a full-length portrait of Sibylle of Württemberg as a mature, smiling, elegant, and thoroughly impressive woman, whose hair was coiffed and embellished into a structure resembling a mixture of a halo and a crown. This made her look more majestic in size and stature, and she would later be remembered for her 'healthy, strong body, good complexion and straight, heroic figure'.[31] Sibylle had always been interested in dress—she owned two French mannequins and a book of costume. She now displayed herself wearing a large, fashionable, perfectly starched ruff with exquisite lacing at the edges and beautiful ornamental jewellery over a doublet sumptuously embroidered with plants embedded in interesting geometrical figures, to create an image not dissimilar to flower beds. This particular emphasis on plants as the basis of her knowledge, and crucial for the role she wished to play as Lutheran duchess, in Figure 16 reveals itself in the detail of a remarkable handkerchief in her left hand. It is listed as *Konfekt-Tuch* in her inventory, and was richly embroidered with large, colourful, and highly detailed plants, which could easily be

Figure 16 Duchess Sybille of Anhalt Württemberg. Oil on canvas, 238 × 136 cm. © Staatliche Schlösser und Gärten Baden-Württemberg

identified by contemporaries. These were not tiny, decorative embel-
lishments, but real phenomena. For the Lutheran duchess, they
featured in place of traditional insignia of rule.[32]

* * *

Soon after Frederick's death, when Sibylle moved from the Stuttgart
castle with its renowned pleasure-garden to Leonberg, she confidently told Heinrich Schickhardt, the duchy's accomplished building master, to create a garden from scratch. How could she conceive
of living without one? Schickhardt (1558–1635) was one of Germany's leading architects and inventive engineers, who had accompanied Frederick on his travels and executed a host of public and
private works throughout his lifetime. Using his ruler and ink, while
on two trips to Italy, Schickhardt amassed precise sketches and notes
on churches, palaces, gardens, bridges, artificial waterworks, fountains, and wells. Even though he kept struggling to learn Latin (first
with the help of a 1598 grammar 'in a special new manner' and,
persistently, aged seventy, with one of Germany's highly popular
self-tuition manuals, which swept the book market and was tantal-
izingly entitled 'For a citizen or peasant, who can only read and
write, to be taught just in 2, 3 or 4 weeks, so that he can afterwards
fill several hundred of pages with correct Latin verse by himself'), the
architect shared a deep interest in practical innovation. This encom-
passed ballistics, the designing of water-pumps for firefighting, rag-
ramming for making paper, oven-constructing to save on wood, bridge-
building, and navigation, as well as minting, spa-building, gardening,
and medicine. Over the years, Schickhardt and his wife collected forty-
two herb books as well as twelve alchemical titles, including one book
with specific advice on how to heal 'harm from sorcery'.[33]

Peasants and artisans were obliged to offer their labour and turned
the 'rough, rocky, infertile' land behind Leonberg's castle into a
pleasurable and useful terrain with fruit trees, flowers, shrubs, a

kitchen garden, and wells.[34] It appeared a marvellous transformation based on Schickhardt's drawing, which Sibylle's son John Frederick quickly authorized. The garden ended with an impressive, Italianate staircase at the centre of its border, opening up into meadows, orchards, and fields beyond. These were filled with successively flowering wild plants and deep colours throughout the year. Schickhardt's open integration of the castle garden into this landscape was pioneering.[35]

Meanwhile a balcony was attached to Sibylle's rooms on the first floor, enabling her to enjoy the colours and scents of the garden. The grounds were also perfectly suited to brief strolls to appreciate plant development more closely. Schickhardt had set out two large quadrangles, each divided into four areas with flower beds arranged in playful combinations of exact geometrical shapes in dynamic patterns. Each centre was marked by a fountain and each corner by a decorative pavilion. His original plans for water basins in the garden's central axis were superseded by an obelisk, set in an octagonal well, and embellished with Sibylle's coat of arms as well as a lion and dolphin, to symbolize power over as well as care for her subjects. This crossroads was planted with pots of bitter oranges, figs, and pomegranate, which were moved into a heated hothouse during the cold months (Figure 17).[36]

* * *

It is tempting to imagine how the small town of Leonberg would have been touched by a different atmosphere during the five years in which Sibylle resided there, from 1609 to 1614. An active as well as cultivated woman, she hired staff, commissioned tableware as well as a bathtub from Katharina Kepler's son Christoph, and entertained her family and guests with rarities ranging from the king of Sumatra's decorative handkerchief to ivories, enormous snails made from mother-of-pearl, as well as a porcelain watering can.[37] She built up

Figure 17 Duchess Sybille's garden in its recent reconstruction © Photograph: Christoph Rublack

her pharmacy and recruited her formidable widowed friend Maria Andreae. Maria had been revered by her husband, Jacob Andreae, a Lutheran clergyman passionate about alchemy, mechanical invention, and the arts. Jacob's experiments nearly ruined the family, but had attracted the attention of Duke Frederick I and brought Sibylle into contact with the older, determined, and highly organized Maria.

Maria Andreae's son Johann Valentin claimed in 1604 to have written *The Chymical Wedding*, a famous Rosicrucian millenarian and alchemical manifesto, and continued to develop far-reaching Christian reform ideas. Under his mother's influence, it integrated herbal medicine by quoting the Sermon on the Mount: 'O blessed are those who work among curative herbs and learn to have faith in God, who feeds and clothes the flowers without any effort on their part'. Maria championed a more sensuous musical strand of Lutheranism, which tempered admonishing sermons by joyous communal singing about natural delights. This strand is exemplified in Paul Gehrhardt's extraordinarily successful hymn 'Go out, My Heart and Look for Joy'. This uplifting Lutheran ode to summer plants ends in an appeal to God to let believers become ever more 'green' until they reach paradise. Such spiritual commitments already led Andreae to believe that a flower's 'pleasing perfume' united people with God.[38]

In 1607, Sibylle had appointed Maria as court pharmacist in Stuttgart, where she soon became known as 'mother of the poor'. 'All of spring', Johann Valentin later remembered, she had spent 'collecting herbs and distilling waters, in summer she made condiments, and the rest of the year she prepared salts and powders for the benefit of the poor.'[39] Maria followed Sibylle to her new residence.[40]

In Leonberg, these two widows ground, mixed, and distilled ingredients from minerals, plants, animals, and humans, ranging from quinces and their home-grown lemons to human hearts, from honey to wolf balm, dog balm, and human balm (fat collected from executed bodies), from 'small sugar brought from England' to golden buttons and 'seven little pieces from a skull'.[41] The castle stood at one end of the town's tightly arranged layout, on the same level as its citizen's houses, and thus was part of what Leonberg life was now about. Sibylle even got Schickhardt, the architect, to build a through passage directly from the castle to the town church, which she furnished with twenty-three paintings and a chamber-pot chair. The tall, well-attired woman in her forties would attend church services seated on a balcony above the laity, and help to embellish the church. Her and Maria's dignified presence must have strengthened the sense that widows did well to be resourceful on their own behalf as well as on behalf of others.

This new life would not extend into old age. Sibylle died unexpectedly in November 1614. Her corpse was instantly treated with sweet-smelling myrrh and a 'joyous' balm oil 'of the Holy Ghost', to renew her flesh and brighten her eyes for when she would meet the

Lord. She was dressed in velvet and laid on a bed of the same cloth. Despite the season, a wreath made from 'all sorts of flowers' was shaped into a cross and put in her hands. Her daily prayer-book was placed to her right. Scattered across her wooden coffin were 'various flowers that were to be had'.[42]

3

THE YEAR OF THE WITCHES

———⊸∞∞⊶———

D uring these same years, Leonberg faced unsettling changes. In 1608, Württemberg positioned itself at the forefront of a defensive military league, named the Protestant Union. The union consisted of Strasbourg, Ulm, and Nuremberg as well as German principalities, including those of the Palatinate and Württemberg. Further revenue to support the union had to be scraped together from the duchy's population of 450,000. As in other towns, Leonberg's population had increased, but the increase came from poor people who often did not own their homes. By 1613, only 286 taxpayers were registered in a local population of over 1,000. In 1608 and 1615, moreover, prices rose dramatically after bad harvests.

Frederick had been succeeded by his son John Frederick, who attempted to appease the local representatives of the Protestant Union, only to risk offending them further by entering the union. The estates and some of his own councillors questioned whether it was right to maintain a military union with Calvinists, and, moreover, whether this was sure to be a defensive league. How and for how long could large armies be afforded? Such discussions lay at the crux of Germany's perennial problem of providing for common defence. The estates disliked the spiralling costs of the Stuttgart court as well as John Frederick's occasional arrogant remarks. One document reveals how the duke ridiculed merchants for their *man-camento di cervello*, lack of brains.

In addition, this well-travelled ruler refused to wear 'traditional', brave, and 'manly' German dress, as his estates demanded. Rather, he took part in the century's dress revolution, which provocatively changed the look of the time. Widely cut, exceedingly comfortable, longer tubular breeches and doublets, galoshes, and oversized felt hats with large ostrich feathers and golden hatbands made far fewer demands on body shapes. These new fashions clad elite men in generous soft fabrics or leather. Gloves, shiny sleeves, golden stockings, sparkling silver buttons, laced ruffs and cuffs, and clusters of brightly coloured silk ribbons were attached for a sumptuous effect, or taken off for popular sportive pastimes ranging from games of balloon (an early form of volleyball) to tennis and pell-mall (a form of croquet). A variety of detachable beards and long hair added to this flowing, confident style, which made the wearer's deportment far more relaxed. This was the 'French mode', sported by *Messieurs* from Flanders to Frankfurt, and adopted particularly passionately by leading Protestants eager to distinguish themselves from constricting Spanish styles.[1]

John Frederick continued his father's role as member of an international elite. He defended his expensive support of alchemical experiments. Such matters were too elevated for the estates to understand, he contended, especially if they kept objecting that alchemists had bad manners and were more likely to attract divine punishment than produce any gold. God revealed his almighty power to this young duke through nature and transformations of matter, as well as books.[2] For nine years after 1609, until the outbreak of the Thirty Years War, the estates did not assemble for discussions, and yet agreed to successive loans which went far beyond what could ever be repaid.

Stuttgart now witnessed the most elaborate court festivities it had ever seen, intended to assert the supremacy of Württemberg's dynasty and confidence in Germany's place among leading nations.[3] During these years, German Protestants strengthened foreign diplomatic relations with Catholic France and Protestant England, which, conveniently, could be made jealous of each other while at the same time both continuing to compete for power with Spain (which could not be allowed to 'master' Europe as well as its possessions in the New World). The marriage of James I's only daughter, Elizabeth Stuart, to the young, powerful Protestant Prince Frederick of the Palatinate in 1613 appeared as a milestone in cementing a European Protestant alliance across the Lutheran–Calvinist divide (Figure 18). It was eulogized as a marriage of the rivers Thames and Rhine, sufficiently strong to submerge 'the pride of Tiber' in the whorish city of Rome.[4] The vigorous Palatinate prince soon was even celebrated as a lion capable of finally finishing off the Habsburg eagle as it kept on striving for universal power and its subjects' servitude, fuelled by its supplies of New World silver. Only readiness to defend Protestantism against Catholics, according to one pamphlet in 1616, could avert the fate of Germans being reduced to 'Spanish sodomites', 'epicurean Italians', or, worse still, to suffer the same plight as indigenous noblemen and commoners colonized in the Indies.[5]

In that same year, the Württemberg court published a lengthy account of spectacular festivities and translated it into English, principally for the benefit of Elizabeth Stuart, whom the modestly sized Protestant courts were anxious to impress.[6] Strikingly portrayed by Nicholas Hilliard with loose, barely combed long golden locks, a forthright gaze, and deep décolletage, the young princess had entered Germany exuding confidence. Her *'blessed presence'*, the Württemberg account keenly claimed, had in fact been the *'chiefe*

Figure 18 Frederick, Elector Palatine, and Elizabeth Stuart as a young couple, engraving by Renold Elstrack, 1613–14, 26,3 × 20 cm © Trustees of the British Museum

cause of the shews'. The account further flattered Elizabeth by recounting the charming entry of three English ladies in low-cut bodices, which demonstrated that '*Womankind doe excel mankind as farre as heaven exelleth earth*'. Württemberg courtiers had become convinced that England greatly esteemed its women.[7]

Even so, at its core Stuttgart's '*triumphall*' 1616 show celebrated Germany for its technological invention of guns and printing as well as its contribution to education and the arts. It featured knights asserting the need for German unity by proposing that those spreading contentiousness and sedition should be killed, before finally cautioning that the love of a country needed to prevail over political considerations.[8] A person dressed up as a monster 'caught on a rope' symbolized a zealous Spaniard, hot-headed Jesuit, and Capuchin, disquieting the German nation through discord.[9] All this illustrated the tension between chivalric heroism, which so powerfully infused anti-Jesuit and anti-Spanish propaganda, and a defensive language of patriotic concord. It reflected long-standing, uneasy debates about the purposes of the Union in the Stuttgart court.[10] The show promoted its own diplomatic goal: to regain a unified Germany without risking a civil war.

Even the most patriotic Protestants, however, were deeply aware of their place in the wider contemporary world of complicated confessional allegiances across Europe. Given the smaller German states' lack of resources, any larger military effort against the Spanish depended on foreign help. German liberties, they realized, could only be preserved through the English and French. Both languages were required and spoken at court, rather than Latin. Benjamin Bouwinghausen von Wallmerode, John Frederick's long-term leading councillor and international diplomat, gained himself rare French regard as '*le plus intelligent*' at negotiations. He regularly corresponded with colleagues and informants from Paris, Prague, London, Florence, Amsterdam, Brussels, Strasbourg, and The

Hague. Wallmerode was the key person to head repeated missions to French and English rulers. These missions devastatingly failed to understand James I's political strategies to steer away from war prospects as religious conflict intensified. But then, few seemed to comprehend that James hoped, up to 1622, that a Spanish match for his son Charles would solve conflict on the Continent.[11]

Keen to impress visitors from afar, John Frederick passionately pursued an elaborate building project of grottoes, complete with an organ, for which quintals of Indian and Mediterranean sea-shells were transported to the land-locked duchy.[12] He employed a full-time grotto-maker as well as a Venetian gondoliere for his artificial lakes. A mounting collection of curiosities consisted of countless treasures from India, particularly expensive decorative pieces made from crystal and semi-precious stones, which, for viewers at the time, united nature and art in the most inspiring manner. The collection also included a whole human skin and heathen gods, while high up on the ceiling hung crocodiles, turtles, and fish.[13]

Lutheran festivities continued. In 1616, a candlelit 'ballet of four continents' dazzled its audience, as twelve dancers clad in national costume suddenly leapt out of large, square papier-mâché heads. Next, another group of dancers appeared, each with 400 pieces of mirror-glass sewn into French-style costumes, and led into a cour-ante in the newest dance style that lasted until midnight. Fine food arrived from Germany and the Mediterranean. Some of it was displayed as elaborate 'show-food', for decorative purposes and designed to appeal to the emotions of any man with a heroic heart, such as an arrangement depicting a mountain on the top of which stood a Turk who had captured a Christian maiden in desperate need of rescue by St George.[14] During the eleven days of festivities and political meetings that took place in April 1616, Germany's foremost Protestant princes and their guests consumed

100 oxen and 480 calves as well as 2,000 measures of grain—a full 3,400 hectolitres.[15]

* * *

Meanwhile, life for ordinary citizens away from court life was harsh. The winter of 1615 had been particularly severe. Philipp Hainhofer, the Augsburg art-dealer, reported that many of the Württemberg vines had been killed by frost 'in the mountains as well as in the valleys'. Cartloads of firewood were transported into Stuttgart every day to combat the excessive cold. In Leonberg, there was no pharmacy to replace Sibylle's and Maria's castle remedies after Sibylle's death in 1614. During the sixteenth century, dukes decreed that there should be four doctors and pharmacists in the whole territory, but Leonberg was not important enough to get one of them.[16] Thus, in 1620, alms accounts would note expenses for items such as 'Maria, blessed Hans Kepplins' little daughter who lives at the old potter woman', who was sent 'two flasks of sorcerer's balm' from the pharmacy in Pforzheim, a town situated 30 kilometres away.[17]

Leonbergers as a whole saw few opportunities to expand their income in these difficult years, so much so that by 1619 some finally complained that their town lay too 'far away from any roads' and trade opportunities. To make matters worse, in the winter of 1618, moreover, the duke reserved a rich harvest of acorns and other pannage in Leonberg's forests exclusively for the wild boars he intended to hunt. In addition, he had constructed scenic lakes on the upper reaches of the local River Glems to create a more pleasing environment for his fellow Protestant princes. Leonberg's gatekeepers were even instructed to check whether people secretly carried acorns into town, to feed to their pigs, as well-fed pigs were an integral part of their attempt to diversify nutrition in winter and not just depend on grain.[18]

Despite such constraints caused by hunting game and limited opportunities for economic expansion, Württembergers—while still suffering during crisis years—coped remarkably well in comparison to other European regions. Tight communal regulations continued to protect a population of small-scale farmers, who survived through a sufficient supply of protein-rich oats, spelt, and eggs.[19]

A measure of the success of this regulated life within tight ecological boundaries is that in Leonberg, on average, only seven or eight people depended on civic alms. In 1615–18, the man entrusted with looking after the poor himself received regular alms of bread and money. So did two widows, two men and two married women. When crisis struck due to severe weather in 1614 and 1615, nearly half of Leonberg's population had to borrow from the town granary to survive, but that granary was full. Between fifty and seventy needy children were fed twice a day with gruel and bread, '*brei und brot*'. Firewood was freely provided, or sold at a reduced price to anyone who needed it.

In the nearby village of Gerlingen, by contrast, seventy-five people received bread, or bread and money—even young couples who were known to be 'hard working' and had children. Lutherans considered that, after the Fall, humans were destined for a life of hard work to sustain their families, communities, and the deserving poor. They absolutely abhorred laziness. Even so, alms extended to the likes of 'Hans Franck, his wife and child who are just wicked do-no-goods when it comes to work', with a grudging acceptance that such people could not be left to starve.

Next among the poor of Gerlingen was the numerous but surprisingly diverse group of widows, including:

> Jerg Weber's widow with three small children
> Hans Vogt's widow with one child
> Agatha Hanns Sautter's widow, an old woman
> . . .
> Stephan Koch's widow, a young wicked woman.[20]

In 1615, in addition to seventy-five destitute people, more than a hundred Gerlingen inhabitants complained of their 'great, unbearable poverty'. They claimed that they had tried to sell their wine or land, which nobody had wanted to buy.

Another village in the Leonberg district even registered several middle-aged artisans who did not own any land. These included 'Hans Reisch, a tailor aged forty with a wife and six small children, owns nothing'. A man named Philipp Schwilckh was described as a 'stone-mason aged sixty with a wife and two strong boys, has nothing except for his craft'.[21] Elsewhere, the list included the lame, people who were known to have been poor for more than twenty years, and those considered very old, for example one man aged eighty.

A final glimpse into this year of crisis is offered by Heimsheim, the only other town in the district apart from Leonberg where the prosecution of witches had begun. The magistrates wrote reports complaining about the 'expensive and troublesome times'. Yet in Heimsheim only eight couples with their children, as well as two widows and an orphaned girl, received alms.[22] Heimsheim lay on a trade route to Speyer and by 1607 earned 469 florins in custom tolls, whereas Leonberg constantly remained in the last one-third of Württemberg's list of income from tolls and, in the same year, collected only 148 florins.[23]

Witchcraft accusations, therefore, were not made in the poorest areas and cannot be explained as a simple scapegoating mechanism in villages by those who felt under particular strain. Accusations concentrated on Heimsheim and Leonberg, the two more urban communities in the district, which evidently felt the challenges of the crisis, but avoided destitution on any significant scale. Leonberg's alms chests even stretched to cover medical welfare, as in the case of an ill widow who was sent to a Stuttgart doctor and then on to a medical practitioner in Wildbad, a regional spa-town.[24]

* * *

Katharina, of course, needed no alms. Yet in that critical winter of 1614 her second-born son, Heinrich the Younger, unexpectedly returned home, impoverished and ill after twenty-five years of service as soldier and imperial guard in Prague. Despite the season, he demanded meat, became angry with his mother when she had trouble providing any, and was the first to publicly slander her as a witch. In the freezing February of 1615, this dissolute son died at his sister's house, in the Heumaden vicarage.

But the word 'witch' had been spoken, and some had heard it. On a hot August day later that year, Katharina faced the accusations. It all began as the glazier, his wife Ursula Reinbold, and her brother, drank wine with Lukas Einhorn, Leonberg's ducal governor. The wine had been fetched from the large, cool cellar below the vast chamber of his four-storey residence. This *Amtshaus* was the tallest building in town, off the market square and close to the upper gate, made even more imposing by its elevated position (Figure 19). Ursula and her brother were sure that Katharina had bewitched her and made her lame. 'Nothing is gained by waiting around for any longer,' one of them was said to have commented. Next, the glazier's wife demanded: 'That Kepler woman has to take her spell away before I die.'

Leonberg's ducal governors had thus far always been wealthy local citizens, whose arbitration cushioned the demands of state regulations and reforms. Lukas Einhorn, a mature man of around fifty, was different. Newly appointed in November 1613, his contract set out how he was to conduct himself as a ducal servant, and to recognize the widowed Duchess Sibylle's authority. Einhorn was to confer with either her or her stewards in any matter of doubt and follow her advice before sending reports to Stuttgart's ducal chancellery. He was to inform Sibylle about any difficulties in matters concerning those who had to be formally accepted as new citizens, and was ordered to evaluate any petition that common people might send to her or her son. Sibylle received quarterly reports on any income, and she herself discussed how wine and grain grown on her land should best be sold. Before holding a local court session, Einhorn needed to

Figure 19 The ducal governor's house in Leonberg, where Katharina was first confronted with the accusation that she was a witch © Photograph: Christoph Rublack

check whether Sibylle wished to send a representative. Like every other governor, Einhorn also swore to be impartial in his judgement about poor or rich, as well as to those he knew, never to accept any gifts, to help protect or extend ducal income, and to respect and publicize Württemberg laws.[25]

Einhorn's office thus had been envisaged as tightly interlinked with Sibylle's position of authority. He was bound in person to her, and Leonberg's castle was located only a minute's walk from his house. Sibylle's death in November 1614, only one year after his appointment, removed this direct layer of communication and control. Burckhardt Stickel, the long-standing upper ducal governor, who had made good after his earlier career as a soldier, had died in 1613. As a result, Einhorn suddenly enjoyed more independence than ever before.

Thus, soon after Sibylle's death, as Einhorn settled into his position and the sense deepened of a prolonged crisis of food shortages in Württemberg, he decided to take accusations of witchcraft seriously in the entire district. So did the local judges. In December 1615, four days before Christmas, Leonbergers watched women from nearby Heimsheim being executed as witches. The executioner beheaded four women (including a mother and her twenty-year-old daughter) with his sword and afterwards burned them. Next, Einhorn pursued four other local females whom the executed women had named as accomplices. During spring 1616, the pastor's widow of Heimsheim was tortured and executed, aged eighty-three, followed by two female pig-herds.[26] Four further witchcraft trials and two executions followed in March and May 1616. During the sixteen years of Einhorn's office, from 1613 to 1629, he led prosecutions which ended in nine death sentences for alleged witchcraft. Seven of these women were executed in 1615–16. It appears that none of these trials were administered in consultation with the ducal chancellery in Stuttgart, as the law required.[27] Only three further executions for witchcraft are recorded in the district's entire history. Einhorn aspired to enforce safety and order in a district which to him, and others, evidently appeared to be under threat.

* * *

Württemberg witnessed no mass trials, as theologians officially held that witches were not capable of *actual* harm, although individual women might still be executed for their pact with the devil. Even so, fears about the effects of witchcraft reached a climax in these years. In Sindelfingen, just 17 kilometres south of Leonberg, another newly appointed ducal governor oversaw nineteen witchcraft trials between May 1615 and October 1616. Twelve women lost their lives, including the sister of a local magistrate. The local executioner became experienced in torturing these special suspects. His equipment at first seemed to magically collapse when he used it on a small, lean old woman, but after more successful applications she confessed fully.[28]

Einhorn, moreover, responded to sustained pressure from Ursula Reinbold's well-connected family. Despite Lutheran preaching to the contrary, powerful communal groups still alleged that witches caused real harm, and their accusations remained a motor of Württemberg trials. Witchcraft was used to explain misfortunes and the shattering experience of *malum*, of something grave, disorientating, and out of the ordinary happening in a person's life.

Ursula Reinbold was desperate about her chronic illness. She had been born in 1568, or thereabouts, and became a citizen of Leonberg through her first husband, Leonhart Holtzing, in 1590 (citizenship could be conferred through marriage). She was three years older than Johannes Kepler, who was himself well into the later stages of middle age.[29] At the beginning of her engagement with her second husband, Reinbold, she had also had contact with Jerg Zieher, a young coppersmith, and a fight between the two men had resulted in their being punished by the town authorities.[30] Ursula's standing was nonetheless increased by the fact that two of her brothers had ducal employment and consequently had personal connections to the court. In 1616, her brother Urban Kräutlin was appointed as doctor for the duke's younger brother Frederick Achilles, and practised as a barber-surgeon in Tübingen.[31] Ursula's other brother served as Leonberg's forest administrator.

This was a significant post. Leonberg's forests were among the most extensive and centrally located in the country. Einhorn and the administrator knew each other well. In fact, the party of Einhorn, Reinbold, Ursula, and her brother—just before they confronted Katharina Kepler—had met in the forest administrator's house together with Frederick Achilles. Einhorn and Ursula's brother closely cooperated to manage the forest as a resource by maximizing revenues, controlling theft, unlawful felling and poaching, as well as keeping count of stags, deer, and hundreds of wild boars and sows for organized hunts. By the end of Duke Frederick's reign, revenue from forests in the district had nearly doubled and the collection of fines from thieves was at an all-time high.[32]

These gains reveal the greater efficiency achieved in local government through closely controlled bureaucratic appointments. Ursula's personal connections, in turn, helped her to pressurize Einhorn as a governor who solely owed his position to the duke and had already shown that he was happy to be tough on alleged witches. Though he should have noted the accusation, informed the local court, and conducted a formal interrogation, Einhorn responded to Ursula's plea by sending someone straight away to fetch Katharina from her small home and ask her to see him at his governor's house.

That summer afternoon in 1615, when she first heard Reinbold's accusation against her, changed Katharina's life. The sixty-eight-year-old widow would have followed Einhorn's messenger uphill through a few cobbled streets in the August heat. Standing in the large reception room of the governor's house, she saw Urban lose control as he shouted at her: 'You are a witch and you gave my sister a witches' brew, look how she is suffering. Now you will work your magic again, but this time to help her.' If she had cast a spell, then she knew how to undo it. Katharina reported that Urban Kräutlin *next* half drew his sword.

According to her family's account, which was never contested, Katharina trembled in shock, but stayed composed enough to respond that it was not legal and right to confront her with such allegations on her own. She was a very old woman and needed protection. How could she help Ursula if she had done nothing against her? God was the right doctor. This whole affair was of the devil. Next time there were any charges against her, she would like to hear them in front of a proper court.

Einhorn then cautioned that violence would not lead anywhere. Urban put back his sword, but suddenly pushed his sister towards Katharina, pleading with her to take back the spell. In desperation, he said he was sure that Ursula suffered from magic, as none of his treatments alleviated her pain. Even so, Leonberg's governor then concluded these emotional scenes by allowing Katharina to go home (Figure 20).

* * *

Walking back home in bright daylight, Katharina no doubt felt fearful and angry. She was unable to protest her innocence on her own; she needed men in the family to step in, or to use male citizens appointed to represent widows in legal affairs. Katharina Kepler immediately informed her son Christoph, then aged twenty-eight, as well as pastor Binder, her only son-in-law. Instantly, they accused Ursula Reinbold of defamation at the civic court on Katharina's behalf in order to stop the rumour from spreading.

Defamation charges were commonly brought to the civic judges' attention. But in Katharina's case the matter went beyond verbal abuse and the ducal governor himself had been led to act in a

Figure 20 Governor Einhorn's coat of arms; *Einhorn* means unicorn. © Photograph: Ulinka Rublack

questionable manner. Einhorn, unsurprisingly, dragged out the process of arranging a hearing, while Katharina's family remained anxious that Katharina and they themselves should be protected from any suspicion of witchcraft. Christoph got involved in a serious, bloody fight with several young men in Eltingen and, on 12 October 1615, was punished alongside others. As was common, any possible insult against someone's family meant that violence between men flared up like wildfire.[33]

In late October 1615, Margaretha Kepler asked for her brother Johannes's help. He only received the letter in late December, and wrote to the Leonberg magistrate on 2 January 1616. Johannes Kepler immediately instructed that it might be best for his mother to leave Württemberg and stay with him in Linz.

* * *

Nothing further happened for a long, uncomfortable period, during which Einhorn waited for further evidence. On 22 October 1616, he finally sent a letter to John Frederick, his 'illustrious, highborn gracious duke and lord'. This was the first time that the duke and his chancellery had heard about Katharina Kepler. Einhorn reported her as a potential witch who had harmed not only the glazier's wife but also local children. This complied with the Empire's Law Code, the Carolina, which demanded that several eye-witnesses needed to have seen a suspect act, and that the accused was commonly thought to have a bad reputation. Einhorn wrote that a poor day-labourer's wife had very recently complained that Heinrich Kepler's widow had hit her twelve-year-old daughter on the arm. This girl had helped the brick-maker's daughter to carry bricks and limestone to the kiln. Katharina had passed by. She hit the girl's arm, and the girl's pain had increased by the hour. Now the child was unable to move one finger. The mother had not yet accused Katharina of witchcraft or sorcery, but had requested an initial inquiry.

The governor was at pains to stress his careful procedure. First, he had verified the twelve-year-old girl's state, and then examined Katharina. He had called on the brick-maker's girl as witness and asked her parents to attend. Katharina denied the charge, but the brick-maker's girl had immediately run up to her parents to inform them about what had happened. The day-labourer's daughter was known as pious and good. She was the kind of girl who would never annoy anyone, or lie. The couple's hard-working boy had already perished. Now the parents wondered whether this 'Keppler-woman' had killed him.

Einhorn's report summed up what he knew about Katharina. He thought that she was over seventy years old and that her husband had left her twenty-eight years ago. Surprisingly to us, he wrote (presumably mistakenly) that she still deemed Heinrich to be alive. She had long been under 'great suspicion' as a witch. The glazier's wife had alleged, 'and desired to die on this', that Katharina had given her a harmful drink four years previously and that she had suffered 'inhuman pains' ever since. Einhorn had wanted to interrogate witnesses the previous Monday. However, as the day-labourer's complaint added to the case he had moved the date. He had wanted to report on events to the duke first, but meanwhile had examined Katharina, threatening her with imprisonment.

She had not confessed anything '*in the slightest*', and so he'd had to let her go, only for her to immediately return with her son Christoph, a pewterer of good repute. She pleaded that he should not believe her opponents. Yet as Einhorn had told Christoph about the further allegations, Katharina's youngest son had 'answered with a great sigh, by God, he wished he could move away from his mother out of town over night – the governor should act as he needed to'. The governor in all likelihood invented these words, as Christoph by all accounts was fully prepared to defend his mother at this time. Immediately after the family had left, Katharina had entered a third time, to beg that Einhorn should not report anything to the duke or else just let the matter drag on a bit. She promised him a beautiful silver cup, before leaving Leonberg to stay with her daughter and son-in-law in his parish in Heumaden, near Stuttgart.[34]

After only two days, the ducal councillors replied with precise instructions: Einhorn was to find Katharina Kepler, imprison her, and, after a day of rest, interrogate her about the incident with the day-labourer's girl and also about why she had left Leonberg. The pastor was to thoroughly examine her piety. Einhorn was to report further at this point and to await advice.[35]

Einhorn acted on these orders immediately. Yet the news was disappointing. A local man, who had just been to Heumaden, reported that Katharina might have left for 'Linz or Prague, where she has a son'. Einhorn suggested that his colleague in Stuttgart should be told to prevent Katharina's escape, especially as the day-labourer's girl was now in a very poor state.

In response, the ducal council immediately gave orders to apprehend Katharina Kepler and take her to Leonberg to imprison her.[36] But, by then, Katharina was gone. Now, more than ever, she depended on her children's support.

4

KEPLER'S STRATEGIES

—— ∞∞∞ ——

If Johannes Kepler had needed to learn anything fast in life, it was how to cultivate support and refute his opponents. He mastered both from an astonishingly young age. In April 1594, aged twenty-three, he had arrived in Graz, a small but impressive Austrian town with elegant arcaded buildings in Italian Renaissance styles, a castle, and famous fortifications against the Ottomans. Kepler once climbed the Schöckl, a nearby 1,445-metre-high mountain on the southern rim of the Alps, which afforded him panoramic views of Hungary and Turkish lands. This was Graz's 'magic mountain'—said to produce hail if anyone threw a stone into its cavities. In fact, a storm had broken loose over Graz as Kepler ascended and he wondered whether he might have irritated the mountain.[1]

Weather conditions interested Kepler as manifestations of the earth as animate organism. The earth could respond to cosmological changes as well, by moving air or producing dense vapours. As Kepler would explain in Book IV of his *Harmony*, just as humans expel winds from the rear, the earth expelled subterranean fires. 'For as the body puts out hair on the surface of its skin,' he wrote, in a passage that Galileo would pour scorn on:

So the Earth puts out plants and trees; and lice are born on them in the former case, caterpillars, cicadas, and various insects and sea monsters in the latter. And as the body displays tears, mucus, and earwax, and also in places lymphs from pustules on the face, so the Earth displays amber and bitumen; as the bladder pours out urine, so the mountains pour out rivers; as the body produces excrement of sulphurous odour and farts which can even be set on fire, Earth produces sulphur, subterranean fires, thunder, and lightning; and as blood is generated in the veins of an animate being, and with it sweat, which is thrust outside the body, so in the veins of the Earth are generated metals and fossils, and rainy vapour.[2]

God's macrocosm, too, was alive and potent. Almanacs linked routine medical treatments, such as blood-letting, to planetary constellations, and people were broadly aware that moon phases influenced the experience of physical pain. Cosmic occurrences, moreover, were understood as God's messages for everyone, and all this engendered interest in observing the heavens among the population at large. Formally, Kepler was employed at the Protestant estates' seminary school for sons of the aristocracy. Yet he soon followed his predecessor's footsteps and offered the estates a calendar with astrological prognostications, advice on when to undergo blood-letting, and weather predictions. After receiving an extra payment for this, he requested a further reward after supplying another calendar in the following year.[3]

This made the estates suspicious about whether or not its school kept Kepler busy enough. During his second year of service, inspectors established that Kepler had at first had few students, but now he had none. Kepler did his best to assure them that aristocratic men were, in principle, destined for the higher mathematical studies that he offered. They did not need to earn a living. This instilled in them contempt for mundane earthly matters and 'imbued' them with a 'special, hidden, miraculous power'. This power might well remain hidden in young people, especially as they struggled with difficult equations, but it would be awakened later in their lives. Luckily for Kepler, the inspectors indeed blamed young people's dislike of mathematics for the lack of pupils for his classes. They commented that he should broaden his teaching to other subjects and be congratulated on his excellent calendars.[4]

On the back of this somewhat reassuring report Kepler returned to Württemberg for half a year, on full pay. He hoped to gain employment back in his homeland and to benefit from a settled religious and political environment. Confessional tension had been rife in Graz for more than a decade and in 1590 had led to violent civic riots by Lutherans against their Catholic overlord. Ever since Kepler's arrival, the adjunct territory of Upper Austria had witnessed peasant uprisings. It was feared that popular disorder might spread. In 1596, the Jesuit-educated Archduke Ferdinand II would reach maturity, and his strict Catholic views were well known.

Kepler embarked on a programme designed to impress and get closer to the Württemberg duke. He first presented Frederick with a prognostication of weather and astrological phenomena for the year 1596, and for this he received a reward. Next, he successfully requested a regular place among the 700 people who daily ate at court, although at the dinner table for middle and lower ducal office-holders, with its separate cook.[5] Having gained a foot in the door of the court, Kepler kept on pleading for patronage and with astonishing speed became a new astronomer.

Hence, in February 1596, the young teacher confidently wrote to Frederick that, after much hard work, God had granted him a 'major insight'. He was going to publish it, but to please the duke also wished to turn it into an engraving of a large silver toasting cup with precious stones symbolizing planets. His letter was accompanied by a drawing. The cup's brilliant as well as witty design fitted courtly etiquette and turned Copernicus's idea of a sun-centred universe into a liquified performance with seven taps. The moon connected to water, while the sun was meant to radiate as a 'delicious acqua vitae' from the centre of the cup, which was to be subdivided into the six orbits, 'that is from the sun's body, which floats *in centro*'.[6] Saturn was 'old wine or beer', Mars was Vermouth. This perfectly suited the taste of Duchess Sibylle, too, who spent much of her time distilling liqueurs and perfecting recipes for the most special aqua vitae (Figure 21).

To keep his name persistently lodged in the duke's mind, Kepler next dedicated a number of poems to Frederick. By July, he judged that the time had come to present the duke with an extraordinarily ambitious scheme: to construct an 'artificial world machine'. It would be magnificently decorated with no less than 1,022 stars.[7] A large, open model of the heavens, this machine was to demonstrate how God had laid out a Copernican cosmos geometrically through the exactitude and harmony of regularly proportioned and numbered shapes.

The model presented the theory which lay at the heart of Kepler's first book, published in Tübingen by autumn of that same year. Enticingly entitled *The Secret of the Universe*, it was distributed by his university teachers, as well as by Kepler himself, to men of influence and scholars of rank—even to the distant Tycho Brahe and Galileo Galilei. An elegant fold-out plate (which had been extremely challenging to produce in print) depicted Kepler's model, and carried a personal dedication for the Württemberg duke as a champion of learning (Figure 22).[8] Flattered and evidently pleased, Frederick sent Kepler a gift of thirty florins, his most significant reward yet.[9]

* * *

Part of the mystery Kepler wished to reveal was that the cosmos presented an image of the Holy Trinity. Rather than an unstable, random swirl of matter, he identified a fixed sun in the middle of the cosmos which symbolized God the Father, around whom everything

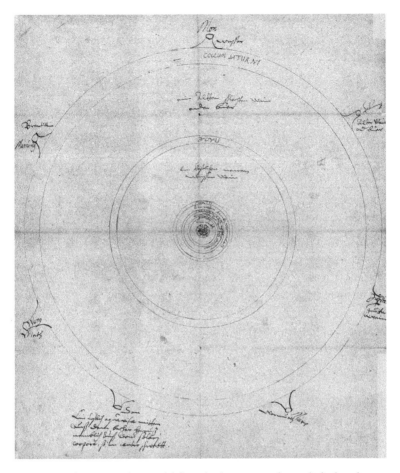

Figure 21 Johannes Kepler, model for a drinking cup with taps linked to the sun in the centre ('a delicious aqua vitae', strong, distilled liquor to revive the spirits), the moon (water) and the planets linked to different types of alcohol, sent to Frederick of Württemberg. Cod. Math. 28, Bl. 2a © Stuttgart, Württembergische Landesbibliothek

else rotated. The sphere of the fixed stars was equivalent to Jesus, and the fixed space in between, he argued, was akin to the Holy Spirit. Instead of becoming a pastor with a parish, the Tübingen graduate turned himself into a priest of the Book of Nature (Figure 23).[10]

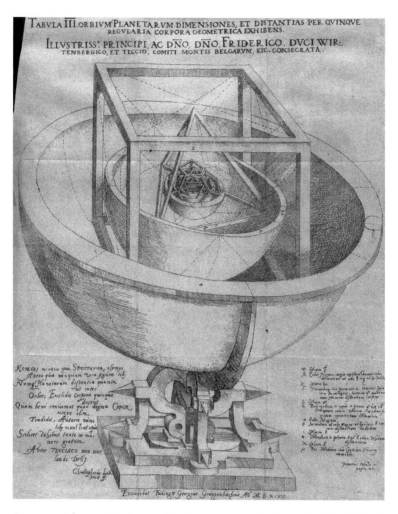

Figure 22 Johannes Kepler, model of a sun-centred universe for Frederick of Württemberg, first presented with explanations on an elaborate fold-out plate in his *The Secret of the Universe*. The model showed that the orbits of the planets resembled the irregular distances from the sun that would be obtained if their 'spheres' were inscribed within and circumscribed by the five regular solids Plato had described in his geometry (cube, tetrahedron, dodecahedron, icosahedron, octahedron). © Cambridge University Library

IMAGO
Clarissimi Viri, Dn.

MICHAELIS MÆSTLINI, MATHEMATI-
carum Artium, in inclyta Tubingensi Academia Professoris:
Anno Christiano 1596. Ætatis 45.

Distichon προσωνομασικόν.
QVIS SICVT DOMINVS, diam profitendo Mathesin?
Non PINGVIS, sed vis mentis acuta tuæ est.
EIVS?

Figure 23 A depiction of Kepler's Tübingen astronomy professor and most important early patron Michael Mästlin in 1596, aged forty-five. Mästlin was a contemporary of Kepler's mother, and Johannes during his early years attempted to cultivate a filial relationship with him. © Cambridge University Library, M. 5.49

The model was not about regularities in a narrowly mechanistic sense. Increasingly, the cosmos appeared to Kepler as a product of God's joyous, intelligent play with ratios of dimensions of geometrical figures as well as physics. Nothing was random. If God had made the five distances between the six planets unequal, this was because he had measured them out with the exact shapes of the five regular solids, which varied in proportion. Irregularity thus resolved into geometrical regularity after all. Humans could understand this delightful harmony through adequate guidance, as they themselves had been formed in the image of God. He had implanted in mankind an ability to respond to divinely created geometrical and numerical archetypes.

From this followed a whole philosophy of social order. If regularities patterned the world, so they could pattern polities and minds. Like the cosmos, nature was God's image, too, and hence imbued with the same features of regularity and play. Whilst regularity led to clear demonstrations and causal analytical explanations, God's play, however, invited marvelling, collecting, deciphering, and more speculative interpretation.[11]

Yet to succeed at courts, a young astronomer required not only a powerful intellect and vision, but also books, ink, piety, and perfect manners. To communicate his ideas, he needed to be a craftsman with manual skill, visual and technical adeptness, as well as have the ability to talk to makers of ingenious machines and take inspiration from their practical, applied conceptual knowledge. He required their help to turn his ideas into concrete objects: this tended to impress dukes far more than highly specialized astronomical books in Latin. Thus, after completing his writing, Kepler not only laboriously crafted a paper model of his artful invention, but himself used a lathe to build the model at the same time as lobbying Duke Frederick to commission a model in metal, and entering into years of negotiations to identify suitable goldsmiths or clock-makers in southern Germany.

Kepler's age was characterized by great enthusiasm for new mechanical arts. These were seen to spur on the religious deciphering of a
perfect cosmic order in God's providentially designed universe.
Kepler was not unusual in aspiring to more than being a mere
mathematician. His aim to reveal God's cosmos and provide guidance for rulers was related to a broader shift in the social and political
context of his profession.[12] Mathematicians and craftsmen engaged
in mechanical, optical, and sound experiments in their intricate
model-making. These arts flourished in Augsburg and Nuremberg,
the two south-German Imperial Cities, and they became world
centres for technical invention and reliability during Kepler's life.

Kepler thought of the heavens as a divinely crafted machine
pervaded by the same spirit as the whole 'world machine'. The
heavens were operated by 'a single, very simple magnetic power,
just as in a clockwork (machine) all the movements from a simple
weight'. The beauty of such physical operations could be demonstrated geometrically and mathematically.[13] If God was partly a
superb mechanic, then the skills of exceptional craftspeople might
get one closer to understanding the principles of physics. Kepler in
turn kept an eye on what counted as the most advanced projects, and
by 1598 reported to Frederick on celestial globes and clockwork.
Everyone knew about the clocks that Francisco Turriano had made
for Charles V. Landgrave Wilhelm of Hesse also owned a celestial
clockwork and Duke August of Saxony owned an even more beautiful one. Kepler also referred to the second Strasbourg Cathedral
clock, completed in 1574, which indicated solar and lunar cycles,
calculated eclipses, and had an automatic cock at the top of the tower
that crowed thrice every day in memory of the temptation of St
Peter.[14] Augsburg and Nuremberg craftsmen, he knew, daily completed 'heaps' of these clock automata (Figure 24).

Still, in Johannes Kepler's view, this extraordinary manufacturing
skill was on the brink of degenerating into absurdities. Objects were

Figure 24 Tobias Stimmer, the spectacular Strasbourg cathedral clock as renovated by Conrad Dasypodius, Stimmer and others between 1571 and 1574, which featured all sacred and secular descriptions of time and provides entertainment through automata. Note the celestial globe at its base, connected to the clock movement, next to it a Pelican, to symbolize Christ as ruler of all eternity. Woodcut 1574, 52.1 × 29.5 cm. © Trustees of the British Museum

becoming too expensive, showy, and devoid of Christian learning. What was one to think about Emperor Rudolph who was having a clock made in Augsburg for himself, so fancy that it was valued at 30,000 florins? Then there was Emperor Ferdinand, who had sent the Ottoman ruler Süleyman a model so heavy that twelve men were required to carry it. Worst of all was one Augsburg invention intended as a New Year's gift for a young Polish king. It displayed a procession of the fat, drunken Roman god Bacchus and his companion Silenus to loud and chaotic music from different instruments.[15]

This was patronage gone wrong. For all the effort that had gone into engineering these most luxurious of luxury toys, Kepler was dismayed that no one had yet produced an automaton to show properly the movement of all the planets. He hoped that Frederick, the Lutheran prince, might seek fame in the representation of *real* phenomena. The ducal clock-maker would be of great value to show nature itself by mechanical means. Hence Kepler, through his writings and models, wanted to render intelligible the nature of regular laws and clear causes in the superlunary world. Observing nature, such as spontaneously generated animals, helped to make sense of sudden celestial change and novelty as reversal of decay. A spirit, Kepler argued, constantly turned superfluous cosmic matter into new and useful forms, which cleaned up the ether. In fact, this spirit was formed of celestial matter and given life by a ray of light from God's countenance.[16] Kepler thus still related his speculations to an accessible language of causes—his interests stood in marked contrast to hermetical traditions fascinated by magic, secrecy, and millenarianism—an occult world beyond rational explanation.

Intent on the need to supply useful knowledge, Kepler endeavoured to demonstrate how applied mathematics would edify Protestant courts in morally defensible ways through clever engineering. Once more, he found recent achievements inspiring. In 1599 and 1602, Adriaen de Vries's astonishingly complex as well as elegant

Mercury and Hercules fountains were completed on Augsburg's market squares. These innovations inspired Kepler to spend years on plans for a water-pump, powered by a spring, which he discussed with Duke August of Anhalt and Rudolph II, before finally offering the elegant finished design of water-works to Duke Frederick in 1604.[17] Such inventive technologies had an immediate impact on everyone (an effect which scholarly books usually lacked, for all the hard work that had gone into them). From the beginning of Kepler's career he had understood this: that in order to impress others and advance his career, his skills as a convincing courtier and his practical knowledge were at least as important as his reputation as a scholar capable of figuring out God's universe.[18]

* * *

This mattered not least because, as early as 1598, Kepler realized that there was little point in asking a Lutheran clock-maker in Graz to start any long-term project, as the Lutheran church ministry in the city was abolished.[19] As Ferdinand of Austria matured and took up rule he was greatly influenced by Archduchess Mary, his militantly Catholic mother from the Bavarian Wittelsbach dynasty, as well as clerical advisers. They were determined to assert Ferdinand's political power and to restore Catholicism in his lands.

This was disastrous news for Kepler, Lutheran schools, and Protestant municipalities. In 1599, for instance, miners, labourers, and woodcutters in a small Austrian town called Eisenerz, who had attacked the papal nuncio and subjected a ducal commissioner to a mock trial, were overrun by a whole army comprising ducal troops, peasants, and Slovenian and German soldiers recruited from the guards in Graz. Soon the town was reduced in status to a mere village. Heretical, Protestant literature was burnt under gallows erected in front of the town hall and the Lutheran chapel was blown up. Ferdinand's men began to systematically destroy Lutheran cemeteries and chapels across Styria.[20] In the same year, Archduchess Mary urged on her young son in a letter: 'My Ferdinand, just ask about the Protestant preachers and if you find one let him be hanged!'[21]

In Graz itself, Kepler was able to watch spectacular exorcisms on women considered to be possessed by demons. The archducal chaplain saw many small as well as tall demons in 'green, yellow and fiery' colours driven from the body of one Maria Eichhorn with thunder and lightning. A young woman called 'Katherle' required exorcizing for months. One devil appeared in the shape of shiny black beetles in her mouth, while another astutely asked for permission to possess the body of the rebellious Lutheran preacher in Eisenerz.[22] All this was publicly staged counter-reformation propaganda. These dramatic scenes were orchestrated by Jesuits and Franciscans, as well as Ferdinand and his mother, who as a widow continued to live in Graz castle, right in the centre of town.

Since 1598, Kepler had been determined to leave Graz. But where would he find employment, and what would happen to his wife's land? Barbara twice became pregnant during the following years, but each time the baby died. By 1599, Kepler began to fear that a 'universal pestilence' might have swept over from Hungary, and reported that he was the first in Graz to spot 'a small cross on my left foot'. Its colours ranged from red to yellow, and its position mirrored the point where Christ had been tormented with a nail. This suggests his anxiety that he might in the same way be martyred for his beliefs. Other citizens found drops of blood on the insides of their hands. Kepler still had to pay off a debt of 200 florins in Tübingen, and repeatedly wrote to Katharina asking her to leave any money owed to him from his paternal inheritance with his former professor, Mästlin, whom he revered.[23] In August 1600, Kepler was told to leave Graz within forty-five days and desperately wrote to Mästlin asking him for a 'small', badly renumerated professorship in any subject. Johannes was already on his way to Prague when Mästlin finally penned his negative reply. All this was alarmingly bleak and, despite all his efforts, he received no invitation from the duke of Württemberg. Finally, when Kepler's fortune turned, it led him towards a Catholic court. The majestic Danish astronomer Tycho Brahe, with his famous prosthetic brass nose (the original being lost through a student duel), invited Kepler to Prague and assured him of his friendship in times of need. On 19 October 1600, the Keplers—Johannes, Barbara, and Regine, her daughter from a previous marriage—arrived in Prague, utterly exhausted. This was two months after thousands of Lutheran books had been burned in Graz to celebrate the town's full conversion to Catholicism, and as Archduchess Mary began to turn Kepler's school into a convent. Almost exactly one year after Kepler's arrival in Prague, on 24 October 1601, Tycho unexpectedly perished—not through poisoning, as has recently been suggested, but most likely through kidney failure or a burst bladder. Emperor Rudolph appointed Kepler as Tycho's successor. The post came with a title which sounded unimaginably grand, to be placed below any of Kepler's future signatures: imperial mathematician.

Even so, Johannes Kepler was under no illusion about his precarious position as a Protestant employed by the Catholic Habsburg emperors. He tried to maintain a relationship with his Tübingen professors, and in February 1601 asked Mästlin to send any letters from the professors to his mother in Leonberg as he planned a trip back home at Easter. He also kept up his relation with the Württemberg court. When John Frederick succeeded his father as duke in 1608, Kepler at once made sure to dedicate a small book to him. The treatise related the astronomer's observations of the planet Mercury in conjunction with the sun, recounting an experiment which had made him run up and down the Hradschin to recruit reputable witnesses. Its preface eloquently spoke about his grief for Frederick of Württemberg, as well as his gratitude for the love of learning cultivated in his lands. In 1609, John Frederick thanked Kepler for his services by sending a silver-and-gold gilt cup worth fifteen florins to Prague (although the astronomer, as telescopes revealed two years later, in fact had observed a large sun-spot rather than the planet Mercury).[24]

In Prague, court politics deteriorated. Kepler saw his future hanging by a thread. Rudolph II was increasingly reclusive, vexed by political decisions, anxious of being bewitched, and torn apart by conflicts with his brother Matthias. From 1601, Rudolph was under intense diplomatic pressure to resign, but remained deeply jealous of Matthias's attempts to gain power. In this stifling atmosphere, Kepler, by 1603, thought about moving back to Württemberg. Rudolph had not responded to his recent writings, and he had received no salary for nine months. In Württemberg, he wrote to a friend, 'I hold a bit of property, my mother resides and so does the duke who granted my education'.[25] Matthias was elected king of Bohemia in May 1611. Immediately, Kepler sent off another petition to John Frederick, this time to desperately ask for his help in securing the 2,000 florins Rudolf had granted him a year previously, as well as to announce that he wished to present himself and serve the Württemberg duke or his wider family as philosopher, scholar, or even in a political capacity. He also pleaded with the widowed Duchess Sibylle, especially as she was now in Leonberg where he still was a citizen and where his 'dear mother lived', asking whether he might serve Sibylle's daughter, as long as there could be some free time left for him to 'speculate and write books'.[26]

Both petitions were supported by ducal chancellors in Stuttgart and forwarded first to Tübingen University, where a committee confidently endorsed Kepler, and said he would fill a teaching position *summa cum laude* (with the highest praise). Next, Württemberg's church consistory considered Kepler's religious reliability.

Here they remembered that Kepler, as a schoolboy and student, had held a Calvinist view of the Eucharist (as a symbolic meal and not an encounter with the body and blood of Christ, which he did not think could be ubiquitous). In 1609, he had formally declared to the duke that, in good conscience, he would not be able to sign the Lutheran *Formula of Concord*, mandatory for everyone teaching in Württemberg. Kepler, they concluded, was an opinionated man, who seemed a Calvinist and as a teacher might slowly pour poisonous ideas into the ears of youth. He would not be offered any position.[27]

* * *

Throughout this period, Kepler needed to find support as a natural philosopher, rather than as a mere maker of prognostications and calculations. He had been rigorously schooled in rhetoric as well as a range of literary styles, to enable him access to a world which valued broad knowledge, quick wit, thorough exegesis, stylized eloquence, and poetic reflection—as well as deft rude epigrams—as the hallmarks of learning. For any scholar, such creativity with words demonstrated achievement and virtue. Ideally, these translated into a patron's regard. The patron might supply a poem to endorse a future publication, or even money.[28]

Elegant dedications to his prognostications and books thus helped Kepler to lobby major Protestant leaders, such as Christian II of Saxony and the Stuart monarch James I as well as important Protestant Imperial Cities.[29] Such gifts were routinely accompanied by courteous letters, with which scholars happily offered their services to render their patrons even more famous as illustrious men engaged in the pursuit of knowledge.

Kepler also left countless entries and autographs in friendship albums, fashionable at the time, which included a motto and coats of arms or other images. He nearly always penned his motto 'Oh the cares of man, how much of everything is futile', to wisely signal his own awareness of human precariousness and transience. This was a cornerstone of humility, essential to counter any allegation that one followed natural philosophical pursuits out of self-interest or to achieve lasting fame.

Kepler made sure to advertise his talents to Catholics in a similar fashion. He sent his calendar for 1597 to a future bishop with a dedication embossed in gold letters.[30] Once his first book was published, polite dedications were printed in several copies, or Kepler paid extra to have them beautifully bound, and was full of remorse when he failed to spend enough time personally overseeing the work of bookbinders to ensure the quality of the production. As Kepler developed into a prolific writer of ground-breaking theories, and gained his position as a Habsburg emperor's imperial mathematician, he presented his writings to some of the most powerful Catholic men of his time. His personal and professional life suffered under these same men—Archduke Ferdinand of Austria, who had expelled him from Graz, received his *Astronomiae pars optica* in 1604. Kepler was careful not to offend Jesuits, the powerful educational order at the forefront of the Catholic Renewal founded by Ignatius of Loyola, which included many keen scholars. Herwart von Hohenburg, one of Kepler's key, lifelong, powerfully connected patrons from the opening of his career, was Bavarian chancellor and close to many well-positioned Jesuits and other Catholics. In 1604, for instance, Herwart instructed Kepler to send by special delivery his most recent publication to the archbishop of Salzburg as well as to one of the wealthy Fugger merchants; his accompanying letter needed to be 'in perfect form'.[31] Like rich merchants, Herwart's Jesuit contacts cultivated far-reaching networks of communication.

Global information now mattered to scholars. Kepler was eager to travel to Sicily, expecting to see 'African mountains', and supported a young assistant keen to study Indian eclipses and stars. His Catholic correspondents related the opinions of Jesuits operating from

China.[32] The mathematician quickly devised his own enterprising techniques to generate comprehensive data. In order to study the eclipse and 'renew astronomy', as early as 1605 Kepler sent out a detailed questionnaire to diplomats and Jesuit connections as well as doctors, lawyers, and scholars across Europe. He claimed that his own observations in Rudolph's pleasure-garden had been hampered by artisans who had not delivered the right instruments and a gardener unable to keep away a horde of courtiers so that Kepler might work undisturbed.[33] Astronomy, he argued, was no abstract theoretical discipline but depended on the senses and quality instruments to generate data—the eye was not superior to such devices.[34] Kepler helped to refine telescopes with friends such as the Prague watch-maker Heinrich Stolle, but never found his research conditions ideal.

Broad networks of information and friendship, in sum, were essential in a period of relatively low resources for research, bitter confessional divides, and political uncertainty. Writing on natural phenomena in this period was animated by fierce disputes about discoveries and theoretical ideas. What we might think of as a mathematical pursuit of 'science' was inextricably linked to constant but inherently precarious efforts to gain attention, by generating, accumulating, and storing new types of factual information on paper with ink. Data needed to be turned into words in order to communicate and defend ideas. This was to prove that all this knowledge really was useful, justified funding for technically sophisticated instruments or printing, and possessed an innovative edge that nonetheless appeared solidly based. Kepler became a recognized scholar through meeting these challenges to an exceptional degree (Figure 25).

* * *

Three strategies helped early modern astronomers to gain attention. It helped immensely to argue that: (1) breakthrough discoveries were

tertium commune in omnibus triangulis, nempe latus a 1, unum nempe quæ-
fitorum, & per hoc latus inquiram angulos ad 1, qui fi lineam a 1 in eundem
zodiaci locum ftatuent (. nifi quatenus ob præcefsionem æquinoctiorum is in
fequentibus temporibus eft promotior). ex eo intellecturus fum , affumptum
a 1 bene habere .

Methodi ratio hæc, quod ut a 1 ad angulos δ. ε. χ. λ. γ. fic a δ. αε. α z.
α λ. α γ. ad angulos 1.

γ a 26.31.36 ♓	δ a 9.22.37 ♓	ε a 25.21.16 ♌	χ a 10.55. ♍	λ a 26.58.46 ♎
γ 1 29.18.30 ♒	δ 1 15.12.30 ♌	ε 1 2. 8.30 ♎	χ 1 2.35.40 ♎	λ 1 20.13.30 ♍
α γ 122.46.54	α δ 155.49.53	α ε 113.12.46	α χ 168.19.28	α λ 136.45.16

Horum finus in diftantias SOLIS & TERRÆ multiplicati, & per affumptam
diftantiam a 1 166700 divifi, produnt finus angulorum. qui additi ad vifio-
nes MARTIS in γ. δ. ablati vifionibus in ε. χ. λ. reftituunt lineam a 1 in hæc loca

γ	δ	ε	χ	λ
29.28.44 ♌	29.18.19 ♌	29.19.21 ♌	29.20.40 ♌	29.20.30 ♌

Debuit in

29.30.51.	29.18. 0.	29.19.36.	29.21.12.	29.22.48

vel in

29.29.51.	29.17. 0.	29.18.36.	29.20.12.	29.21.48

Nimirum non aliter differre debuerunt loca quinque, quam quanta eft dif-
ferentia præcefsionis æquinoctiorum .

Vides autem ex fchemate , fi cæteris manentibus , breviorem affumferis
a 1, venturam in γ δ. in confequentia in ε. χ. λ. in antecedentia, non tamen
ubique æquali fpacio. At fimul hoc feceris, nocueris in δ.χ.λ. profueris in γ ε,
Contrarium, fi prolongaveris . At confonum eft, errorculos hosce diftributos
haberi

S

at stake; (2) that their implications were relevant for everyone; and (3) competing ideas could conclusively be proven wrong. This, however, made sceptics notoriously wary of inflated claims from enthusiasts carried away by their findings. 'Heaven is God's book, which we must leave to him,' one English cleric commented in 1601, cleverly observing: 'To what end has God placed us so far from the stars, if with astrolabes, staves and quadrants we can do all things as if we were nearer?'[35] Demonstrations with new instruments appeared as a further promising strategy, but could just as easily fail. In 1612, for instance, Melchior Goldast, then Saxon envoy at the Prague court, was formally invited to lunch with a party of six men, including 'Kepplerum mathematicum' (Kepler), and, following the meal, was made to peer through a telescope. With palpable distaste, Goldast instantly reported that this mathematician had 'boasted to have found a new world in the moon, which is supposed to be much bigger than this habitable world of ours. He thinks we will be put there after the Resurrection.'[36]

Apart from the unsettling question of how astronomy could be reconciled with Scripture, even its most exciting results met with significant scepticism about what constituted sufficient evidence, especially since many natural philosophers, among themselves, either aggressively disagreed with or only superficially took note of each other. A wider public of interested academically trained practitioners, particularly physicians and pastors, vigorously published their own views on nature. Insults abounded. One clergyman, for example, wrote that those belittling astrologers were 'coarse fools, absurd dunces, grunters, cyclopses, who look at nature with calves' eyes.'[37] This whole world of intellectual thought can, to experts, appear as nothing but a 'confused mixture of learned exchange, invective and irony'.[38]

Kepler once again stood out. True, he did at least once call an opponent a Cyclops (one-eyed, unclothed monstrosities), but in his major Latin tomes he successfully developed strategies for communicating his radical astronomical ideas convincingly and politely. He trained himself to unpick arguments implicit in virulent rebuttals of astronomy in order to discuss and oppose them with care. These techniques helped him to scrutinize what constituted evidence and a consistent body of propositions. He then authoritatively argued that evidence needed to be read critically in its historical context, with philological detail in mind.[39]

By the time Kepler published his *New Astronomy* in 1609 he had adopted a characteristic style of his own. It was rooted not only in extensive reading, but also in the lively world of verbal exchanges with other members of Rudolph II's court in Prague. The *Astronomy*'s prologue repeatedly dwelt on the hard, extremely specialized work required to arrive at conclusions. The body of the text anticipated readers' critical responses, and was carefully constructed to 'block as many of those avenues as possible'.[40] Aware of the charge that he might invent novelties to gain fame, Kepler showed in detail why the puzzling planetary motion of Mars could not be represented by standard mathematical tools. A rhetorically compelling exposition set out why other arguments provided no alternative. Finally, he left no doubt that a religiously based commitment to truth underpinned his work as a sincere and devout scholar.

During his early thirties, Kepler had therefore equipped himself with the ability to imagine exactly what others thought and might object to in his argument. He knew how to demonstrate, in detail, where others went wrong and vigorously pre-empted criticism. These scholarly tools would prove crucial for the astronomer's ability to counter the most damning allegations he had ever faced. His ability to write for an audience, aware of critical crossfire which could only be fought off by a rigorous method and dense argument, would now turn into a survival skill.

5

A FAMILY RESPONDS

Katharina Kepler would eventually admit to having offered the ducal governor a silver cup. This was her first mistake—not trying to bribe a governor, which must have been common enough, but trying to bribe Einhorn, a recent arrival in Leonberg, who owed his position to the duke and someone who had already allowed the Reinbolds to threaten her. Katharina's cup would come up again and again, gleaming out from the court records, just as silver shone out among Leonberg people's domestic belongings. Most people owned wooden as well as thick clay plates, spoons, and cups; solid iron pans, spoons, and candle-lights; clay oil-lamps; sometimes green or white glasses for drinks; and matt pewter jugs, plates, salt-cellars, candle-holders, and half cuirasses, which easily took on rust.[1] Glass and clay broke, while washed wood looked dry and faded. Silver only needed polishing to show one's reflection. It stored value, and was used instead of money. Schickhardt, Duke Frederick's architect, beautifully illustrated twenty pages of his own inventory, listing when he had received presents (of gold and silver goblets, jugs, and small barrels) for what kind of building work and which gifts he had sold or handed on (Figure 26).[2]

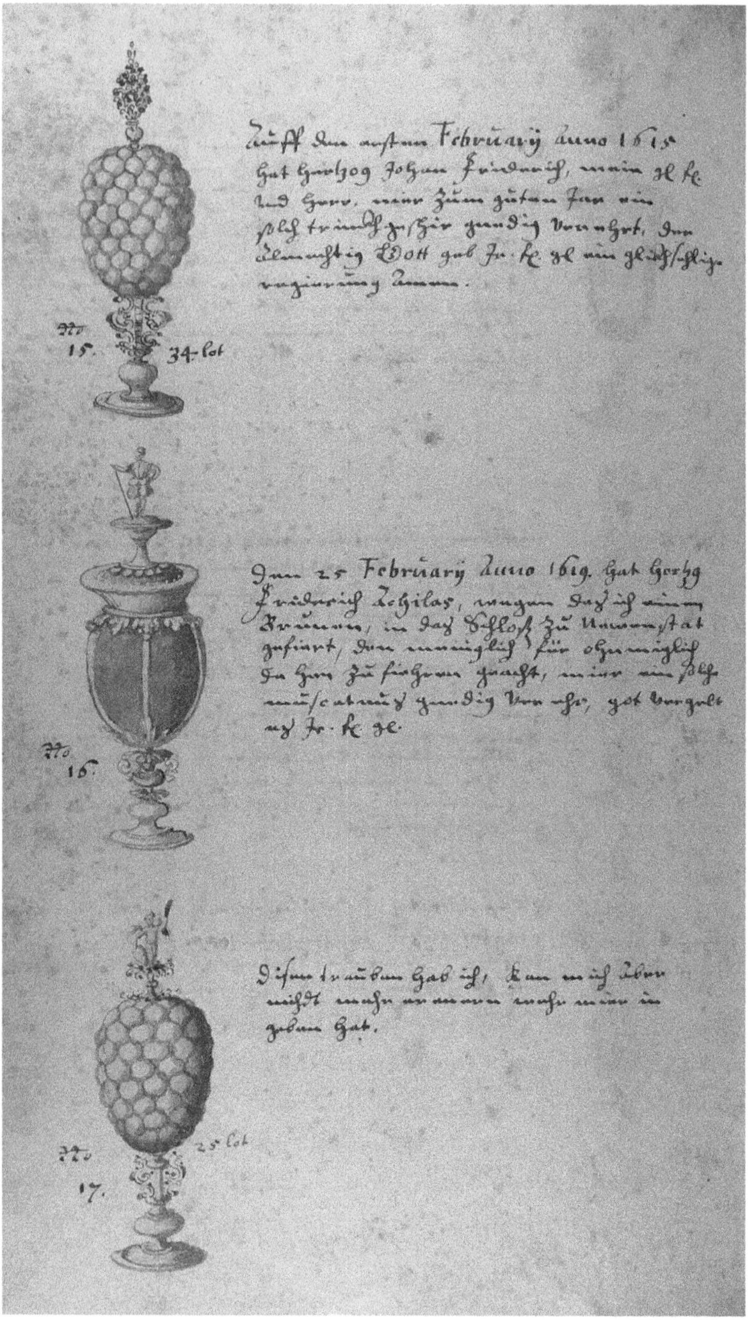

Figure 26 A page from Heinrich Schickhardt's inventory-book which lists the drinking cups and goblets in his possession and where he received them from and for what services. Interestingly, he was unable to identify who presented him with the final item. Cod.hist.fol.562, 152v. © Stuttgart, Württembergische Landesbibliothek

Stones and plants were traded across long distances for fashionable objects in silver. In 1631, one widow from the well-off Besserer family left gilded coins and a lynx tooth set in silver—said to fight epilepsy—as well a gilded mistletoe, corals, and a silver case for a date stone, imported from the Mediterranean. Date stones promised protection from lightning, and one craftsman managed to amass fifty-five healing stones as well as two silver-plated wolf's teeth (to ward off evil and sleepwalking).[3] As the price of silver had dropped through New World supplies, even Leonberg craftspeople were able to acquire some silver goods. For example, when Barbara Schifer moved to a home for the sick and elderly in 1577, she bequeathed a silver cup to her sister and husband, the baker, in addition to a small plot of land.[4] The potter Stoffel Bulling's inventory in 1603 included two silver-plated wolf's teeth, one silver-plated date stone, and four silver-plated spoons. A clue as to how he might have received such prized possessions is the godparents he managed to enlist for his children—the Margrave of Baden and Landgrave Maurice of Hesse. Wealthy people regularly became godparents to children of the lower orders, and gave money and expensive gifts to foster loyalty across social divides (Figure 27).[5] In 1610, even a shoemaker left behind one cow, two pigs, and 'two high silver cups gilded with gold at the top'. Had these cups perhaps been received in connection with his office as lay judge in the criminal court for over two decades?[6]

Naturally, the silver possessions of Mathis Plüderhausen, who had preceded Einhorn as Leonberg's ducal governor, were extensive. In 1621, his house on the market square stored trunks with one gilded bunch of grapes, one gilded lion with a shield, one gilded goblet and cup, two silver glasses, fourteen silver cups, one silver pot, a silver ship, one silver salt cellar, nine silver spoons, and one pair of knives.[7] How would such a state official have responded when a godchild or their kin was accused in court? Had he been bribed with some of these fourteen silver cups, and quite possibly others he had already given away?

Figure 27 Silver-gilt child's bauble, set with wolf's tooth, to ward off illnesses, south German, seventeenth century, 11cm × 4.5 cm. © Victoria and Albert Museum

In offering Einhorn a silver cup that she had stored for a time of crisis, Katharina probably simply did what people in trouble always had done to sway governors. She had made an appointment to see Einhorn and guarded the cup under her woollen gown, rather than show it to him straight away. Einhorn alleged that her children Christoph and Margaretha offered him similar gifts on separate visits.[8] What an official might have customarily accepted as a gift was now labelled a bribe to indicate Katharina's guilt.

The cup further testifies to her relative wealth. This explains why the day-labourer Haller confidently paid a scribe to petition that some of Katharina's property should be used to support his family whose 'children had been badly affected by her sorcery'.[9] In early December 1616, on receipt of this request, ducal councillors told Haller to rely on the poor chest. Even so, they requested a full list of Katharina's possessions and prohibited her from selling anything. By this point, Katharina was regarded as a fugitive; she was to be arrested upon her return in order to establish whether or not she was a witch.[10]

* * *

But where had she gone? Katharina now lived mainly at her daughter's house, in Heumaden's vicarage, and had leased her land to her youngest son.[11] This was a common arrangement between widows and children, in advance of the latter receiving their share of all property after the parents' death. The redistribution of fields, meadows, vineyards, and vegetable plots occurred slowly, which ensured that Württemberg parents retained as much power as possible over independent children. It tied children to their parents' money and expectations, imposing a regime of diligence and thrift to ensure that they maintained what would eventually be their own. Children cultivated the leased land for a wage or for part of the produce. An old, widowed mother would receive money and would be sent grain after it was threshed and milled, as well as grass that was cut, hay from a barn, and barrels of pressed wine.[12]

After bringing in the harvest, Christoph collected his mother from his sister's house in order to travel with her far to the east, over Württemberg's frontiers, to Johannes Kepler, who now taught at a tiny school in the Lutheran enclave of Linz. This Upper Austria provincial capital was situated on a trade route 240 kilometres south of Prague and lay on the River Danube, but lacked any postal service to Prague, Graz, or Vienna. Expensive messenger services had to be paid for—with the cost based on the weight of the letter.[13] In addition to teaching, Kepler reluctantly surveyed mountains and villages to map Upper Austria. This justified his title as 'district mathematician'.

A woman like Katharina Kepler in all likelihood would have had to walk to Linz, as she could not ride, nor indeed afford to rent a horse (and those with carts avoided taking on passengers). She must have begun her journey on the busy, and thus relatively safe trade route south from Stuttgart to the city of Ulm. From Ulm, Katharina travelled by boat on the Danube through Catholic areas in the south-east, and on to Passau. Leaving Bavaria, the boat reached Upper Austria. Kepler himself once completed this slow, cramped journey, becoming infested with lice on the way.[14]

Although Katharina was accompanied by her youngest son, this must have been a severely demanding trip for a woman of her age to undertake during the freezing winter. Characteristically, she managed the journey staunchly. She fell ill, however, as soon as she arrived in Linz. Away from her home, and bereft of control over anything she owned, Katharina now depended on her kin to send their supplications to John Frederick, duke of Württemberg.

* * *

German princes governed as personal rulers as much as heads of increasingly bureaucratic kingdoms. A literate population either sent written supplications by post, or, even better, handed them over directly to a ruler. But they always had to be in writing, so that they could be answered by administrators and then be retained in the kingdom's files. Maximilian I of Bavaria (r. 1598–1651), the powerful and deeply cultivated leader of the Catholic Renewal in the German lands, thus was known to accept supplications from his 'poor subjects' every morning on his way to church in Munich. Peasants travelled for days to catch his attention. Women were prominent among these supplicants and in return for clemency might undertake to pay for an annual mass at a shrine, just as they were used to asking Mary and the saints for help— and thanking them in turn.[15] The notion that spiritual and secular authorities could be asked for help was therefore just as deeply rooted in people's minds as the idea that reciprocity underwrote such exchanges.

What might Lutheran women offer in return for being listened to? The glazier's wife Ursula Reinbold sent her own supplications to Duke John Frederick. She promised in one long sentence never to 'forget Your Princely Grace's lady wife's and children's temporal and eternal well-being and to plead for a Happy Reign to god the Almighty in my zealous prayers and Lord's Prayer'. She signed: 'Duly and humbly awaiting your gracious resolution. Your poor, ill subject. Ursula Jacob Reinbolden's wife in Leonberg.'[16] In return for her zealous prayers, she wanted Katharina imprisoned.

* * *

At the time of his family's crisis, Christoph Kepler was a young man in his late twenties. The accusation against his mother disrupted a steady, regular life, a state for which Christoph must have longed, given his unusually disrupted childhood. In 1612, aged twenty-five, he had married the daughter of Eltingen's mayor. This matched him with a woman of exactly the same status as his mother when she had married. Christoph benefited from the flourishing of his craft during the following years (by 1626 fifty-five pewter masters practised their trade in thirty-one of Württemberg's small towns).[17] Christoph had earned himself good money by working for Duchess Sibylle—who paid 173 florins for a bathtub he crafted for her.[18] In summer 1613, as his wife was pregnant with their first child, Christoph purchased the back part of a house opposite the town hall on the market square. This fine address was opposite the house that his parents had first moved into when they came to Leonberg. This move reasserted the family's standing in the social topography of the town.

The purchase of the house required 150 florins to be paid up front, the rest—275 florins—in annual instalments. Christoph shared the building with a young tanner of white, refined leathers for gloves and shoes. Both young craftsmen ran their workshops for luxury goods on the ground floor. There was a reception room on the first floor to the back and two small bedrooms, with a view to the barn at the rear, two pigsties and Kepler's dungheap. The tanner kept his own treasured manure on the market square.[19] Yet this did not put customers off the gleaming, soft leathers nor Christoph's pewter-ware. For five years, the Keplers nestled in their home with their only daughter, shaping plates, candle-holders, tankards, tubs, wolf-teeth amulets, and perhaps even toys.

As Christoph fought for his mother's honour, he also expressed his own wish for well-earned stability in life. In January 1617, the Stuttgart chancellery received a long letter signed by Georg Binder, pastor in Heumaden, and Christoph Kepler, citizen and pewterer in Leonberg, addressed to Duke John Frederick as their 'gracious prince and lord'. The letter referred to the beginning of the unhappy affair, into which they and their 'dear old over seventy-year-old mother and mother-in-law' had been drawn. The petition set out a step-by-step account of the accusation and tried to impress upon the duke that the Keplers considered themselves a class above the Reinbolds.

The family explained that they had not willingly ventured into a vengeful lawsuit to settle local enmity. Rather, the pastor and pewterer had taken to the law as a last resort. Katharina had first dismissed Ursula's abuse that she was a witch as 'mere words and women's talk'. She and her family had decided not to 'clean themselves on a sooty kettle'—that is, to assert their honour against disreputable people—and hence initially had not sued for defamation. But in the end they had been left with no choice but to defend their honourable name.

Christoph Kepler and his brother-in-law immediately cast doubt on Ursula Reinbold's good character. The glazier's wife, they alleged, was hated by everyone and known as a whore; she had even been imprisoned for illicit sex. Ursula had been seen in perfect health by everyone at many events such as weddings and church fairs. Even if she really were ill, the Keplers argued, her condition doubtlessly resulted from her unruly sex life and mistaken medical advice. Ursula Reinbold had used forbidden, 'devilish' things, rather than proper medicines, which, furthermore, she had got from disreputable people such as the Stuttgart officers in charge of vagrants, and from quacks visiting local markets.

To make these claims convincing, the Keplers drew on detailed information. Only three days earlier, they explained, Ursula had asked one of these 'run-around chaps' (as they referred to the visiting quacks) to come to her house and had taken his medicine. The man had subsequently been imprisoned because of his 'forbidden arts'. She had similarly consulted a man who had claimed (in Stuttgart and other places) that he knew how to eliminate hunchbacks and goitres. The man had killed several of his patients. Ursula had felt that her heart was about to be pushed out of her body after she had taken his medicine, and only her brother's skills had kept her alive. Aware of all these circumstances, Katharina's family had not taken the accusations seriously, but had asked the ducal governor to intervene and tell Ursula to stop defaming them.

They explained their resort to legal action by emphasizing a turning point in the story: the incident in the governor's house.

Ursula, her husband, and her brother, along with governor Einhorn, had drunk far too much and requested Katharina to appear before them without any male legal representative. Ursula's brother had put Katharina under intolerable pressure. After the Kepler family had finally decided to formally accuse the Reinbolds of defamation, the Reinbolds, as much as Einhorn, avoided legal hearings by cancelling dates.

Just before the date that had finally been agreed for a hearing, the son of the knacker Haller and his wife had entered the scene. Both were known to be thieves and had been punished for theft some years earlier. The knacker's wife was also known for dabbling in magic and medicine. These disreputable people claimed that Katharina had hurt their children. Einhorn had picked up the charge and asked for the ducal councillors' permission to order Katharina's immediate arrest because he was worried that a legal hearing would implicate him for acting rashly and in a partisan manner on Reinbold's behalf. Katharina's home had been closed off and all her possessions had been recorded. This brought much 'dishonour and mockery'. In any case, the letter went on, the most valuable objects in the house belonged to Johannes Kepler, appointed as imperial mathematician in Linz.

The writers, therefore, left no doubt that the Reinbolds and Hallers could not be believed because of their bad reputation, while the ducal governor could not be trusted. They forcefully argued that Einhorn favoured people who wanted to 'line their own pockets' through 'unfair justice'. The governor had endangered the life of an old woman without any evidence.

The Keplers further implied that the whole community was on their side. 'Everyone' in Leonberg, they wrote, doubted that the day-labourer's girl really had a problem with her arm. 'Everybody', moreover, knew that the girl's parents had lost all their property through being spendthrifts, then had started to steal, and now secretly consorted with the Reinbolds.

The attack on the reliability of the witnesses was followed by the final point in the case for defence: Katharina had not run away because of her bad conscience, but as a result of the 'imperial mathematician's' advice. She lived with him at 'an honourable rather than an unknown place, as a result of the treatment she had received'. She would return, and be willing to appear in court with a representative. All the family asked for was to be allowed to continue with their defamation charge in the proper manner.[20]

The Keplers, in their letter, presented a world divided between honourable people of good judgement, the group to which they clearly belonged, and their enemies. The latter consorted with shiftless, marginal, nomadic liars. They were ruthlessly interested in their own gain, and should not be protected by the law. Yet in their letter the Keplers offered nothing in return for seeking the duke's grace, not even gratitude. Neatly penned in Binder's handwriting, their account covered pages and pages. Effective supplications, however, were usually crisp as well as far more polite and subservient in tone. Advice books on letter-writing set out at length how much care one needed to spend on any correspondence of this kind.

The ducal councillors simply noted in what an 'ugly way' the Kepler family spoke of the governor and the Reinbolds.[21] It is unlikely that they passed on such a letter to the duke. Audacious rather than gracious in tone, this intervention may actually have harmed their case.

* * *

Yet at the same time, still in January 1617, the ducal chancellery received another, perfectly judged petition, written less tidily, in thick ink, but with a far longer opening address:

> *His most illustrious Highborn Gracious Prince and Lord. Your princely Grace can be assured of my poor subservient service at all times. Gracious Prince and Lord.*

Johannes Kepler elegantly expounded his awareness of how princely support had enabled him to achieve his position, how he would always be aware of his duty and debt to his fatherland, and wished nothing more than to serve it with his mathematical skills. He underlined his complete loyalty to the dukes of Württemberg by writing that he had never once missed an opportunity to praise them. Any esteem he gained for his work, the astronomer continued, would reflect not only on those who employed his services, but on the Württemberg dynasty itself.

These words were carefully calculated, as all courts were keen to be lauded as patrons of art and learning. Might they be mere flattery? In order to demonstrate that these were not just empty words, Kepler cleverly enclosed a sheet from a recently printed report on his eagerly awaited *Rudolphine Tables*, highlighting a passage obediently expressing his thanks to the dukes of Württemberg. Kepler knew how to skilfully balance the need to appear as a humble servant, while also projecting confidence in his abilities and influence.

He knew, Kepler now pressed on more forcefully, that due to his mathematical expertise and impeccable behaviour he could always rely on the support of many German as well as foreign potentates, and hoped that the same was true for his relationship with John Fredrick. Only after this careful exposition of his achievements did Kepler succinctly refer to his mother's case: she had been badly defamed, and the ducal chancellery had issued a series of dangerous orders just before witnesses were to be heard. Kepler did not request that the duke intervene primarily for the sake of his mother. He himself needed support as one of the duchy's internationally successful scholars: to 'graciously save and protect my otherwise rather well known good name against the threat of great mockery and abuse'. The mathematician added that he had been forced to remain in Linz for the moment, but had appointed an advocate to represent his claims. He affirmed that his 'dear mother' was innocent and had been pressured into this lawsuit to defend her honour, life, and property.[22]

The argument was clear enough: Kepler saw that his own reputation and good relationship with the dukes of Württemberg was at stake. His good name reflected on theirs, and he could shift his loyalties entirely to foreign patrons, even though the *Rudolphine Tables* (his most important work) were not yet published in full. The case against his mother was based on defamation and she was certainly innocent.

* * *

In addition to sending this formal petition, Kepler also posted a long personal letter to Sebastian Faber, the ducal vice chancellor. Kepler had probably met him at court in Stuttgart or Prague, when Faber had represented Protestant Union interests to Rudolph II in 1609. A lawyer by training, Faber remained in his post as vice chancellor up to his death in 1624 and was one of Württemberg's ablest senior officials. Kepler realized that Faber would be closely involved in decisions concerning his mother's case, as he presided over meetings of the judicial council in the upper part of the Stuttgart chancellery building. The upper council had swollen from nine to about twenty men, most of them lawyers, in charge of major legal disputes in the duchy. Faber might review difficult cases together with other senior advisers and the duke in sporadic sessions of the Privy Council. Faber had shaped important policy decisions in the duchy for nineteen years. Kepler knew that now was the time to use this connection, not least to make sure that his petition to the duke would actually be read.[23]

Kepler wrote frankly to Faber about his own feelings of deep despair. So far, he had always enjoyed a good reputation. Now, Kepler continued, with considered use of a somewhat dramatic expression, this 'thunderstorm' pushed the ship of his life against 'dangerous cliffs'. His mother was no more than an old woman who talked too much and was guilty of other habits that were 'very widespread' in Leonberg, such as curiosity and ill-will. But she did not deserve to be treated in such a cruel, unfair, and undeserved manner. 'All damage', he explained, fell from his mother onto him. It is clear from Kepler's letter as to how much anxiety about the case gripped all the men in the family. He reported that his younger brother Christoph had told him how the conflict arose. Christoph had first been involved in a quarrel over some business with Ursula Reinbold and accused her of a licentious life. Katharina had joined in. Now Christoph was afraid of governor Einhorn and of upsetting the local council, especially as he had just bought his citizenship. Binder, his brother-in-law, feared losing his parish. Kepler made light of his oldest brother Heinrich's public defamation of their mother as that of a soldier too well 'practised in quarrelling'. Women's incessant gossip had done further damage. He accused Einhorn of misconduct. Finally, Kepler informed Faber that he had appointed legal advocates for himself and his mother in Tübingen, Stuttgart, and Leonberg.[24]

At the end of January, the chancellery received yet another supplication, this time from Reinbold, the glazier. He alleged that Christoph Kepler had helped his mother escape, had removed her most valuable property, and had threatened Reinbold with prosecution that would reduce him to beggary. The glazier lamented that this was bound to be his fate anyway, as his wife was now too ill to help with any work.[25]

* * *

On 29 January 1617, three ducal councillors responded to this increasingly complicated case. Kepler's pleading worked. Katharina was no longer under arrest and was guaranteed safe passage for her return to Leonberg. Einhorn was not to imprison her, but only to interrogate her as to whether and why she had touched Haller's girl, why she had promised Einhorn a silver cup, and why she had left the country. Einhorn was then to forward her responses to the chancellery and await further instructions. Meanwhile, Katharina's son Christoph and her son-in-law should keep all of Katharina's property under their care.[26]

Five weeks later, Christoph Kepler and Georg Binder complained that no date for a legal hearing had been set.[27] The chancellery, in turn, firmly ordered governor Einhorn to start proceedings even in Katharina's absence.[28] Town scribe Kern, who acted as commissioner in the case, now duly informed Katharina's legal guardians of a date when witnesses would be heard. The trial seemed about to begin.

Women needed male guardians to act for them in civil or criminal courts. The men read out all documents, explained their meaning, and obtained the woman's consent before proceeding. The guardian first appointed for Katharina was Bertlin Oberlin, her next-door neighbour in the small house she owned in Church-alley, which Einhorn had locked up. Her second, far more influential guardian, was Veit Schuhmacher, a seventy-five-year-old saddler. A respected man, he had just served as mayor in 1615–16 and had been criminal court judge since 1585. A man who had grown in wealth over his lifetime, Schuhmacher was only a little older than Katharina. They would have known each other for decades. He, too, was beginning to feel his age, so much so that in 1619 he would request leave to retire from all his obligations on account of his 'very old age and other difficulties'.[29] But for now, the saddler acted as Katharina Kepler's adviser.

Binder and Christoph Kepler meanwhile kept up the pressure on Einhorn. They reported to the chancellery that he was still refusing to start proceedings without Katharina and was the 'cause of all this confusion'.[30] The next day, on 28 March 1617, ten ducal councillors impatiently wrote to Einhorn ordering him to make a start on the case, even if Katharina had to be represented by her male guardians until she returned.[31] Still, nothing happened.

* * *

April 1617 found Johannes Kepler in Prague. He sent a long letter to Regine, his stepdaughter from his first marriage, who had grown up in the city, but now was a woman in her late twenties and lived elsewhere. At the beginning of their time in Prague, he had still instructed his first wife Barbara to keep 'Regerl (Regine) busy sewing' and indoors. They had looked for a Protestant husband for her, ideally a quiet man with pleasant features and noble appearance, cheerful and 'military' in expression rather than melancholic.[32] In 1608, Regine had been married to a representative of Frederick IV of the Palatinate. Now she was pregnant for the first time. Kepler, anything but the cold, reclusive scholar he has often been portrayed as, related to her in a letter who had died in Prague, who wished to remarry whom, or what some of Regine's peers had been up to. Kepler was an empathetic man and valued as part of social circles. Hence he reported that Frau Poltzin, a noble woman of 'Austrian elegance', married to an imperial councillor in whose house Kepler stayed, passed on greetings, but sent sad news. She was gravely ill and had lost her youngest son as well as a daughter three months before. Kepler was immersed in intimate personal affairs at this time, catching up with Prague friends and being invited to a number of weddings by his male and female acquaintances.

Friends as well as family were central to Kepler's life. Just the previous Christmas he had asked his younger brother to transport a large parcel for Regine, as Christoph returned to Württemberg after having taken Katharina to Linz. Did Christoph ever resent being assigned tasks by this famous older sibling? Johannes recommended Regine a good book of midwifery and instructed her to avoid beer, but to drink wine regularly. He let her know that his sister

Margaretha was very ill, and deaf in one ear. Even so, she was caring for the oldest girl left behind by Heinrich, their disreputable brother. Although she never bore any surviving children, Margaretha must have been under considerable strain in the Heumaden vicarage, and hardly able to cope with their mother as well.

The pressure began to take its toll on the Keplers, not least on Johannes. When he had to see the emperor in Prague, he had left Katharina at home, where she remained gravely ill. Susanna, his second wife, was once again pregnant. She had lost three babies soon after they were born. Their only surviving child was two-year-old Margaretha Regina, lovingly nicknamed Maruschl. But Maruschl was now mortally ill and during the past six months had gone blind. Kepler in his letter to his stepdaughter worried that Maruschl might have perished already. He nonetheless planned to travel back to Württemberg with his mother on his return from Prague. In that case, he promised, he would surely pass through Regensburg to visit Regine and leave her some 'old things' he still kept for her.[33]

Johannes Kepler arrived back in Linz on 26 May. His Genevan assistant, Gringallet, arrived shortly after, and they settled back into work while Katharina was at home and Susanna in the last month of her pregnancy. On 31 July, they celebrated the birth of a new baby. It was a girl, and the first one in the family to be named after its grandmother. 'Infans: Catharina', reads the moving record. Johannes and Susanna wanted to please Katharina. One local widow and a 'Freyin von Herberstein' served as godparents. Weeks later, Maruschl, who had suffered from a bad cough throughout the summer, finally died of consumption and epilepsy. Baby Catharina would survive for little more than six months.[34]

Johannes lived through these births and painful deaths while still completing major academic work. In late August he planned to travel to Württemberg to return his mother to Margaretha. However, Katharina left by herself in September, while Johannes addressed a further petition to Duke John Frederick, stressing once again that his mother had not arrived as a fugitive. Rather, she had hoped to convince her oldest son to return with her to Leonberg and take action on her case. To avoid any sense of bias, Kepler stressed that he was well informed. He had talked to his siblings and learnt from them as well as from 'impartial honourable people' that Katharina was innocent and had always conducted herself as a 'Christian, honour-loving woman'. Writing to the duke, Kepler still stoutly defended his mother's life and name.

* * *

By now, Kepler was meditating on what it was that had made an accusation of witchcraft plausible and he noted his conclusions in his letter to the duke. Kepler's scholarship was not just based on pure maths and observation, but on using words to resolve rival sets of hypotheses, to analyse motives and causes, and to engage in historical reconstruction. These same rigorous strategies informed his letters and supplications to save his mother's life.

Trained in classical methods of obtaining proof and rhetoric, he engaged with complex constellations of facts, confidently advancing three interrelated causes to explain her accusation. How could an old widow find herself accused of the ultimate crime of heresy and harm? First, he identitied 'no other cause' than:

> [S]he has had to defend herself among the common rabble during the twenty-eight years, during which she has lived without help and as a widow with her many immature children, has scantily fed herself, improved her land, and defended her interests, and sometimes been drawn into various quarrels, unhappiness and enmity.

Kepler detailed Katharina's social situation—what it had meant for his mother to be a widow with two young children while still trying to keep her property. He described her as a woman who had suffered the emotional consequences of having to stand up for herself in the community.

Kepler's letter noted a second cause for the accusations, and he became the first person to link his mother's vulnerability to the new ducal governor's readiness to take up witchcraft accusations. He observed:

> Which is why, when a few years ago, under Your Princely Grace's current governor in Leonberg, several witches from the district were taken and brought to justice, much talking, murmuring and inquisitiveness arose among the superstitious and especially the women folk about whether such people might also live in town.

The third point in Kepler's letter was that those fearing witches in their own community targeted women who 'in the view of the young, vile world have lived too long, and have in their old age become morose, as in the all too common unchristian proverb: quickly to the stake with the old women'.

'Quickly to the stake with the old women,' resounded Kepler's charge in the supplication! This was an effective polemic against an irrational witch-hunt. Nor was his argument far-fetched: 'New advice on revealing old witches' read the heading of a legal opinion co-written by Tübingen university lawyer Johannes Halbritter for the Austrian government in 1594.[35] Not every witchcraft trial stated the age of the accused, and accusations had often been building up for many years. It is therefore impossible to say for certain how many of those on trial were 'old' women, but it seems as if as many as 85 per cent of women formally accused of witchcraft might have been over forty. At forty, women were generally regarded as well established in life, just like men. Then perceptions diverged. Men were commonly thought to be at their peak a decade later and, at seventy, thought to be an old man; whereas popular verse on the stages of life saw women rapidly decline: 'At fifty a grand-mother/ At sixty age-worn.' Sixteenth-century images and sensationalist cheap prints began to elaborate the scary figure of the witch as old, envious, heretical hag, keen to rave at the Sabbath.[36] Many contemporaries thought these women invited hatred. Their physical changes were connected to troubling emotions. It was feared that old women were envious of other people's beauty, fertility, or riches, and hence wished to harm them. The interest in classical literature popularized the view that old people were despicable as they were poor, decrepit, ugly, and weak—but only old women were thought to bring bad luck. Images of the stages of life represented women as completely 'disfigured' from the age of seventy on. Such perceptions coexisted with the idea that old women could be 'wise' due to their experience, but it must have been difficult for mature women to accept ageing with humour and grace. The fact that fewer people lived to a very old age also made such women seem peculiar.[37]

For Johannes Kepler, these three elements—enmity against his mother due to her social situation as widow, a new governor ready to act, and pervasive cultural fears of old women—made perfect sense of his mother's ordeal. This fatal constellation of underlying general causes might equally operate elsewhere. A towering intellectual, he had identified how the German persecution of witches worked.

His mother, Kepler pointed out, was now over seventy and almost the oldest woman in Leonberg. Before the recent quarrel with Reinbold she had enjoyed a good reputation, but her opponents now reacted furiously to the fact that Katharina had once reminded Ursula of her illicit behaviour and public punishment. Like the rest of his family, Kepler implicitly alleged that the Reinbolds had teamed up with the day-labourer and his wife in revenge.[38]

Given such circumstances, Kepler explained that he felt himself 'obliged by God' to look after his mother, but had been unable to leave Linz to take her back to Leonberg. The River Danube had been frozen that winter. Next, the emperor had called him to Prague in February. While he had been away, his mother had been so severely ill that everyone had thought she might die. As the date for a legal hearing had been moved several times, Kepler had not thought it appropriate for his mother to return after she regained her health. This, he was at pains to stress, was not because of any misgivings about the duke or his Stuttgart councillors. Their good faith was not in doubt. He simply worried about taking Katharina back before any 'honourable' witnesses had attested to her innocence. His mother was an imprudent woman well advanced in her years. She could not be exposed to her enemies, or be forced to incur useless expenses, especially as she was now prohibited from drawing on her capital. As ever, Kepler was anxious to guard his finances.

At the same time as stressing his mother's mental feebleness, Kepler insisted that her behaviour had been entirely normal. She had notified her guardians, the mayor, and the governor of the fact that she had begun to live, intermittently, at her daughter's in the Heumaden vicarage, as well as of her trip to Linz. She had travelled to her oldest son, with whom she had already stayed several times before. Her greatest concern had been to receive his advice on how to respond to disreputable people 'living off Leonberg alms'.

The petition ended with the request to allow Kepler and Katharina's legal guardians to administer her land in order to prevent any loss of value as well as to use her capital to pay legal and living expenses. Kepler pledged that he would mortgage whatever was necessary from his own property as well as his inheritance portion from his grandfather, father, and brother Heinrich, should the Reinbolds and Hallers successfully request compensation. His paternal inheritance was still part of Katharina's possessions, but had been precisely detailed in the town records in 1609.[39] Now he wished the defamation suit against the Reinbolds to continue so that it could be brought to a swift conclusion.

* * *

In response to Kepler's letter, John Frederick told his ducal governor Einhorn to allow Katharina's children and guardians to look after her land and use it as capital to cover her living and legal expenses, but also to let the chancellery know immediately if any witnesses suspected Katharina of doing them any harm.[40] On 8 November 1617, it was decided that Katharina Kepler's legal guardians were to sell her house in order to provide her with an income. 'The siblings', the document continued, 'will know how to mutually liquidate what *Herr* Kepler has otherwise lent his mother or she owes him for living expenses.'[41] *Herr* was only used for the astronomer, as it was a highly privileged term of address.[42]

By November, Kepler reported that he had followed his mother back to Württemberg in October, while reading Galileo's father's writings on musical theory. He was in his native land during the joyous celebrations of the first 100 years of the Reformation. His friend Hebenstreit, in Ulm, had just restructured the school for 600 boys to be even more academically challenging, and announced a whole week of Latin orations to commemorate Luther as the man who had brought light to Germany.[43]

Kepler had little reason to join the celebrations. His stepdaughter Regina had died after giving birth to her child in October. Meanwhile, the date for a legal hearing in his mother's case kept being moved and manipulated by the Reinbolds. Katharina had spent a full three months back home in Württemberg, but nothing had happened. As a 'dutiful child', Kepler stressed that his mother really did not have the mental or emotional strength—or money—to continue in this situation. Indeed, he urged, there was real danger that she might lose 'not only her senses but her life before its time'. The Reinbolds might easily manipulate her into further 'rash words, rage and impatience', as they knew how to exploit Katharina's 'imbecility and great age'. Kepler imagined that Reinbold would be pleased that he had travelled at his own expense to Württemberg for nothing. Even the Tübingen higher court of appeal's (*Hofgericht*) demands to proceed with the Keplers' civil defamation charge against the Reinbolds had been so far averted.

Given this intolerable situation, Kepler planned to take Katharina back to Linz by winter. He ended his petition by pleading with familiar, urgent rhetoric to John Frederick as 'father of widows', to support his 'deeply afflicted and confused' seventy-year-old mother. The letter was signed humbly, in the hope of being rewarded with empathy and grace:

> your subservient and obedient poor servant and country's child, Johan Keppler, now the Roman Emperor's and the laudable estates of Austria on the Enz's Mathematician.[44]

His mother would return only if the duke demanded that she should.

* * *

Once again, the imperial mathematician's skilful writing secured success. In November 1617, the chancellery told Governor Einhorn that Kepler was entitled to take his mother back with him to Linz. Reinbold would have to pay a fine of ten florins if he did not attend the next hearing or tried to move its date. The chancellery would review any legal documentation before a verdict was reached.[45]

A preliminary hearing was concluded in May 1618. Einhorn informed the chancellery that, surprisingly, Katharina had not travelled back to Linz with Johannes, despite having permission. Ursula Reinbold meanwhile asserted that there had now been enough legal testimony to make it as clear as day that Katharina was a witch. Katharina, she insinuated, had flippantly asked Ursula why she had 'made such a fuss about the drink' when she, Katharina, had 'just gotten hold of the wrong jar'. Even Katharina's own son Heinrich said that his mother had 'ridden a calf to death and prepared him a roast dish from it, he himself wanted to accuse her before the authorities'. Witnesses had told her so. Katharina, Ursula added, was now in the Heumaden vicarage, but preparing to escape again to Linz. Articles 44 and 206 of Emperor Charles's law code for the German lands were clear enough with regards to fugitives and their property. Ursula pleaded that Katharina be taken to Leonberg and imprisoned until the legal proceedings were finally completed and she could be properly punished.[46]

Yet the chancellery merely ordered that the local court should reach its decision and then, as usual, present it to legal experts at Tübingen's law faculty as well as at the Stuttgart court before making it public in any way. In summer 1618, the chancellery appointed a man called Melchior Nördlinger from Merklingen to head the local commission. A full hearing of witnesses was only arranged in October 1619. This, however, would result in a 280-page document that cast serious doubt on Katharina's reputation.

6

MOVEMENTS OF
THE SOUL

⸺〰⸺

As Johannes Kepler lived with his mother in Linz and waited for the interrogations to take place in Leonberg, he confronted his deeper fears and feelings about Katharina's personality and about how his relation to her could be seen. His mother was an old widow, but was she also partly responsible for the accusation against her? Kepler during this time kept revising his major work, the *Harmony of the World*. As the accusation against his mother moved into its decisive phase, he became one of the very first scholars to introduce psychology as a subject in the contents page of a book. Just before witnesses were interrogated, he wrote in the *Harmony* that he and his mother had little in common. Kepler argued that neither the stars nor hereditary factors fully determined personalities. Social factors, biological sex, and individual moral choices were the key to explaining his mother's accusation. He did this to defend his own reputation, even at the cost of dangerously blackening Katharina's. The case moved him on emotionally and intellectually. It enshrined his view that astrology was of little value in explaining behaviour

Figure 28 A richly coloured broadsheet about the 1618 comet in the heavens, 41.4 × 50.5 cm. © Trustees of the British Museum

and forced him to search for new answers to questions about what made individuals differ from each other or influenced their actions.

* * *

In the late sixteenth century, people usually explained personalities through astrology. Astrology formed a routine part of elite education, and was part of many universities' curricula. Kepler, too, had learnt to cast horoscopes and predict the weather in Tübingen as part of studying mathematics, which in turn was integral to studying theology and the arts. During his career, he went on to compile a vast collection of more than 1,170 horoscopes for over 850 individuals. Although commissions from clients near and far provided him with welcome additional income, Kepler also collected horoscopes and data from a broad range of other practitioners in order to study them. When news reached him of an illness or the death of a particular person, he updated his records in order to verify his predictions. Horoscopes of famous, or ordinary, ill-fated people, such as a woman executed in Tübingen for infanticide, were closely scrutinized for patterns and causes.[1] This immersed him in contemplating many different biographies. It made him curious about others. Anything but a distant academic dissociated from ordinary lives, he mined this information as a tool of empirical observation, so as to understand human nature through the movements of the stars.

The mathematician first seems to have completed cursory notes on the birth horoscopes of his family, compiled after he returned to Graz from the Württemberg court in 1597. Johannes was still unmarried at this time. These private notes described his grandmother in Weil der Stadt as filled with envy and endlessly creating confusion, and his father's father (Sebald) as thirsting for power and wealth. His father's horoscope revealed his immoral and rough character traits. Katharina was described as addicted to quarrelling, sharp-witted, and unpleasant, although Kepler showed some sympathy for her having to hold her own against her parents-in-law and abusive husband.[2] Kepler added no further information about his mother's life after 1589, when her difficult marriage ended. If his notes on the personalities of his relatives seem acerbic, a fellow student, for instance, hardly fared better, characterized by Kepler as a 'suspicious, over-critical' man, 'impulsive, bitter, bad-tempered, bad-mannered...', though talented and able in his judgement.[3]

The negative sketches of his parents, therefore, were not considered all-encompassing assessments by Kepler nor do they reveal his relationship with his mother for his entire life.[4] Rather, they highlight a son's ambivalence towards his elders, which was widely shared. Cardano, the sixteenth-century astrologer who came from a wealthy background and was partly raised by wet-nurses, wrote in his biography that his mother was of quick memory and wit, a 'fat, devout little woman' who was quick-tempered and less loving than his father. Such comments highlight the peculiarly exacting type of character analysis that astrology encouraged in its most intelligent practitioners. For men like Kepler, the whole point of astrological thinking was to identify weaknesses and tensions in a person. It was much the same when contemporaries went to weekly sermons expecting to be berated. The convention in sermons as much as in horoscopes was to focus on failures. In turn, the mental world of men who believed in astrology could be one of arresting psychological observation, which at best led them to accept imperfection and a permanent gulf between ideals and actual behaviour. It encouraged an outlook on life as a permanent struggle for some degree of self-control.[5]

Kepler's remarkable, lengthy analysis of his own personality, completed in 1597, bears this out. Oddly, he referred to himself in the third-person singular throughout: 'This person' (so Kepler introduced himself), 'had been destined to work through towering intellectual problems, ranging from history and chronology to theology, poetry and mathematics.' Their 'order of difficulty', he opined, 'deterred almost anyone else'.

The young Graz schoolteacher, barely twenty-six years old, who was not yet Kepler the imperial astronomer, regarded himself as an intellectual Hercules. He suffered accordingly. This fate, he complained, lay at the root of his most unflattering characteristics. He was painfully aware of tensions between his social expectations and actual behaviour. If one changes his description back into a first-person narrative, this is the kind of character trait that a dismayed Kepler revealed: 'despite a strong desire for human company, I refrain from it'. A tendency to hoard things likewise worried him: 'I keep all sorts of insignificant pieces of paper I have written and doggedly hang on to books of all kinds which I have been given, as if they could be of future use.' Although pleased by his ability to engage in complex thought, Kepler worried that he communicated his views in a way which made it hard for others to follow.

Such insights rapidly led to sharper self-criticism: 'Too tenacious in matters of money, tough in my economy.' A troubled passage explored this further. Was his preoccupation with money primarily motivated by his fear of poverty? Or by a keen sense of its necessity and use to gain respect? Mercury in the seventh astrological house, he continued, had caused his resistance to hard work. Luckily this was balanced by the sun's position. Still, Kepler continued to emphasize his deep hatred of disciplined work. Then there was his taste for starting new projects before finishing old ones. Added to a hyper-critical attitude, he confessed, was a tendency to lie and deceive.

His lack of tact and thirst for fame made things worse. Why, Kepler asked as he peered into his soul: '1. do I only cherish true fame? 2. Why so much?' What he dreaded most in life was 'really and truly, shame'. These reflections led to further considerations of why and how these terrible traits manifested themselves. Even some of his positive characteristics, he noted despairingly, such as a general friendliness or happiness, were always misinterpreted by others.

This, in short, was a young man's convoluted self-scrutiny, revealing inner turbulences rather than a solid sense of self. It went on to list names of enemies from his school days onwards, and musings about why he thought so much about himself in relation to them. He recalled a relationship of 'tender love' with a fellow student, which had nonetheless remained 'clean' in action, and was marked by bitter, constant quarrelling as well. Kepler concluded that he was like a spoilt domesticated dog (*Haushund*), desperate to gain favour from authorities, but always unhappy with himself, keen to bark and bite anyone who took something away from him or displeased him in other ways.

Kepler conceded that he had some virtues for which he was well regarded. He had no really major failings in his relations with others, and was always considerate to old people. In its final paragraph, his Latin text tailed off, unfinished, into a cascade of questions: 'How to explain this? Where does this come from?' Even so, and luckily for the historian, Kepler kept this astonishing self-analysis in that hoard of papers he could not bring himself to throw away.[6]

* * *

At the beginning of his time in Graz, then, we encounter Kepler as a deeply self-conscious and ambitious scholar who explained his behaviour in astrological terms. Yet soon after, when his life took its astonishing turn, Kepler changed his views on astrological prediction.[7]

At their most elaborate, astrological predictions used the twelve houses of the zodiac to predict a plethora of outcomes, ranging from material success to disease, through marriage to the number of children a person would have. Parents commonly paid for a horoscope when a child was born, and submitted to an astrologer a list of questions about all these aspects of the child's future life. Specific illnesses were predicted for precise years, just as a future husband's profession seemed determined. Kepler's collection, for example, included one birth horoscope cast by an anonymous astrologer for a girl called Eleonara, probably in Kepler's collection because she had been born in the same year as him. The anonymous astrologer's characteristically cursory comments ran as follows: 'I think her husband will not die of a natural death, but is going to be a soldier. Further, she will not have a good face and suffer damage to her eyes.'[8]

In Prague, Kepler's writings began to vigorously reject this popular practice as a blunt tool for prediction, on which it would be foolish to base one's life.[9] He likewise rejected the idea that the heavens conclusively inclined a person to live in a particular way.

By contrast, Kepler became interested in setting out how the stars affected a person without discounting other factors, such as human choice, variation in character, and individuality. These other dimensions were lodged in the human soul. They were influenced by socio-economic, political, and cultural circumstance, as well as random accidents. Kepler further regarded people's physical constitution as both naturally given as well as influenced by human behaviour, such as eating or drinking habits.[10]

In 1611, for instance, he wrote to Rudolph II, who for years had failed to take determined political decisions, and thus had driven his brother Matthias into rival action, and could no longer call any territory his own: 'I have often reported to his Majesty with all due deference that the heavens in themselves can do nothing.'[11] Rather than asking Kepler to predict whether a Hungarian war would succeed through cosmic change, Rudolph should take political measures which were sure to prove beneficial for the country.[12] The emperor, he explained, had fatally 'imbibed'—that is, absorbed—some recent bad constellations to such an extent that everything with which he now tried to ameliorate the situation with his brother only made things worse. This made Rudolph himself yet more deeply unhappy. Kepler thought that the heavens presented stimuli, to which some people responded more than others. Kepler's firm advice was that the emperor switch off completely from these torturous worries about the fraternal divide. He needed to take political action rather than wait for a more beneficial heavenly constellation.

A proper horoscope, Kepler further insisted, depended on correct data. He told Rudolph that with regards to the Ottoman sultan—the emperor's enemy—he could not make precise predictions as he did not even possess, for example, the sultan's date and hour of birth. Astrology needed to be precise and, he now thought, comprehensive and comparative. The only way forward was to observe patterns of what types of behaviour had actually been caused by heavenly constellations across different countries and throughout history.[13] Like good medical practice, Kepler argued, astrology was a justified pursuit only if it was grounded on layers of experience, time, and good interpretation. Quick diagnosis was for quacks, and he was well aware that some attacked astrology as superstitious magic and even sorcery. Astrology proper could slowly grow into a professional science only if it reflected on mistakes and uncertainties, as well as on the relationship between general patterns and individual variations.[14]

This new scientific approach was remarkably transparent as well as open-ended. Kepler likened the extraordinary extent of variation in human behaviour to fruits and flowers that had an irregular number of five, nine, or eleven leaves. His watchword was 'individually'—and he wanted to identify interesting specific divergences. Kepler explained these divergences through the fact that God had left some aspects of creation undone, to be shaped by fortune and circumstance.[15]

After 1610, Kepler nonetheless felt sure that a character or soul was deeply influenced by heavenly constellations during the first four months of life. Like many of his contemporaries, he thought that astral rays infused the terrestrial world (including humans) with spiritual 'impressions'.[16] As everything created by God was good,

Kepler was certain that this whole process could implant only positive qualities, such as a shared human sense for musical harmony and geometry.

Subsequently, a person's soul could be stimulated by particular heavenly constellations. However, any bad behaviour resulted from human sinfulness, which warped God's beneficial design. This was rooted in mankind's general frailty after the Fall. Yet it was also a matter of life choices and life circumstance, with God's help in making humans distinguish good and bad.[17] Nothing evil, then, was predetermined. In an extraordinarily optimistic summary, Kepler concluded that the character implanted by nature kept the reins on a life.

On the whole, he thought in 1610, things went the way that God regarded as best.[18] Yet even for God, the interplay between human agency and circumstance, Kepler quickly conceded, was a complicated matter to control.[19] Moreover, the stars had not been created to gain mastery over men and rule over them day and night. The more a person struggled to be good, the more he or she succeeded.[20] Here, once again, was that sense that people were to some degree involved in creating their own destiny.

Kepler at the same time believed that parents fundamentally shaped their children. His *Harmony of the World* commented on the way in which a 'father creates a son, and a son another, each one resembling him'.[21] In addition, the astronomer regularly referred to the common idea that a woman's imagination could imprint itself on the foetus 'during the whole pregnancy', to shape a person's appearance and character. In popular belief, a mother's imagination was understood to be awakened in particular by excessive desire or fear. If a mother was overly keen on strawberries, for example, a child might have a bright-red dot on his or her face, or a baby might be crippled if its mother had been frightened by malformed people. Paracelsus (*c.* 1493–1541), the early medical chemist invigorated by Protestant reforms, developed this into a broader concept, according to which pregnant mothers were powerful creators, imprinting much of what they saw on the foetus.[22] Kepler seems to have followed these Paracelsian ideas as they regained prominence after 1600, and certainly thought that physiognomies generally bore a mother's imprint. In 1602, he noted that a baby still 'kept much of the mother's conceptions and feelings and mixes them with its nativity (i.e. horoscope)'. Whether a person became 'ethically good or bad' was also not decided by a horoscope.[23] From at least 1610 onwards, therefore, Kepler held that a child's upbringing generally mattered, although he never discussed in detail what effects certain forms of upbringing and childhood experiences might have. Yet by acknowledging factors such as education and choice as relevant to understanding a person's life and ethical choices, Kepler's astrology opened up social and individual psychology in pioneering ways.

* * *

Perhaps the greatest challenge to the idea that heavenly constellations might completely influence human character sprang from the view that masculinity and femininity created fundamental differences. What we call 'gender' played no role at all in the explanatory framework of astrology. Yet it was central to the symbolic system by which contemporaries made sense of most aspects of their world, including science. Many entities in Kepler's intellectual sphere of mathematics, music, and knowledge about nature were classified as either 'male' or 'female'. This was anything but a neutral world of factual communication. Kepler's *Harmony*, for instance, reflected on melodies and affects attributed to tones. Drawing on the writings of Galileo Galilei's father, Vincenzo, Kepler thought the musical interval to be immensely important. Admiringly, he commented on its 'daringness, élan, courage; it is like a soldier, masculine and dashing'.

Musical tones, Kepler insisted, could only be ascribed to one of two sexes. A third would be unnatural. There were major and minor tones which created corresponding effects: 'just as the wife has been predominantly created to suffer and the man to act, especially in procreation, thus a minor serves to express passive female characteristics and a major the active male ones'.[24] One was hard; the other soft. This difference between the major and minor third corresponded not just to the difference between men and women in physical height, but also the 'strength of the soul in the sexes'. In fact, so much did Kepler stress that femininity was self-sufficient, incapable of creation, and made to suffer that he developed the image of the minor third as a hen: 'she always ducks like a hen on the ground and is ready for the cockerel who jumps on her. These are the causes of the effects in the tones and tonal ranges of the primary system starting with G'.[25]

Like Pythagoras, Kepler held even numbers to be female, and odd numbers to be male. Calm, steady, and thus quintessentially female qualities could, at best, lend themselves to a peaceful and friendly state. Yet, in fact, they were always precarious and thus easily descended into weakness, anxiousness, and lament. Just as the cockerel needed the hen, so Kepler thought that in real life women and men needed to be mixed proportionately to avoid boredom—men would enjoy women's beauty and women would be guided by male authority.[26] Courage and daring, Kepler agreed with the French philosopher Bodin, were cardinal virtues—and obviously embodied by men.

Within this patriarchal mindset, Kepler generally described soldiering with great admiration. Soldiers epitomized audacious men of action. We find no direct comment on Kepler's traumatic relationship to his father who had kept running away from the family to be a real soldier, other than by idealization. Passionate though Kepler was about advancing religious peace, these positive evaluations of soldiering revealed a central tenet of his age, which continued to revive

Roman and medieval chivalric ideals. In his dedications to Rudolph II he kept using military metaphors to describe his enterprise, in order to dramatize the importance of his work and impress on Rudolph the urgent need to be paid his salary in order to hold out in a besieged castle, or enlist new soldiers, and successfully finish the campaign. In 1604, this kind of plea naturally led on to Kepler wishing Rudolph a victory in his own, extended, battle against the tyranny of 'barbarous' Ottomans.[27] Long after knights had been replaced by armies of foot soldiers, the *miles* (or chivalrous soldier), could still be honoured as a distinct social figure. When reflecting on himself, Kepler prized his own bold mind as analogous to the boldness of soldiers. In his self-description, he had fantasized about how brave a soldier he would have been, quickly drifting into reverie about the nobility of violence: 'the good soldier is not driven to his profession because he desperately enlists once he has consumed his possessions. There is anger in him, a permanent search for cunning, agility, impulsive and surprising attack, and perhaps luck would not be lacking either.'

Yet Kepler had known from a young age that he would never be able to go out in a gleaming cuirass to vent anger or fall in line with commands. Indeed, his physique confronted him with a contradiction to his ideas about men and women. Like Katharina, he was small and lean, so much so that Kepler even described his youthful body as unsuitable for sports and manual labour.[28] In a student theatre production in 1591, the twenty-year-old was selected to play Mary Magdalene because of his slight, graceful figure, and promptly caught a cold after performing on Tübingen's market square. Even three years later, he and his family had to concede that it was easier to imagine him as a teacher than in a pulpit—as parishioners associated solid, bearded manliness with authority.

If anything, these physical traits became more marked with age. Kepler's life was marred by illness and failing eyesight, which some took to discredit his astronomical observations.[29] Even in 1604 he noted that he could not recognize the faces of men approaching in freshly starched, multi-layered wavy ruffs, though he used this inadequacy to explain how images formed in the eye through movements of light. His decision to remarry in 1612, after his first wife had died and left him with two young children, further caused him to consider his body, age, and manhood. Kepler set out that he had first considered choosing a widowed matron. Aged only forty-three, he perceived himself as a 'philosopher whose age of manhood has already passed its zenith and is on its descent, whose effects have been calmed, and whose body by nature is sapless and soft'.[30] He and other advisers worried, for instance, about the height and athletic stature of a younger woman from Linz who in other respects was considered a possible match.[31] By the time that an exhausted Kepler was considering the tenth marriage candidate he was once more thrown back on his thin, sapless, delicate body, which contrasted with the said candidate's small, but excessively fat, features.[32] In the end, he chose a woman he had previously considered, number five in the sequence of potential candidates, a girl called Susanna, whose parents were carpenters. Following their premature death, she had received a disciplined education in a religious school that took in poor orphans. This was not a strategic alliance to increase (or even match) his wealth, honour, and status, yet Kepler wrote with relief: 'her features, manners, physique are adapted to mine'.[33] Kepler fixed the wedding to coincide with the eclipse of the moon, 'in which the spirit of astronomy is hidden'—the heavens could influence life for those who were receptive, but did not determine it.

* * *

Because of his delicate body, Kepler had always regarded himself destined to be a scholar. He differed from women, he mused, chiefly through his well-educated, balanced mind. He also cultivated a sense of his exceptional humoural dryness (whereas women were associated with wetness and cold), so much so that he confessed to liking dry bread and bones, and thought that his later love of 'exceptional Rhine wine' made him sick because it induced too much fluid. From a young age, Kepler disliked water on his body, in such a way that was peculiar even for his time. This became an issue in his first marriage: 'On 29th May', he wrote in 1605 from Prague, 'my wife ruthlessly forced me to finally and for once wash my body.' Kepler tried to keep super-dry. His unease about his masculinity meant that he remained correspondingly anxious to keep women away from any involvement in his work. Intellectual exchange, let alone mechanical or experimental help from a female, would threaten his reputation for unique achievement as a man of the mind. Unlike other natural philosophers, Kepler did not exchange letters with clever high-born women on scientific subjects, nor did he raise his older daughters as humanist miracle girls, in the way that Thomas More, for instance, had done. By contrast, his son Ludwig translated Tacitus with him, and he worried about where the boy should best study. Kepler maintained a clear belief that women's nature prevented them from fully comprehending God's order through reason. 'A wife', he resolutely observed in 1612, 'has and keeps her honour according to her birth and behaviour, she must not help her husband at stargazing.' Fantasizing about his future fame, Kepler immediately spelt out what this meant: none of his wives could claim any share in his reputation, 'which I (will) enjoy in far away countries or after my death'.[34]

Yet as a scholar, Kepler carried out much of his research at home. He vividly related his impatience with his first wife Barbara when she had entered his study at unsuitable times to ask him about household tasks. The door of the study marked their different realms, and Kepler made a point always to speak in Latin to guests on matters of theology and philosophy, so as not to confuse and frighten his wife with troubling ideas, especially since she had already developed a melancholic disposition. Nor did he show her foreign books.[35] As the couple settled into life in Prague, Barbara became acquainted with the astronomer Tycho Brahe (who, in the Austrian fashion, she called Diho Prei), knew the men in his service, talked to them about pay, and took a friend to walk up to the emperor's garden and listen to roaring lions in his zoo. She noted Tycho's instruments in the gardens and, in a rare surviving letter, told Johannes about all these items of news.[36] Her husband wanted her to limit rather than develop this curiosity. The fact that Rudolph was unmarried presumably meant that she never set a foot inside his palace and was unable to see his collections. This was a peculiarly male court—there was no confident empress to shape the court's exchanges with the nobility and the city, just a mistress and erotic paintings. Kepler, in turn, was not confronted with highly learned women at court. His extensive musings on a second marriage reveals that Kepler valued a woman's humility, simplicity, industry in house-holding tasks, thrift, patience, pleasant features, health, and loving behaviour towards his children. These qualities he had come to value more than money or a family name. They also promised to cause least trouble for his professional ambitions and sense of masculine superiority.

As a married scholar, Kepler practised his Lutheran commitment to a legitimate family, heart-felt love, and regular sex.[37] A good Lutheran wife was meant to be a receptive, subordinate, but actively supporting companion for her spouse. Susanna embodied this idea. She also was less rigidly submissive and suffering in the marital bed and, in this, Kepler later in his work adapted a famous analogy by Virgil: 'when the womb of the earth received rain it was like the womb of a happy wife who had pleasure' and 'supported her spouse through suitable movements'.[38] Rain was like male semen, but it needed to fall on fertile ground. This observation strengthened Kepler's objection to the view that the earth was merely inanimate, receiving matter, without any part in or dialogue with creation.

Intellectual practices and academic spouses' lives alike were informed by these time-bound cultural ideas and experiences, which made ideas about masculinity and femininity matter for accounts of creation.

In contrast to the Catholic, unmarried Galileo (who kept a mistress), Kepler never fathered illegitimate children, and during his whole life hardly ever lived alone. He moved from home to boarding schools for boys and then to university life with fellow students, and Tübingen professors and their wives—and then established his own family as soon as he could afford to. Helped mostly by a single male assistant, his research took place while babies were about to be born or about to die, while children played in front of the house or lay sick in their beds. Kepler instructed his children in religion. He lived through his first wife's diseases and looked after the complicated financial matters relating to his stepdaughter Regina. Guests were welcomed in his homes. Alongside the professional institutions for which he worked, the family stood at the centre of Kepler's life.

Although Kepler began to live in a world far removed from Leonberg, he never renounced his family ties. He named his first-born son Heinrich, when his father was already dead, and there was no direct need to please him. He could have chosen the name of his maternal grandfather, who had provided Katharina with a loan to support Johannes's degree. The horoscopes he sketched for his kin document Kepler's particular fascination with patrilinear, not matrilinear descent. His collection included not just Kepler's paternal grandparents, but paternal uncles and aunts, as well as all of his siblings.[39]

His relationship to Katharina, too, was sufficiently strong for her to travel all the way from Leonberg to Prague to visit Johannes's new family in 1602. She would have celebrated becoming a grandmother and seen her son's slight figure walk up the steep hill to the imperial castle in his starched ruff and black gown. As we have seen, he thought several times of returning to Württemberg, closer to his 'dear mother'. For years he would write letters to Katharina, which his sister Margaretha or the local schoolmaster read out to her. She would dictate letters in return. Margaretha knew that she could count on her eldest brother's help when she wrote to him about the allegation of witchcraft against their mother.

* * *

Kepler proved reliable, despite being frantically busy with research. Sheltering Katharina intermittently in Linz, and as the Bohemian Revolt shook the Continent, Kepler continued to work hard on the five books of his most important work so far. The *Harmony of the World* was dedicated to James I as a man who had unified three crowns, 'extinguished' any memory of wars and dissonances between his kingdoms, and seemed destined for 'greater works'. Kepler's view was that a council should be held to reunite the church and restore its early Christian simplicity alongside peace in Europe. He kept fighting against his excommunication in Linz as an alleged 'Calvinist'. The *Harmony* included what we now know as Kepler's third and final law of planetary motion. Kepler had finished its five separate books over many years, but still added new parts, examples, and observations. In December 1618, the first sheets of book five, on astronomy, metaphysics, and 'most complete harmonies of heavenly motions', were printed locally to advertise the work through Kepler's best-known area of expertise (Figure 29).[40]

The other four books were printed in the following six months to July 1619, and they demarcated what was now the far greater scope of his ambitions as a natural philosopher. Typical for his time, Kepler regarded knowledge as revelation about a unified, sacred world rather than a separate, secular system. Book three was prefaced by a quote from Proclus, the Greek philosopher who had held that mathematics created order and harmony in everyone's manners and characters. Mathematics was an ethical and transformative discipline, which

Ioannis Keppleri

HARMONICES
MVNDI

LIBRI V. QVORVM

Primus GEOMETRICVS, De Figurarum Regularium, quæ Proportiones Harmonicas conftituunt, ortu & demonftrationibus.

Secundus ARCHITECTONICVS, feu ex GEOMETRIA FIGVRATA, De Figurarum Regularium Congruentia in plano vel folido:

Tertius propriè HARMONICVS, De Proportionum Harmonicarum ortu ex Figuris; deque Naturâ & Differentiis rerum ad cantum pertinentium, contra Veteres:

Quartus METAPHYSICVS, PSYCHOLOGICVS & ASTROLOGICVS, De Harmoniarum mentali Effentiâ earumque generibus in Mundo; præfertim de Harmonia radiorum, ex corporibus cœleftibus in Terram defcendentibus, eiufque effectu in Natura feu Anima fublunari & Humana:

Quintus ASTRONOMICVS & METAPHYSICVS, De Harmoniis abfolutiffimis motuum cœleftium, ortuque Eccentricitatum ex proportionibus Harmonicis.

Appendix habet comparationem huius Operis cum Harmonices Cl. Ptolemæi libro III. cumque Roberti de Fluctibus, dicti Flud. Medici Oxonienfis fpeculationibus Harmonicis, operi de Macrocofmo & Microcofmo infertis.

Cum S. C. M^{ti}. Priuilegio ad annos XV.

Lincii Auftriæ,
Sumptibus GODOFREDI TAMPACHII Bibl. Francof. Excudebat IOANNES PLANCVS.

ANNO M. DC. XIX.

Figure 29 Johannes Kepler, title page of *Harmony of the World*, with its fourth part on psychological matters. © By permission of the Master and Fellows of St John's College, Cambridge

moreover guided the individual towards a proper understanding of the best principles of political rule and practice. Kepler ended with a political discourse setting out which form of rule was destined to be harmonious and most beneficial. It concluded with an extraordinary prophetic statement: 'I myself indeed, if it should seem good to Him that I should not die but live, shall in the following books declare the works of the Lord.'[41]

Book four continued with the most speculative part of Kepler's religious natural philosophy. This, as the completed edition's title page would explain, was a book that is 'METAPHYSICAL, PSYCHOLOGICAL, AND ASTROLOGICAL'. It dealt with 'the mental essence of the harmonies and on the types of them in the world, especially on the rays which descend from the heavenly bodies to the Earth, and on its effect on Nature or the sublunary and human soul'.[42]

Here was Kepler's attempt to work out the manifestations of harmonic relations in the world and to argue that the earth possessed a soul. Kepler reiterated that he had been particularly impressed by the fact that pregnant women could transmit impressions of people and things they saw onto the foetus. Cleft stones—such as slate, quartzite, or sandstone with their interesting textures—similarly replicated unusual appearances of 'soldiers, monks, priests, kings', as if the earth could have seen them. In just the same way, gems and crystals frequently replicated the five regular geometrical bodies created by God, the world's maker.[43]

This earth reacted not only in ingenious and beautiful ways, but it could suffer illness. It digested and breathed. It was connected to the macrocosm of planets and carried within it the image of the circle of the zodiac. From here, Kepler naturally moved on to discuss astrology. He once more refuted the view that heavenly constellations at the time of birth determined a person's life.

After living for months with Katharina at his home, Kepler now inserted a startling personal paragraph to his astrological writings.

This was most unusual in scholarship of this kind. Continuing to argue against the idea that a horoscope determined a person's life, Kepler could think of no more extreme example of differences in character than himself and his mother, even though they had been born under the same aspects. First came a sentence which still obscured that it was Katharina he had in mind: 'I know of *a woman*', he began:

> [W]ho was born under almost the same aspects, with a temperament that was certainly very restless, but by which she not only has no advantage in book learning (that is not surprising in a woman) but also disturbs the whole of her town, and is the *author of her own lamentable misfortune.*

Having made this extraordinary allegation (Figure 30), he then revealed that he was writing about his own mother. Was this calculated, or did it spring from a lack of control as he reworked his text and found himself too emotionally involved? It is impossible to know. But he wanted to convey that he and his mother were different, and this led him to reflect on the relevance of gender and the power of social as well as political institutions in shaping a life. A person's character was therefore not just to be understood in theological, metaphysical, or cosmological terms, but also as a historical and social phenomenon. It mattered whether you were a man and had access to higher education. It mattered whether your parents were rich or poor. In many ways these were obvious facts, but no one had yet spelt them out in this way. Typically, Kepler focused on a causal analysis, which conventionally compressed complexities into numbered key points:

> First, then, there was added to the aspects of the planets the daily imagination of my mother during her pregnancy, whose mother-in-law, my grand-mother, an enthusiast for popular medicine, which was also practised by her father, was an object of admiration; secondly, there was added the fact that I was born a man, not a woman, a difference in sex which the astrologers seek in vain in the heavens. Thirdly, I take from

CAP. VII. averat trinum Saturni, Sol & Venus juncti defluebant ab isto, applica-
bant ad illum, utrobiq; Sextilibus, defluebant & à quadrato Martis, ad
quem Mercurius proximè applicabat; Luna ad ejusdem trinum ibat, o-
culo Tauri proxima, etiam in latitudine: oriebatur autem 25. Gemino-
rum, culminabat 22. Aquarij. Triplicem configurationem ejus diei
partilem, Sextilem Saturni & Solis, Sextilem Jovis & Veneris, Quadra-
tum Mercurij & Martis prodebat auræ mutatio; nam post gelu dierum
aliquot, eo ipso die tepor ortus, glaciem solvit, pluvias dedit.

Exceptio contra A-strologiam.
Neque tamen hoc uno exemplo omnes Astrologorũ aphorismos
defensos & confirmatos volo; neq; cœlo transcribo rerũ humanarum
gubernacula, imane quantum adhuc abest philosophica hæc observatio
ab illa stulticia, seu malis insaniam dicere. Nam ut hujus exempli vesti-
gia premam; novi fœminam ijsdem penè natam aspectibus, inquietis-
simo sanè ingenio, sed quo non tantum nihil proficit in literis (non mi-
Quæ effi-ciuntur a circumstan-tijs rerum sublauariũ, non funt adscriben-da sideribus
rum hoc est in fœmina); sed etiam totum turbat municipium suum, si-
bique author est miseriæ deplorandæ. Primùm itaque accessit aspectib?
Planetarũ, imaginatio diuturna matris prægnantis, cui socrus, avia mea
medicinæ popularis, à patre etiam excercitæ, studiosa, erat admirationi;
accessit secundò quòd vir natus sum non fœmina; quod sex? discrimen
frustrà quærunt Astrologi in cœlo: Tertiò corporis temperaturam à
matre traho, studijs magis aptam, quàm alijs vitæ generibus; Quartò res
erat parentibus non ampla, glebasc. aberat, cui adnascerer, adhære-
sceremque: Quintò aderant Scholæ, aderant exempla liberalitatis
Magistratuum in pueros studijs aptos.

Animi qua-litates cum planetarum qualitatib? consentiũt plurimum.
Hic intersere, rursùm ex Genesi, Planetarum discrimina in qualitatib?. Nam si Anima lux quædam est; discernet etiam Martis rubore à
Jovis candore, Saturniiq; livore: itaq; fatendum est, magnum auxilium
ex Marte, non tantùm, ut priùs, ad industriam; sed etiam ad acrimoniã
ingenij, quæ consistit in vi ignea, videasq; præcipuos Philosophiæ natu-
ralis, & Medicinæ peritos, sub aspectibus idoneos Martis cum Sole Mer-
curioque nasci: quia nimirùm majus requiritur acumen, major soler-
tia ad eruenda Naturæ arcana, quàm ad reliqua vitæ negocia, studiaq;
ijs deservientia. Largiar etiam amplius aliquid; ex Jove esse in cœli Medium elevato, quòd magis delector Geometriâ in Physicis rebus expres-
* Stipem hic aliq Sa-tyricis no-stris. Nam
sâ, quàm abstractâ illâ, & Saturni siccitate præ se ferente; magis in quam
Physicâ, quàm Geometriâ: et quòd Luna gibba in clara fronte Taurinæ
constellatione, impleat Animæ Phantasticam facultatem imaginibus:
ut apparet, egestas ip-sos premit, qui jocum meum unâ hujus simi-lem ex li-bro de stel-lâ novâ, jam aliquoties intra XII an-norum cur-riculum ru-minarunt.
quarum tamen multas Naturæ rerum consentaneas reipsâ expert? sum,
velut ex Procli * Paradigmatibus delapsas. At si jam de eventu studio-
rum meorum loquar, quid quæso porrò invenio in cœlo, quòd ad illum
vel leviter alludat? Philosophiæ partes non contemnendas à me, vel de
novo erueras, vel emendaras, vel planè perfectas esse, fatentur periti: ac
mea hic sidera fuere, non Mercurius orientalis in angulo septimæ, in
quadrato Martis: sed Copernicus, sed Tycho Braheus, sine cujus Ob-
servationum libris omnia, quæ nunc à me sunt in clarissimâ luce collo-
cata, sepulta jacerét in tenebris: non Saturnus domin? Mercurij, sed Cæ-
sares Augusti, Rudolphus & Matthias, Domini mei: non Planetarum
hospitium, Capricorn? Saturni, sed Austria superior Cæsaris dom?, ejus-
demq;

my mother my bodily constitution, which is more suited to study than to other kinds of life. Fourthly, my parents' means were limited, that is to say there was no land for me to be born to and cling to. Fifthly, there were schools available, there were examples available of the liberality of the magistrates to boys who were suited to study.[44]

Johannes Kepler clearly at times felt resentful of his mother, so much so that he decided to distance himself from her for the learned audience whom he hoped would read his book, by alleging that she was the 'author' of her misfortune. In contrast to Kepler's petition to the duke, Katharina in part appeared an individual wilful agent, guilty of some of her choices and sins, if also a victim of her sex and circumstances. At the same time, he surprisingly revealed a family history of Kepler men and women in his paternal ancestry who had been interested in healing. As always, he underlined that his body had a similar make-up to his mother's. Still, his formal education made him a different person who cultivated a good will rather than evil. Kepler clumsily struggled to protect himself in case Katharina was condemned in a criminal trial, which at this point seemed more likely than not.

* * *

In 1619, he began to present his magisterial tome to high-ranking governors and academics. Several prayers concluded each part. In defiance of the fact that Württemberg churchmen in 1611 had alleged he might stir up too much trouble, *Unruh*, in their Lutheran university, he asserted his religious voice. In fact, Kepler now claimed to be a prophet tasked with revealing God's cosmic harmony for the benefit of mankind.[45]

This ambition once more underlines why he had to distance himself from his mother as much as defend her. In April and June 1619, Kepler had received letters from Christoph Besold, his old Tübingen friend who had risen to become one of six faculty professors of law, and with whom he had kept in touch. Kepler had asked him for his legal opinion. Besold agreed that his mother's trial was a grave matter. It had many possible consequences and no clear outcome. The Tübingen law professors—and thus he himself— were likely to be consulted about how to proceed if the Reinbolds managed to turn the civil defamation suit that the Keplers demanded into a proper criminal trial in which Katharina herself stood accused. Besold assured his friend that he would instantly use his own contacts to the ducal councillor, Bidembach, and the vice chancellor, to ascertain whether a criminal trial might still be prevented.[46]

7

THE TRIAL CONTINUES

Besold's fears that there might be a criminal trial against Katharina were realized. On 9 November 1619, six witnesses assembled in Leonberg's town hall at eight o'clock in the morning. Five were local women: the wife of a tailor, the wife of a barber, and the wife of a carpenter, as well as Benedict Beittelspacher's wife and the daughter of a man known as Schnitzenbastian. They were asked to put their right hand on their hearts and swear on their soul, God, and eternal life, to say nothing but the truth. The only male witness merely had to lift three fingers and swear. Given the gravity of the charge, Christoph Kepler had requested that these solemn 'physical' oaths be made, as opposed to merely verbal oaths. He had asked Dr Matthias Hiller, a member of the Stuttgart chancellery, to supervise proceedings. The matter at hand was no longer the Kepler's defamation charge against the glazier's wife Ursula Reinbold, but the Reinbolds' counter-claim for 1,000 florins in compensation.

Evidently, the Reinbolds had received legal advice on how to construct their case. The glazier represented his 'dear' wife with a much enlarged list of forty-nine accusations. These recounted the, by now familiar, charge that Katharina had asked Ursula to enter her house in 1613 and had given Ursula the drink which had instantly wrecked her health. This allegation was now strengthened with further, shocking, information, which followed the Imperial Law Code teaching on what constituted convincing evidence. Katharina, the glazier disclosed, had learnt witchcraft from an aunt in Weil der Stadt. Contact with any previously convicted person could count as powerful evidence, but even more so if that person was a relative. Katharina Kepler, the Reinbolds alleged, had lived with this aunt for some time, until the woman had been publicly burnt for her craft. In addition, the Reinbolds repeated the claim that Heinrich Kepler, Katharina's second-born son, had been convinced that his mother had ridden a calf to death by getting on its back, in order to cook a roast for him. Even more alarmingly, Katharina had tried to entice a young woman to come with her to the Sabbath (Figure 31). She had thus tried to teach witchcraft, which the Law Code recognized as further evidence of a person's guilt. Katharina had repeatedly driven her husband from home, so that he had perished miserably in war, and had also harmed other men, women, and animals. According to the Reinbolds, she had then tried to escape from Leonberg—a further fact which the Imperial Law Code recognized as supplementary legal evidence to prove a suspect's guilt.[1]

Dr Hiller, the legal prosecutor, regarded such testimony with well-honed judicial reserve. He was determined to establish reliable information and was aware that Katharina might only recently have acquired her reputation as a witch, whereas the Law Code required it to have been thoroughly established for many years. He relied on the six tools of Roman Law to establish circumstance (who did what, where, when, why, and by what means), and therefore insisted that all witnesses needed to specify the exact day and hour when Katharina had apparently acted illegally, as well as who had seen her do what. The Imperial Law Code required at least one acceptable eyewitness report to justify torture. The code treated only

Figure 31 A depiction of a nocturnal Sabbath at a desolated place, attended by whole 'rots' of new witches who arrive on their pitch-forks, dragons or goats to teach each other sorcery, feast and drink without measure, have sex with the devil or dance with cats, snakes, toads and owls. After many years of such practices, they drive to hell with their devils. Broadside, *c.* 1630, based on previous images, 23.5×27.9 cm. © Trustees of the British Museum

men as fully reliable (except if they were already known to be a partial or a personal enemy).

The Keplers in turn provided Hiller with a long list of precise questions. They aimed to undermine the Reinbolds' allegations point by point. What was the name of Katharina's aunt and when was she meant to have been burnt? They knew of no such woman. The family also cast doubt on the Reinbolds' reputation. First, they questioned Ursula Reinbold's sexual history. Was it not true that a coppersmith named Georg Zürn had had sex with Ursula before she had married, and that the glazier Reinbold in fact had married her for her money, even while she was still in prison and known to be a whore? Was there no clear connection between Ursula's lasciviousness and childlessness? Then, the Keplers commented on their own brother Heinrich. There was no point in denying that he had called his mother a witch. But was it not normal for a soldier to talk rudely and was it not more likely that Heinrich himself had slaughtered a calf and then accused his mother of riding it to death? Finally, the Keplers objected to some of the witnesses in advance. The saddler, for instance, was a person well known to exaggerate.

* * *

Among the twenty-one witnesses, the German schoolmaster might appear particularly reliable. Some years earlier, he reported, Katharina Kepler had been constantly pestering him to read out letters from or send greetings to Johannes. One day, she had entered his house through locked doors as he and his wife were having their dinner. Katharina had demanded that he should write a letter to be sent off to Linz then and there, though he no longer remembered its contents.

Similarly, Katharina had asked the schoolmaster to come to her house ten years earlier and read out several letters. It had been a Sunday, and he had wanted to go to church. Yet Katharina had detained him, pressing him to drink some of the good wine she had in her cellar, to thank him. As he was not thirsty, he had only sipped from the pewter mug, but Katharina kept prevailing upon him to drink more. Another woman joined them, swallowed most of her wine and had become so ill that she later died. The schoolmaster had begun to feel pain in his thighs the following day. Next, he could only walk holding on to sticks. Now he was almost lame.

A woman named Dorothea Klebl also appeared to be a perfectly trustworthy witness. Born and raised in Leonberg, she was married to the local marksman. She knew that her age was roughly thirty-three and she carefully replied to questions. Her answers revealed surprising as well as legally damning information. Five years earlier, she had employed a young local seamstress to carry out some needlework. Just before this time, this girl had worked for Katharina Kepler, who had once urged her to stay overnight. Deeply disturbed by the events which had followed, the girl had confided in her new employer.

The woman Klebl relayed what the girl had told her. 'Close to midnight', the girl had said, Katharina had risen from her bed to 'roam about' in the main room of her house. As the seamstress woke up, she asked: 'Why do you roam about in the chamber instead of lying in bed?' Katharina replied: 'Would it not please you to become a witch (*Unhold*)?', promising the young girl 'joy and debauchery beyond measure'. On earth, Katharina had declaimed to the girl, there was 'neither joy nor spiritedness'.

Klebl continued to repeat apparently verbatim how this strange nocturnal exchange continued. The seamstress had worried: 'If you have a lot of joy and voluptuousness in this world, you will have to pay for it eternally.' Katharina had instantly dismissed such pious concerns. 'There is no eternal life,' she had brutally stated: 'when man dies, he perishes, like senseless beasts'. The seamstress had nonetheless insisted on the message she had heard in Lutheran sermons, catechism classes, and school for so many years. 'The pastors', she retorted, 'preach that the one who believes and has been baptised will live for eternity.' Those who 'do not believe will be damned'. Katharina had responded darkly that the only reason for having pastors was that people could safely cross the streets when visiting one another instead of fearing violence.[2]

How are we to treat such an astonishing report? Nobody thought that Klebl was untrustworthy. Everything she said was taken to be a plausible account of how an evil person might act. She testified under oath, and was told that God would punish her if she lied. In Klebl's version of events, Katharina spoke with the voice of nocturnal pleasure, against a moral dullness that had drained women's lives of fun and surprises—the pangs of excitement, one might imagine, that a woman of any age might feel when she saw a handsome man and felt like flirting and flying towards him. According to this account, Katharina's reasoning was not even linked to a positive vision about how civil communities could be allowing for female desire and spiritedness. Its darkest element was the idea that citizens were full of individual hatred against each other and were unable to live safely together. The clergy fulfilled a functional role of basic peacekeeping. Ordinary citizens were seen as latent murderers, in a joyless society kept together by invented religious ideas. It was the force of such broad and destructive social visions which made the figure of the woman as a witch so deeply unsettling. Witchcraft allowed ordinary men and women in tightly regulated communities to speak about fears so terrifying that they otherwise could never have been voiced.

Many Württemberg people experienced life as a path to eternity (or damnation for those who did not adhere to Lutheranism or behaved sinfully without repenting). Pastors used sermons to illustrate why God was so angry with his flock and required immediate repentance. This produced pervasive concerns about individual or collective divine punishment, and explains why many communities felt such a need to permanently exercise control over individual behaviour. 'All punishment and plague', the saddler repeated, 'comes from the Lord.'[3] People prayed to attract God's grace, but sin was believed to threaten every minute of their lives. Fear of punishment was projected onto others. Tellingly, the Leonberg schoolmaster revealed that he had not spoken of his suspicion before as he suspected Katharina might have been God's tool to punish him with lameness for his past sins. If the devil used people as his instruments to act on earth, so might God.

* * *

Alongside God's providential punishment, a son's hatred for his mother must have ranked among the worst of this period's anxieties, perhaps so powerful that it was almost entirely taboo. Biblical stories, of course, contain a remarkable amount of sibling hatred. The popular story of the prodigal son illustrates family disappointments. Yet no Christian story provides ways of thinking about what happens when a child viciously takes against his own mother, as Katharina's second-born son had done.

Heinrich had always been a demanding child and brother. Johannes Kepler wrote fully about his brother in his early horoscopes. From childhood onwards, Heinrich had suffered from epilepsy— one of the most feared illnesses at the time.[4] A person was diagnosed with epilepsy if seen losing control in terrifying attacks of trembling and falling. Sometimes foam built up in the mouth, and their thumbs turned inwards towards the hand. Epileptic children appeared unpredictable, like wild animals. They were often kept out of the sight of pregnant women, who, it was believed, would be so shocked that they could 'imprint' similar cramps on the foetus. In addition, just like Heinrich, many of those afflicted suffered from respiratory problems, which at their worst threatened to suffocate them.[5] It was difficult to find apprenticeships and work for epileptic teenagers, and Heinrich's masters gave him regular beatings.

By 1589, the year their father eventually left the family for good, Johannes recorded that the father had driven his second-born away, threatening to sell him.[6] Pushed out from home, Heinrich the Younger travelled to Austria to embark on a series of precarious short-term employments. He moved on to Hungary to fight against the Turks, and then returned to a living baking bread and singing in the streets of Vienna. For four years from 1590, while Johannes thrived academically, his brother was a servant, sometimes homeless, a beggar, a robber, and a drummer for an army regiment. After being robbed in Cologne (by a band of thieves called cockerel-feather, *Hahnenfeder*), he returned home. Johannes Kepler stayed with his mother in July 1593, presumably to help her with the harvest. Listening to his brother, he tried to help him as best he could. Johannes wrote a brief letter to their grandfather Sebald to let him know that Leonberg's pastor had talked to the ducal governors and they had been willing to arrange some kind of position for Heinrich. As these plans would need at least eight days to be finalized, Johannes was anxious for his brother to stay, in the meantime, with his grandfather in Weil. This would ensure that the Leonberg upper governor could not change his mind on account of Heinrich's behaviour, which clearly made him a liability. Johannes added that Heinrich was 'of no use to his mother'.[7] Katharina at this point would have had two young children—little Christoph (aged six) and Margaretha (aged nine). Johannes was a student. To have a difficult twenty-year-old descend on her in summer, when her farm work was as its most intense, was doubtless demanding.

In 1597, Johannes Kepler again wrote on Heinrich's behalf, this time from Graz. Heinrich had visited a tavern in the town of Bruck fourteen days earlier to drink, and had stayed overnight. In the morning, he left behind his passport on a table near the window. Although he had properly paid the innkeeper and left the customary tip for the maidservant, they had not forwarded the document. Following his brother's pleading, Johannes thus asked a high-ranking local acquaintance whether he could do anything in the matter, so that Heinrich could continue to travel.[8]

In Prague, once again Johannes helped Heinrich, this time to become an imperial guardsman. Johannes was an important figure and his appeal on behalf of his brother could not be dismissed. Accordingly, for the first time in Heinrich's life, it seems, he managed to hold down a job for eight years. He married and had two daughters. But, in 1613, as soon as Johannes left Prague, Heinrich felt so ill and poor that he sought care from monks in the convent of Ammerbach: he persuaded Johannes to write to the emperor pleading for a payment. As he converted to Catholicism, Heinrich was then assigned a monastery that would take care of him as his health further deteriorated. His wife seems to have died or disappeared. Yet as he presented himself at the monastery, its monks refused Heinrich entry. It is easy to imagine just how frustrated and angry he must have been as a result.[9]

By 1615, Heinrich had left his two daughters with Johannes in Linz to return to Leonberg on his own. Worn out at forty-two years of age, he complained to others about the permanent feeling of cold he had suffered as the emperor's guard.[10] He arrived at Leonberg's gates on a frosty winter weekend. Everybody had baked as much bread as they needed for the week, as was the custom. Gaunt cows stood in cold stables. The baker's wife reported that Katharina had knocked on her door on a Saturday evening to ask whether she could have a little drop of milk because her 'son had come and desired to eat [*sic.*] milk'. Since the baker's wife had not been milking much at the time, she sent Katharina on to another neighbour, whom she knew had bought new livestock. Katharina, however, insisted. The baker's wife had finally given her milk. By Sunday morning the baker's wife reported that their calf was ill. The old cowherd of Eltingen instantly diagnosed that it suffered a 'bad sickness'. The baker's wife was told that she should simmer good herbs and feed the calf with them as well as spread the mixture along its back.

One week later, the baker's wife was kneading dough at Ursula Reinbold's house when the latter complained how Katharina's drink had made her ill. Instantly, the baker's wife made the connection: 'Well, well, she has also come a lot into my house, the day my calf was ill, I wonder whether she has been riding it.' This was reported to Governor Einhorn. By the time Katharina heard about this charge, she angrily challenged her neighbour: 'Are you telling people that I have ridden your calf to death?' 'No', the fifty-year-old baker's wife replied with great force, 'but if I knew that you had done it, I would beat you down with a log.'

Such testimonies bear out the extent to which people in this society were woven into each other's lives. They helped each other, knocked on doors, cared for each other when illness afflicted them, worked in each other's houses, shared drinks, and, sometimes, feared the worst of each other. An honourable Lutheran baker's wife evidently had no trouble imagining herself violently striking down an old neighbour.

Heinrich himself had told the baker's wife that things were not right with his mother. The baker's wife enquired of him as to whether he had not received roast meat and presents from his mother (in fact, Katharina had asked to roast meat for her son in the baker's wife's oven). At this Heinrich exploded, and became a liability to the family in ways that Johannes had always feared and tried to contain: 'The devil should feed on the roast,' he exclaimed. Anything his mother had ever given him, he claimed, she had 'brought over from Weil der Stadt'—the nearby town where his grandfather Sebald lived, as if this meant that she neglected him. He demanded extraordinary motherly care and was to be endlessly disappointed. When the baker's calf finally died, Heinrich felt certain that it was because his mother 'was not right'.[11] On 17 February, Heinrich passed away at his sister Margaretha's home, the vicarage in Heumaden.

* * *

Once a woman was seen to be a witch, many people believed that she could transform herself into other creatures. One of the saddler's neighbours thus pointed out a cat crouching upon a barn and said that this was Katharina.[12] Some men blamed Katharina for driving her husband away. A 'proper, honest wife, who valiantly keeps her husband well', they said, would not have a man leave her.[13]

Fears soon attached themselves onto Katharina more easily. The butcher, for instance, had felt pain in one thigh and suffered from blurred vision 'as if there was fog in front of his eyes' after Katharina merely walked past him one day. He knew that anyone who could harm could also heal, and also that the way to get help was to beg such people three times for help in God's name. So he murmured to himself, 'Katharina, help me again.' Next, he washed himself with his own urine and also put a urine-soaked cloth over his thigh. Urine was believed to be nature's precious distillation from the human body. After these treatments, he said that he had felt fully recovered from her magical attack, and in court was anxious to stress that, above all, he had surely received God's help.[14]

A tailor, who worked in Katharina's and other people's homes, similarly knew how to protect himself against evil. He always blessed himself as he rose up in the morning and lay down at night. When two of his children became seriously ill, Katharina taught his wife words to say during 'full moon in the church yard under the open sky'. But this was no secret female knowledge—he already knew the words himself.[15] Lutheranism could envelop ancient ideas about how to ward off evil or draw supernatural power into daily life, so as to avoid misfortune. Religious prayers and rituals provided a sensation of agency against malice and formed part of men's as much as women's survival tactics.

This was why it was all the more shocking when these common tools seemed to fail and an identified witch was perceived as too wicked to undo her own spells. At this point, she became someone the community might feel licensed to denounce. Suspicions were passed on from generation to generation, so much so that one thirty-year-old woman reported a story she had heard from her parents about Katharina from twenty-five years earlier. They had told her that in 1590, just after Heinrich had left, Katharina had asked the forester to help her put manure on the fields, the all-essential treatment for her soil. He had been too busy, but in turn had worried that she, in revenge, had made one of his pigs go wild and die.[16]

As a widow whose two oldest sons had lived far away for many years, Katharina relied on help from others. She had no horses to do any carting, and this meant asking wealthier people for favours. Eight years earlier, the district scribe, for instance, had declined Katharina's request that his servant should fetch her one cartload of hay. Instead, he had instructed the servant to get the horse ready and transport hay into the master's stable. Mid-way, at the shepherd's house, the horse had suddenly become unusually weak. It drank from a well. Its throat began to swell. After a few days, the precious horse had recovered 'with God's help'. There was no clear reason to blame Katharina, but the scribe had never forgotten the event.[17]

Some parents who had lost children, and never lost their deep sense of pain, sought to attribute blame. The tailor remembered that Katharina had dropped by his house ten years earlier to offer advice about his ill children. She had been 'leaning over the cradles and children' just in order to kill them, he said. There was no doubt in his mind that she should be examined under torture to reveal her 'devil's art'.[18]

Another man felt similarly convinced of Katharina's wrongdoing. Donatus Gültlinger, a man in his fifties, affirmed that even if he was given the whole of Leonberg's 'Angel'-mountain in gold he would not lie. The truth, he said, was that Katharina had told him herself on the market square that she had mistakenly mixed up her jugs of wine and herbs when inviting Ursula Reinbold to her house.

* * *

There is little sense in all this evidence, however, that Katharina was regarded as a specialized healer who was paid for her recipes and advice. She was once referred to as a midwife (*Wehemutter*), but local records show that she was never approved for this important communal position. Like most people, she could draw on a rich diversity of local herbs and plants, as well as a range of ingredients traded at markets. With age, she would have accumulated experience, which was believed to be all important in understanding the endlessly intricate effects of drugs. A few of Württemberg's small towns sustained their own pharmacy, while a host of specialized practitioners offered advice for more complicated or persistent symptoms.[19] The day-labourer's wife Haller, for instance, paid for a prescription, bought herbs, and then made hot baths for her son to take for nine days, during which no stranger was to look at him.[20]

The question was how to distinguish between good and bad medicine. Johannes Kepler, as we have seen, agreed that good astrology was very much like medicine in its character, as inductive art which required observation, experience, and analysis. Medics, he wrote, needed to listen to what 'old women' would tell them about the virtues of herbs, but without taking on all of their superstitions. Experts observed symptoms, therapies, and, with 'reason, time and experience' learned to distinguish general principles from particular circumstances that could influence an illness. Proper medical experts, in addition, studied the many different properties of the same type of herb and thus identified essential knowledge. Astrologers similarly learnt from peasants. Yet this did not make a peasant an astrologer, or an old woman a medic, except if she was a *Pharmaceutria*—a pharmaceutic expert distinguished by sufficient experience.[21]

Kepler's view thus allowed for the possibility of lay expertise and endorsed that particular types of sciences needed to build on common knowledge. Other men of his age, such as the French jurist René Choppin, even thought that 'simple old peasant women' outdid medical savants, while Robert Boyle urged his readers to be 'a little more curious to take notice of the Observations and Experiments, suggested partly by the practice of Midwives, Barbers, Old Women, Empericks, and the rest of that illiterate crue'.[22]

In everyday life, it remained common for men and women to simply offer their advice and anything they found useful, whether this be herbs, sayings, amulets, stones, or by touch. Katharina Kepler was no exception when she followed the medical principles of sympathies and correspondences, and offered a 'fire-stone' to cure like by like by drawing heat out of one woman's body and by utilizing the stone's attractive powers. (Basilius Valentine's rediscovered writings positively endorsed the medicinal properties of fire-stones as did the most recent medical literature.)[23] At other times, Katharina might leave herbs to soak, to turn into a paste and be smeared on the feet or other parts of the body to re-establish a flow of blood or other substances which had got dangerously stuck.[24] Such common Galenic treatments tried to restore a humoural balance of fluids. These treatments were often linked to spiritual elements that called on divine help. More often than not, many of these cures proved effective.[25]

* * *

There was, however, one exceptional thing that Katharina Kepler had done: she had asked for her father's skull. Skulls ranked among the legally recognized means of sorcery and could render anyone dealing with them under suspicion of being a witch. The interrogator tried to establish what exactly had happened. Allegedly, Katharina had entered the baker's house announcing to his wife what a 'stately thing' it was for a person to possess their father's skull. The baker's wife had already heard from the gravedigger's widow that Katharina had asked him to dig out her father's head and bring it to her. She wanted to turn it into a drinking cup, and knew a man who had done the same.[26] A witness called Hans Gülttlinger reported that the gravedigger had been sitting at home mending his shoes when he told his nephew that Katharina had intended to send this drinking cup to her son in Prague.[27] She imagined that the skull would be mounted in silver, but had dropped the whole idea once the gravedigger made clear that he would have to inform the authorities. Leonberg's gravedigger at that time was a man named Martin Häller. He remembered how around eighteen years previously, when he was a fifteen-year-old boy helping to dig a shoemaker's grave, the former gravedigger had told him that Katharina had seen him about her request, promised a good reward, and said that she wanted to send the skull to Prague.

Why would Katharina Kepler have thought of such a seemingly bizarre gift? As we have seen, a deep fascination with the arcane was fundamental to the world in which Johannes Kepler moved. It coincided with the period's interest in 'rational' measurements of shapes, time, and space. 'Herein lies his Majesty's brain' reads the engraving on a silver vessel in Rudolph II's tomb, while the most precious of three rings with which the emperor was buried was made of carefully chosen gemstones in rectangular mounts with zodiac signs in between.[28] The melancholic emperor was attracted to objects that had a magical, mysterious, wise, or witty quality. Characteristic examples of his collection of strange and intriguing things were Arcimboldo's *Reversible Head with Meats*, a painting that turned a composite head into an image of two hands revealing a platter of meat, and a Nuremberg goldsmith's vessel made from a rare rhinoceros horn, which was sold to Rudolph because it was 'meant to be good against poison'. Among Rudolph's most prized possessions was a unicorn's horn, which alongside other items in his extensive cabinet of curiosities supported him in his claims for universal knowledge and imperial magnificence. Most of these objects had protective properties.

Rudolph's tastes were widely shared at the time. Skulls, of course, were ubiquitous symbols of the vanity of earthly pursuits. Contemporary still-life paintings, such as Pieter Claesz's *Vanitas Still Life*, represented skulls and assorted bones in such a realistic and shocking fashion that these painters must have worked from real specimens.[29] For cabinets of curiosities, skulls were closely observed and carved in ivory, which naturally looked like bone. There was great interest among learned people in classical sources that described how Germans and other people had used skulls as drinking vessels in hero worship or ancestor cults. In Wales, worshippers went to the small village of Llandyfan to drink healing waters from what they believed to be the skull of St Teilo, a bishop in the sixth century.[30] The idea that drinking from a skull was a protective or empowering ritual was, therefore, a connection that was just about within the realm of the possible at the time.

Skulls, moreover, were used to make medicines. Leonberg's castle pharmacy, operated by the ladies Sibylle and Maria, contained a 'little bag with seven pieces of a skull' in one of its drawers. They also owned glasses of human fat, taken from the bodies of people who had been executed. This was another ingredient used in medicines, as it was believed to preserve the person's vital forces. In 1609, Joachim Tancke (1557–1609), an anatomy professor in Leipzig, explained to Duke Moritz of Hesse-Kassel how the body of a healthy man who had died violently could be turned into 'quite a precious' mummy. Tancke was a follower of Paracelsus, exchanged letters with Johannes Kepler about musical harmonies. He explained that the mummy would avert illness through the healing power of intact tissues, which counteracted putrefaction.[31]

This partly explains why German executioners and their wives typically worked as healers, as they provided access to these magical properties. Johannes Hartmann (1568–1631), who took up the first professorial appointment in chemical medicine at Marburg University in 1609, noted how in 1615 a hangman sold him a wandering monk's blood. He used it to produce the *mumia aurea*, the vital force on which 'sympathetic preparations of most Paracelsian physicians' focused to regenerate the body of man.[32] Even monks, it seemed, retained some uses for Protestants.

At courts, meanwhile, the cult for ewers, bowls, jugs, cups, and drinking vessels of all kinds of material was at a height. These were common gifts and provided further opportunity to use prized metal-workers, play on learned references, and make ingenious innovations for mounts.[33] It is entirely possible that Katharina had been inspired by an object she had seen during her own stay in Prague. Many specialized craftsmen displayed their innovative wares, and burghers living in the New Town area owned objects similar to those found in the cabinets of curiosities.[34] Later in the trial, Katharina testified that she had seen two of these skull drinking cups at a provisor's house in Tübingen as well as one in another Tübingen home, presumably when she had visited Johannes as a student. She had also heard drinking rituals from skulls mentioned in a sermon.[35]

Sometimes gravediggers found a skull that was used for magical purposes on site: in 1619, a Württemberg pastor reported that the gravedigger had found one inscribed in ink with the words Boach, Sarrith, Lucifer, and marked with cross-hatching.[36] Evoking the devil and—presumably—evil spirits was clearly not at all what Katharina had in mind, and she certainly seemed to think that Johannes would appreciate her present. This suggests that she hoped that he would identify with her side of the family, through the memory of a grandfather he had known well, lived with inter-mittently, and by whom he had been financially supported. The drinking cup perhaps ultimately expressed Katharina's wish that her local, peasant origins could be connected to and gain a presence in

Johannes's courtly life in Prague. All the same, her request was remembered locally because Leonberg people clearly drew a line when it came to digging up human remains of an honourable Christian in order to turn them into a decorative object.

* * *

Taken together, all of the depositions provided a mish-mash of contradictory evidence. Katharina appeared hospitable and helpful to some, but pushy and dubious to others. While several witnesses were sure that Katharina needed to be interrogated under torture and had done much harm, others presented far more ambiguous assessments as to whether their physical symptoms might be linked to any of her deeds. Those who were sceptical deployed a clear set of common sense criteria to make causal connections. Barbara, the butcher's wife, for instance, said that Katharina had not touched her husband on the day that his symptoms began—and he himself even added that the whole matter was dazzling and deluding, and 'hence he could not know it'. They were both careful not to associate themselves with the Reinbolds' campaign to turn their experience into evidence against the accused.

Some witnesses even showed solidarity. Katharina's sister-in-law, who was now a fifty-year-old widow and lived locally, testified that Katharina's maidservant had once brought her some herbs, with which she had fed her animals. They had fallen ill, but perhaps because of some insects in those herbs. Other people who had looked at the animals felt sure that at least one of them was touched by evil. Still, each of them had been cured by medicine, 'soups and fruit'. In contrast to other witnesses who reported on this story to blame Katharina, her sister-in-law could see no evidence for any intentional harm.[37] Agnes Werner felt unsure that Katharina's husband had necessarily left Katharina out of anger. Moreover, she asserted, 'he would have been sure to save his children from knowing' about it.[38] So how, then, were any of the community meant to judge his motives?

'God in Heaven will know best', another witness firmly concluded, echoing what Lutheran pastors had cautiously preached for many years: instead of blaming others, and perhaps blaming the wrong person, people were to think about their own sins, try to behave as best as they could, and leave it to God to separate wheat and chaff on the day of judgement.

Appolonia, Hanns Schmid's wife from the village of Höffingen, even recounted that whenever she had visited Leonberg over many years, Katharina had always invited her in for drinks and a meal. She had never once felt ill. Aged fifty, she was now short of breath and suffered from a bloated body. But she really could not blame Katharina for that, as she had been sociable with her long before it had happened.[39] Common people were thus perfectly able to critically assess the evidence. Their scrutiny kept accusations low. It also prepared the ground for Kepler's final defence.

As for Ursula Reinbold's reputation, it turned out that she had indeed been fought over by two men, and that her other suitor had later left Leonberg. Everyone was aware that she had not had any children. This, most of all, cast doubt on what kind of woman she was. A hallmark of Lutheran womanhood was to sustain regular sex within marriage, avoid contraception, experience the pain of childbirth, and rear pious children. Since all women were believed to be heavily tainted by sin and characterized by their lack of reason, they could raise themselves to be considered honourable women only by how they behaved. It mattered how they spoke, dressed, how well they cleaned, worked, how endlessly busy they were, and how selflessly they cared for others. In Reinbold's case it was not clear that she had ever cared for anyone else, except for jointly working with her husband.

* * *

In mid-January 1620, the whole record of inconclusive interrogations was sent to the Stuttgart chancellery. The glazier soon worried that the Keplers might wish to delay proceedings and keep Katharina at her daughter's house, waiting for the mother, 'an old wench', to die.[40] By late March, the duke received an appeal written in Katharina's own name. She, too, wished her case to be concluded, promising to 'earn' grace for Duke John Frederick through her 'poor prayers to God'. The document is signed 'humbly Catharina, blessed Heinrich Kepler's widow at Leonberg'.[41]

8

OTHER WITCHES

———⊗⊗⊗⊗———

Religious and political trouble in Europe had mounted since the beginning of Katharina's trial. Frederick V, the Calvinist ruler of the Palatinate, was crowned king of Bohemia in autumn 1619, and promised to turn the country into a military Christian 'bulwark' against the Turks (Figure 32). But Emperor Ferdinand II was determined to defend Habsburg lands for the Catholics. A war challenged the Holy Roman Empire's whole framework of cooperation between territories of different faiths. In Lutheran territories, anxieties about Jesuit deceptions and Spanish tyranny, as much as about Calvinist conspiracies, rose up at once. The empire's well-honed mechanisms aimed at creating a culture of religious compromise, prosperity, honesty, and justice were now under threat.[1]

In this climate, the very title of Kepler's *Harmony of the World* was intended to be a political statement. If the Brandenburg pastor Schaller was among those confessional polemicists who expected a *ruina mundi*, a downfall of the world, then Kepler calmly and confidently insisted on a harmonic world and non-confrontational religious behaviour, even in the wake of the Bohemian revolt.[2]

SERENISS. POTENT. PRIN. FRIDERICVS D.
G. BOHEM. REX, COMES PALATINVS. RHI . S.R. I.
PRIN. ELECTOR . DVX BOIAR. MARCH. MORAV. DVX. SILES.
MARCH . LVSAT. ETC.

Figure 32 Frederick, Elector Palatine, as King of Bohemia, with Prague in the background, engraving by Matthäus Merian, *c.*1620, 35 × 26.3 cm. © Trustees of the British Museum

This eirenic project now attracted obstacles as if by magnetic force. By June 1619, the old, experienced Palatinate councillor Christian von Anhalt had convinced many fellow Protestants to favour a military confrontation with the Habsburgs. Württemberg's court was split into different factions. One remained loyal to the emperor in Vienna and worried about the Heidelberg Calvinists. Another happily imagined a Protestant push for the imperial crown and a new European order defined by cooperation among England, the Estates General, France, and German Protestants. A third faction pondered how Habsburg weaknesses might be exploited within the German lands. As ever, the problem remained as to how to find the means to provide for common defence. Duke John Frederick wrote to his estates in April that the Habsburgs would now descend on all Protestants after triumphing against the Bohemian estates.[3]

In July, for the very first time Württemberg estates recommended a large-scale military recruitment of 12,000 mercenaries. Many feared that a 'Spanish monarchy' would revoke religious peace agreements. In a radical shift of policy, Duke John Frederick, who possessed no military experience, informed Christian von Anhalt that he was keen to lead troops into battle. Even Sebastian Faber, the duke's trusted adviser, began to adopt the rhetoric of 'Spanish danger' and thought that if a Protestant had obtained the Bohemian crown this had to be 'God's will'. New, divinely created possibilities presented themselves. Guards were reinforced across the duchy. Frederick's homeland in the Palatinate would certainly need to be defended in case of a Habsburg attack. 'Reason of state', John Frederick explained to the English diplomat Henry Wotton, tied him not to 'suffer a stranger to be his neighbour'.[4]

As fears of instability gripped Germany, Leonberg witnessed further witchcraft trials. Shortly after Katharina's file had been sent to Stuttgart to await a decision, two other women stood accused in Leonberg's town hall. For three years there had been no witchcraft trial in the entire district. Now, the same jury was alert and ready to proceed quickly.

On 21 January 1620, three Leonberg councillors and two citizens watched the executioner torture an old widow. A resident of the local home for the sick and elderly, Margaretha Frisch had not confessed to any charges, but she seemed alarmingly ignorant in matters of religion. The documents remain silent about how she was tortured. At the very least, the executioner would have shown Margaretha his tools in order to frighten her. Then, he would have progressed to real torture by applying thumb- or leg-screws, or by tying the woman's arms and legs together and pulling her off the ground on a rope which was attached to a wheel. Those accused of witchcraft and other crimes were left hanging on this rope for between seven and fifteen minutes, their bodies brutally stretched. Further measures were rare in Württemberg, but would include repeatedly pulling up an offender, or using heavy weights on the legs, so that the body was painfully stretched up as well as down.[5]

In the afternoon, after the executioner (*Henker*—hangman, as he was officially called) had finished his work, Margaretha fully confessed that the evil spirit had met her twenty years previously, while she collected firewood. She and the devil had had rough sex in the middle of the Sindelfingen forest and several times afterwards, despite the fact that her husband then had still been alive. Abandoned in pleasure, they would often dance in the woods. *Black Caspall* was her 'suitor', dressed in black and standing tall on his goat-feet. Carried away by delusion, she had only noticed these after some time. He had told Margaretha to harm several people and no longer to worship God. In return, Caspall promised her wealth, 'considerable' trade, and fine food and drink. He gave her a salve to smear onto a long stick in order to make it fly. Margaretha feasted and danced at the Sabbaths, where she recognized four other local women, three of them from the care home, as well as the old coppersmith's wife, who lived in the poor house. Her night flights ended when the salve was all used up.

As the law required, Governor Einhorn, the pastor, and the civic scribe read these confessions back to Margaretha Frisch the next day. She now denied some details and withdrew three women from her list of playmates. The men found her obdurate and evil. After one further night in prison, she died. Even her guard, a woman nicknamed 'crooked Agnes', had no sense of what the cause might have been.[6]

Margaretha was buried below the gallows, on a hill outside Leonberg, where the ashes of the witches who had been burnt in 1616 had long dissolved into the soil. After the Heimsheim hunt, a widow from the village of Eltingen had been released after not confessing to anything during torture. A Heimsheim potter's wife was tortured in 1617, but likewise did not confess.[7] In 1620, Einhorn and the court were in no doubt that Margaretha Frisch had intended to mortally injure others. Had she not perished in prison, Margaretha would have been the first citizen of the town of Leonberg to burn, and the first witch to die after the winter of crisis in 1616.

Governor Einhorn was responsible for nine out of at least twelve death sentences for witchcraft in Leonberg's entire history. Yet his predecessor had already sentenced two women to death in 1612 and Einhorn did not obsessively hunt witches after 1616. Leonberg was not gripped by a panic—in fact its local women, on the whole, were well protected from accusations. Every decision in cases of witchcraft involved local judges. From 1620, it also involved local jurists, the pastor, scribes, and ducal councillors. None of this was Einhorn's sole preserve. All these men were shocked when a woman such as Margaretha told her terrifying story about wishing for the 'good' life of evil. She had slapped people so that they were lame.

No relative lobbied for Margaretha Frisch, even though a son and a sister lived nearby. Everyone knew her by the first name of her deceased husband, Martin. She was Martin's *Greta*, as if she still belonged to him. Some had been suspicious of her for many years, in Leonberg and elsewhere, so much so that children might be held away from her when she visited a house. Legally, such suspicions could then be represented as 'common opinion', even though many other people were less certain about such allegations. Margaretha herself had already formally complained years earlier that she felt unfairly targeted—and she clearly felt under enormous pressure. The trial established that she had twice angrily slapped a twenty-year-old maidservant who was aware of her reputation. She had also touched a cow after exclaiming how beautiful it was and enthusiastically patting it with her hands. The cow had subsequently suffered unusual pain. Finally, Margaretha had encouraged her prison guard to feed his pig on the food she had left uneaten. This pig had likewise exhibited strange symptoms. Both animals had subsequently recovered, while the maidservant had been unable to work for a time. Margaretha had eventually recommended a successful recipe against the maidservant's headaches: simmer cherry kernels in vinegar and afterwards use a veil to press them onto the head.

Had Margaretha cast a spell and was she now prepared to take it away? The maidservant's father testified cautiously that he was unaware of the widow's bad reputation, but could not be sure she was innocent either. Hanns Nestler, an advocate, declared that Margaretha's sister was married to his brother in Sindelfingen. He was seventy-four or seventy-five years old and had heard about the suspicion against Margaretha ever since becoming a Leonberg citizen. Surprisingly, this aged advocate also acted as occasional vet. Two months earlier he had been asked to help Hans Beutelspacher's sick cow. As she recovered within an hour, he remained unsure about whether her illness had natural causes or not. But he was certain that some Leonberg animals were attacked by sorcery. Four months hence, Oberwiert's calf had clearly been touched by a 'night damage'. He had also seen the civic guard's pig, which trembled, tried to dig itself into the ground, and pushed its snout against walls. The pig's tongue seemed to have been smeared with lard. There was no doubt that it, too, had been 'badly' attacked, although it likewise responded to his treatment within twenty-four hours.

All this confirms that people's common sense knowledge was frequently informed by distinctions between what was known and what could be proved. Some people were remarkably scrupulous about relating observed phenomena to natural or supernatural causes, as well as being thorough in collecting evidence. Many kept registering evidence for someone's propensity to be a witch, recording magical occurrences over years, and even decades, weighing up different indications, and prepared to leave their conclusions open until further proof emerged.

Another Leonberg citizen, who was eighty-three, related how a full fifty-three years earlier he had suffered terrible pain below his knees for twelve weeks, and not been able to sit, lie, or stand. Even so, he had never suspected Margaretha of being the cause. Jacob Stoll, a vintner, who only knew that he was 'over seventy years' old' was interrogated next. He and Margaretha's first husband had been close friends. This meant that they confided in each other, enjoying a 'special trust'. One day, Margaretha's husband had secretly told Stoll that his 'manhood' had completely disappeared. He was impotent. Four months later, he died. Stoll was at pains to stress, however, that his friend had not feared sorcery nor suspected his wife in any way.

Seventy-year-old local judge Michel Stoll remained cautious, too—it was 'far too difficult', he testified, for him to know whether or not Margaretha had caused disease in animals through sorcery. His wife agreed 'by her conscience' that she was unable to say whether or not the maidservant's accusations were true. The stakes were high. If an accusation proved wrong, instigators were likely to be charged with the costs of a trial. Witnesses were reminded that any false testimony they might knowingly supply would attract

God's great anger during their earthly life and provide Satan with their soul straight after death.[8]

Sixty-year-old Lucia Dreher, who belonged to one of Leonberg's wealthy families, was more suspicious. A resident of the local care home, she had witnessed how a man had publicly insulted Margaretha, calling her a witch and a beast. Margaretha had not rebutted the accusation. When asked why she was not protesting or taking him to court, she had merely replied that this man was not 'good' enough for her to bother with. To Lucia Dreher, this seemed strange—as people usually defended their good name.

The care home's cook, by contrast, quickly concluded her testimony: she was very busy with her cooking and did not care much about rumours. Aged around twenty-three, she had worked at the home for six years, and reported factually how the maidservant had returned to work after having been hit about twelve weeks earlier. She suffered increasing pain. The care home's maid in charge of animals had nothing to add either.

Alleged witches were hence victims of some rather than all of their neighbours. Next among the witnesses was Walburga Haller, the forty-six-year-old day-labourer's wife, who was also in the forefront of those accusing Katharina Kepler as a witch. She immediately reported that she had known 'forever' about the 'very bad suspicion' and 'great rumour' against Margaretha. And it was she who finally supplied a new piece of damaging information. Once, the pastor's maid had told her that Margaretha had entered the vicarage before church on a Sunday morning. She had asked to see the pastor's wife, who had recently given birth and was still resting. The maid had been suspicious, as such visits were never made on Sundays, least of all to a pastor's house. So the maid quickly moved the cradle to a corner in the chamber where Margaretha would not be able to touch the baby. After she left, Margaretha had instantly boasted to an acquaintance that she had visited the pastor's wife and brought a gift, and thus had gained privileged access to a person of local influence. Haller asserted that 'everyone' suspected Margaretha of witchcraft.[9]

In response to these divergent testimonies, Einhorn and his court decided to commission a legal opinion from a local lawyer instead of the law faculty at Tübingen's university. This proved cheaper, swifter, and safer. Was there sufficient evidence to call in the hangman with his torturing tools? Phillip Jacob Weihenmayer, the Leonberg doctor of jurisprudence to be addressed as 'honourable and highly learned *Herr*', duly conceded that, according to the legal literature, a bad reputation in itself did not justify torture. But he firmly advised that the case of Margaretha Frisch was different. She had not understood any of the pastor's questions about basic doctrine and religious practice (no report on this interrogation survives) and appeared to behave suspiciously in several respects. Hence, Weihenmayer concluded that he had no 'concerns' whatsoever about her 'sharp questioning'—the close examination which followed torture.[10] Four days later, Margaretha Frisch was dead.

* * *

If anything, the witness testimonies drummed up against Katharina Kepler made for far more alarming reading than the charges that emerged in the case of Margaretha Frisch. The latter had never given her own recipes or drinks to anyone, and she had only touched one maid and two animals, who had recovered through treatment. Katharina, by contrast, was meant to have caused lasting suffering. She had already admitted to trying to bribe Einhorn and had behaved very strangely by asking the gravedigger for her father's skull. If Margaretha had confessed to her pact with the devil, how could Katharina Kepler not be expected to do the same? Had Margaretha's case not shown yet again that torture led to truth and could save a community from further harm? Was it not logical to shake out words from those concealing evil secrets?

In Einhorn's and the judges' view, the case of the next woman tried and executed for witchcraft in Leonberg certainly confirmed such an impression. Lena Stüblerin was a widow who lived in Mönßheim, on the western fringe of the district's territory.[11] She was examined on 26 January 1620, only a few days after Margaretha Frisch's death and while Katharina Kepler's file still awaited its decision. Stüblerin was accused of cursing some villagers who had refused to help her out. It was said that she knew how to make bad weather by darkening the sky, and had threatened to burn down the local bath-keeper's house. Allegedly, she had harmed several humans in the course of many years. Ulrich Broll, a ducal chancellor whom Johannes Kepler would challenge in 1621, did not hesitate to authorize Lena's torture.[12]

Lena at first denied all charges. After her torture, however, on 10 February, she freely confessed. Much of the detail would have alarmed the judges. She confessed that she had once walked back from Pforzheim with flax for spinning when she had first met the devil and his dog next to an oak tree. This dog had sometimes floated in the air like a ghost. Eighteen years ago, she told, she had been collecting wood on a mountain near her village when a handsome man had approached her. He asked: 'Do you want to be mine?' Lena cautiously answered that she needed time to think the proposition over. But Barthlen, this evil spirit, had returned twice more. The third time he told her that she had to do as he wished. She should wait for him at night with a lit candle and afterwards attack humans. One night, a light had appeared in her chamber, like a ghost. She had vigorously thrown her distaff at it. It now seemed as if the devil was inside her, Lena confessed. Once she collected firewood at the castle mountain with her daughter, and suddenly took an old piece of cloth and told her daughter that she felt like strangling her with it for behaving badly. Lena kept having strange visions. Next, she saw a large number of men and exquisitely dressed women with veiled faces, right in front of her. The devil had been there, too, and comforted her by saying that he could see that Lena did not really want to hang her daughter.

Further on in Lena's disturbing confession, the scribe tersely noted: 'Yes, she was sorry to confess that she had submitted to the dreaded devil.' During eighteen years, Lena and the devil had had sex at home in her bed seven times. Confession number six revealed that Lena had killed the bath-keeper's child through illness, while number seven admitted her fatal attack on a man. Next followed the account of how she and three local women had tried to 'make weather' on the Castle Mountain but had been prevented by God. In this account she said that as the devil had never given her a salve she had not flown anywhere. A poor little witch, she'd had to walk to and from meetings on foot. Her further attempts to make weather by ingeniously using children's hair and spreading a girl's urine over a courtyard had been fruitless.

Moreover, Lena said that she felt dominated by other evil women. Another time when she had been collecting wood, six or seven more experienced witches from the next village had joined her and ordered her to do as they wished. Then, suddenly, their faces had turned into black caps. They sat up on a thorn-hedge. Lena had only been able to watch their extraordinary transformation. After three hours, they let her know that in a month the witches would hold an Imperial Diet in a local forest. They ruled their evil empire through political summits just as the German government did! Lena accordingly was not allowed to tell anyone about what happened at this event, but now admitted that all her life she 'had been a big witch'. She had not received the Eucharist for three years. When the local pastor had registered her persistent absence and finally insisted on her attending communion, he had been unable to force the host into her mouth.

The executioner first beheaded Lena Stüblerin by sword and then pulverized her corpse to ashes in February 1620. Her final words are recorded in Leonberg's 'blood-book' (*Blutbuch*) of sentences in criminal trials: she was sorry to have wasted everyone's time by withholding the truth for so long, and grateful for the merciful punishment of being beheaded first rather than burnt alive.[13] Apart from Katharina, she would remain the last witch to be tried in Leonberg for the following eight years.

* * *

Most rumours and accusations that circulated in the streets of towns and villages remained mere talk, even though disputes about whether a person could be judged honourable, fair, and trustworthy could sear communities. Everybody used local courts to settle rumours and restore peace. This meant that the legal sphere and institutions of local government were deeply enshrined in people's lives. Every person's reputation was seen in relation to at least the previous generation of their family. In August 1619, one Leonberg woman was said to have insulted a member of the dyer's family who had died more than twenty years earlier. Honour had its own genealogy, past and future, and this made it vital to fight for a family's good name.

Social status was not the only crucial element in these cases. Courts were also used by inferiors as a means to make a formal complaint. So, for example, a servant complained that the son of a citizen had thrown his hat in front of pigs, ruinning the hat and the hat-band, but was refusing to apologize. In 1620, the wife of the esteemed stonemason Jeremias Schwarz was punished for dishonouring a male citizen. Fines were annually recorded in the alms records. Channelled into charity, they transformed enmity into fellow feeling. Katharina herself was never once accused of dishonouring anyone, even though this charge was common. In 1620, for instance, the wife of her legal guardian was punished with a fine for verbal insults, as were another woman and a young girl.[14]

Records from local court sessions in 1619 and 1620 open a window onto a community that experienced further strains on resources and relations as it was drawn into the Thirty Years War.

Feelings hardened. In the worst confrontations, people began to be accused of being inhuman and demonic. Jerg Zieher, the Leonberg coppersmith who had once had an affair with Ursula Reinbold, for instance, reported in April 1619 that the cowherd had beaten his daughter and called his wife a witch as well as accusing the smith of forging three penny coins. In the end, the poor cowherd was imprisoned in the local tower as he had no money to pay a fine, while the coppersmith's family was assured of its good name and provided with a written copy of the verdict.[15]

Craftsmen and other middling people commonly paid for copies of such documentation to prove that any insult against them had been legally 'undone', as the formula went. For every testament, a rhyming formula confirmed that the words were written into the book so that they had *Macht und Kraft* (strength and power).[16] Paper documents affirmed people's sense that conflict was contained. They helped to distinguish, for example, an insult that someone was a witch from the enduring charge that someone had done harm because they *really were a witch*, as Ursula Reinbold alleged against Katharina Kepler.

Local legal practices provided assurance and were flexible. Middling people of equal status, for example, sometimes merely used the court to make peace. Thus, in October 1619, when Christoph Kepler stood in front of the lower court for quarrelling, he quickly affirmed that he only had the best, that is 'honourable, kind and good things' to say about the Stoll family. Kepler's small conflict with young Hans Stoll, whose cousin in fact sat among the judges, had simply resulted from anger and 'perhaps a drink'. The Stolls in turn similarly confirmed their high regard of Christoph Kepler, and no trace of what had actually been said during the quarrel entered the written record.[17] Settlement in this case meant keeping silent.

In these times of mounting external pressures, Leonberg faced new demands as a community.[18] Citizens were now required to help to secure town gates, as times 'were so dangerous' due to the Thirty

Years War. Many people met economic shortfalls by working harder. The rope-maker who lived on the market square was reported for unloading wine during church on Sunday. Shoemakers, butchers, saddlers, ropemakers, and bakers used Sundays to sell their wares in the district—a sign of how artisans tried to increase their income by working longer hours and widening their distribution. Few people went to church on Friday, especially the artisans, because they worked. Stoffel Schmid did his threshing late at night by candle light. The barn had caught fire and everyone had to stop it spreading.

Leonberg looked and felt different in the crisis years. The bath-keeper failed to cultivate his vineyard, and so did others, for viticulture required much labour and yielded smaller returns than work on the fields. Wood theft abounded in the winter of 1620, and an unlucky man from the poor house was caught stealing wood. Another man even dug out cabbage from someone's plot and stuffed it in his breeches to take it home. The custom's officer complained that many goods went undeclared. Those responsible for welfare complained that charity payments, which were collected every week from citizens, were now only given in counterfeit coin, which was almost useless due to the hyper-inflation which followed the widespread debasement of silver coins with copper. Some individuals were singled out for their meanness. Jeremias Schwarz, the sculptor, was reprimanded for not donating any alms in church for two years.

There was increasing misrule. 'Crooked Agnes', who had guarded Lena Stüblerin in prison, played the zither in Leonberg's suburb for an unruly dance where much blaspheming went on. The cowherd and a butcher had a big fight with loud swearing at the upper gate. Affairs in the tailor's house were 'annoying' by day and night, and a furrier was 'shouting about'. Many family lives were marked by problems. Hans von Sachsenheim wasted his own and his children's money on gambling, excessive eating, and drinking. Endriß Franken had left his wife, and she was unable to cultivate their vegetable plot.

Neighbours complained about damage from weeds. Old Michel Riltlinger wanted his son-in-law to settle debts. Stoffel Bauer hit his wife, even when she had just given birth, drank and feasted, and failed to provide his children with clothes. Marx Christman's wife swore like a fishwife and wished her husband to have an accident when he went to work in the fields. Christman hit her very badly, but had then overslept instead of going to prison as he was ordered. Lorenz Sporer's oldest boy suffered from leprosy, had to be separated from other children, and was not even suitable for work as a day-labourer.

Some cases were so frightening that they could neither be silenced nor easily solved. Allegations that a citizen or even a relative was involved with the devil would be part of the accusation. By the end of October 1619, Zieher the coppersmith and his wife had stood once again in Leonberg's town hall. The reputable Severin Stahl and his wife accused Zieher of shouting that Stahl was the devil's god-father. Stahl retorted that if Zieher said such a thing, then he himself should be a devil's man and have an unchristened child.[19] In 1620, another man got completely drunk, roamed about furiously, and when he returned home he abused his father and brother. Finally he shouted that his stepmother was a witch and his father should have been burnt twenty years ago. Witchcraft was certainly not perceived as an exclusively female crime, even in a community like Leonberg, where only women were ever formally accused. Everyone regarded witchcraft as heresy, which could run among both men and women alike. This made Johannes and Christoph Kepler so vulnerable as they awaited a decision in Katharina's trial.

9

KATHARINA'S IMPRISONMENT

———— ∞∞∞ ————

As witnesses arrived to make their depositions about Katharina in 1619, Christoph Kepler, through the thick, frosty glass roundels of his first-floor room, might have watched their dark figures moving early in the morning across Leonberg's market square to the town hall. The year before he had moved from the rear of the building, with its unappealing view, to the privileged front elevation. Life was cramped outside as much as inside. In front of the house was a dungheap. Goods were unloaded on the market square, customers entered the ground-floor workshops, and animals roamed at the back, among stored craft materials and agricultural produce. At least twice that we know of, Kepler lost his temper when several carts blocked his access to the back of the house and he burst out swearing 'for heaven's sake', only to be duly reprimanded at the local court.[1] The Keplers still shared the house with the tanners, who had moved to the back with their four little boys and girls. While the young tanner's family multiplied, Christoph and his wife lived with just one daughter for many years.[2] A baby girl named Anna had perished shortly after her birth, in 1618. Only in 1619 did

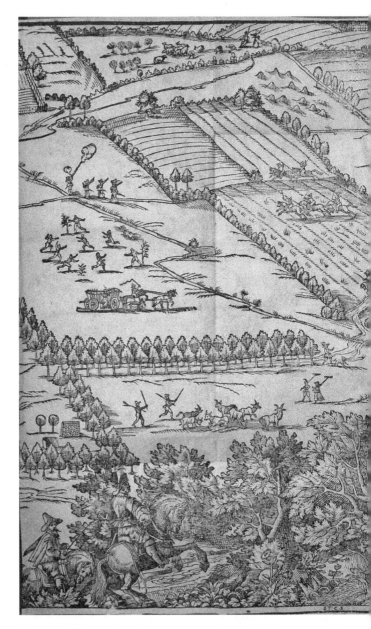

Figure 33 This woodcut depicts townsmen being drilled to run and shoot on the upper left, as well as men and women who harvest or travel in Württemberg. Detail of woodcut in Johann Bauhin, *De aquis medicatis nova methodus*, 1612. © By permission of the Master and Fellows of St John's College, Cambridge

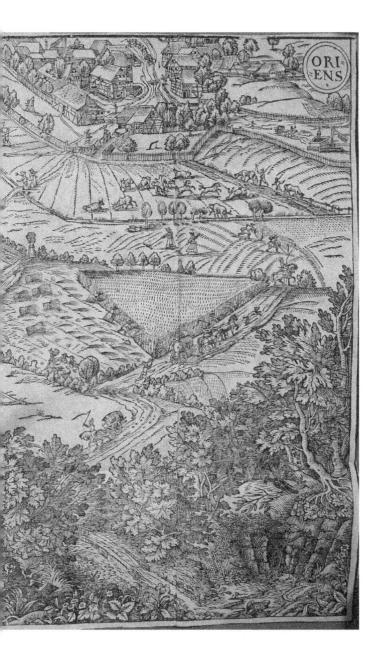

ORI
ENS

six-year-old Agnes get another sister. She was called Margaretha. Was it mere coincidence that Christoph never passed on Katharina's name?

Growing up the son of a widow, Christoph Kepler had achieved much. Reaching his thirties, and despite ongoing investigations against Katharina, the pewterer was entrusted with significant civic responsibility. In 1618, as the duke recognized the urgent need to train men for military defence, Kepler was appointed to the salaried task of drilling local men on weekends (Figure 33). Duke John Frederick pressured his estates to buy gunpowder and to professionalize shooting exercises. Loading and firing a musket could involve up to twenty separate actions, and had to be practised on moving targets.[3] If Württembergers were not drilled, John Frederick warned, 'poor, inexperienced people would be delivered onto the slaughtering racks' of a looming war against the Habsburgs. Moreover, if he failed to recruit citizens for defence tasks, he would need to recruit many mercenary soldiers from Catholic lands at great expense.[4]

This new task of training military men connected Christoph to his father's profession (although he was unlikely to even remember Heinrich, who had disappeared when he had been only two years old). The task proved difficult, as the local men lacked any sense of discipline. They had little sense of duty either. By 1620, 'Corporal Christoph Keppler [sic]' complained that one of his men had joked that they all looked ridiculous during their drilling sessions, like 'hangman's lads' running 'into each other' when they marched and turned.[5] Physical control of this kind was alien to them. In 1620, Christoph once more lost his temper and swore badly at the men, only to be fined yet again. In court, he repeated that most men avoided training and found the most far-fetched excuses. Like other Protestant states, the duchy realized that it would need to keep on relying on mercenaries, especially as the war escalated that year.

At home, Christoph Kepler began to take care of men who were similar to his father and soldiering brother. In 1620, for instance, he looked after an ill soldier until he was transferred on, and in the same year he took care of soldiers who had finished their duty elsewhere.[6] In spring, leading Württemberg diplomats finally came to understand that England would not offer military support to Protestants on the Continent. Duke John Frederick nonetheless retained his determination to help the Calvinist Palatinate, at least within the empire's boundaries. By June, he was determined to ride into battle himself.[7]

There would be more soldiers for Christoph to manage in the following months. By August 1620, Ambrogio Spinola and 25,000 soldiers marched from Brussels to the Rhenish Palatinate, while general Tilly crushed Protestant rebels in Austria. In November, Frederick V of the Palatinate lost the Bohemian crown during a fight that lasted barely two hours at Prague's White Mountain. Ferdinand once more triumphed, and Johannes Kepler later received news of the barbarous execution of rebel leaders, among them the anatomist and natural philosopher Jan Jessenius, whom he had known for many years. Jessenius's tongue was cut out prior to his being decapitated.

Meanwhile, that same summer, Christoph Kepler's life shifted. The Stuttgart chancellery had made up its mind. On 7 August 1620, his mother was first imprisoned in Stuttgart and then led to Leonberg for the beginning of a formal criminal trial. All the family's pleading had been in vain. Christoph felt horrified. It seems that he could imagine only too easily the civic guard fetching the seventy-three-year-old, now nearly toothless, small, white-haired Katharina from one of Leonberg's prison towers, to take her on a chain or rope to the town hall, right in front of his house.

His reaction showed that he could not bear to think of the shame. He may have been among those watching the executioner behead and burn Lena Stüblerin in February that year. Every German execution was staged by local governments as a communal event, to admonish everyone and make them pray for a poor sinner's soul in eternity. Could he imagine being in the crowd to watch his mother's corpse being laid on tightly stacked wood? Christoph wrote to Duke John Frederick at once, proudly relating that he had honourably learned his trade and even practised it with 'particular fame'. The past five years of investigations against his mother had already been 'extremely painful' to live through. Now he feared 'people's open contempt'. Christoph Kepler demanded that Katharina's trial should be conducted elsewhere.

The Leonberg judges and Governor Einhorn supported his request with 'particular pity'. A special bell was customarily rung from the town hall for the opening of criminal trials. The judges agreed that this custom would dishonour the pewterer—everyone would know that his mother was on trial. She might well be tortured and executed. Nothing could be worse for Kepler than for this to take place not only in his home town, but in front of his house. Christoph Kepler, the judges stressed, had always been faultless and diligent in his conduct, and acquired his special expertise in his craft by visiting many towns and territories during his wandering years. His wife and her family had an honourable name, as her father had been Eltingen's mayor for twenty-seven years.

Stuttgart's chancellery officials were also sympathetic. They granted, on the very day they received it, Christoph Kepler's request to change the place of Katharina's imprisonment and location of the trial.[8]

* * *

Margaretha Kepler had written to the duke before her brother, while her mother was still imprisoned in Stuttgart. Margaretha, too, was alarmed about the beginning of a proper criminal trial. For the first time she pleaded in her own name. She wanted to protect her mother and wrote how shocked she was to see Katharina imprisoned in Stuttgart. 'I can report on none of the things of which the Reinbolds accuse her in this long legal process', the pastor's wife wrote determinedly, 'but only how she had always instructed me to fear God and be mindful of all the best virtues and thus has herself always behaved in a Christian manner.' She asked to save the old woman from the harshest form of imprisonment—the Stuttgart 'thieves' tower'. This was one of Germany's thickly walled, bare-brick prisons, with nothing more than straw on the floor, and meals of water, a little wine, and gruel, to be taken in the company of female pickpockets and robbers.

Margaretha, too, was successful in her plea. The Stuttgart governor was instructed to find a more tolerable prison before Katharina's transfer to Leonberg. Margaretha and her husband were requested to present themselves at the Stuttgart chancellery at seven o'clock in the morning.

The siblings all knew that their mother might face torture. Margaretha stood outside her mother's Stuttgart prison cell and continued talking to her as the civic guard took Katharina away for an initial interrogation. Margaretha urged Katharina: if she had 'done something bad, she should say so, but spare her and her brother and family in Linz, and not put such shame on all of them'. They were haunted by the fear of being dishonoured for the rest of their lives. She encouraged her mother to withstand torture and tried to calm her. Even if she were stretched, Margaretha said to her old mother, this would only be one 'bad hour' in her life. Katharina wished her daughter to come back and talk more, but the civic guard reprimanded the women and said that any visiting time required the ducal governor's permission. Katharina was later questioned about what she had intended to say to her daughter. The seventy-three-year-old confidently replied that she had just wanted to give Margaretha one florin to shop for eggs and food that she could cook. As matter of fact, she said, she was unable to 'cope with bad food'.[9] This is one of the very few times that we hear Katharina Kepler's voice. She was practical and wise to insist on good, basic food—the eggs and oats she was used to and which had helped her to reach such an old age—to keep physically as well as mentally resilient. She still wanted to make decisions about her own life.

* * *

Stuttgart's ducal governor had been trying to arrest Katharina since late July. During late spring and into summer, Katharina had mostly stayed with Margaretha in Heumaden, but still enjoyed her independence, had looked after her health, and had spent money on herself. She had travelled towards Ulm in order to take a cure in one of the Württemberg baths, but then fell ill and spent some time in the city of Esslingen. Once she had recovered, she returned to the Heumaden vicarage. Johannes Kepler alleged that Binder, her son-in-law, was now so upset by the whole affair that he did not want to see her face again and told Katharina so.[10] Even so, she stayed on.

In the ducal chancellery, meanwhile, doctors Groll, Kölz, and Rösch, as well as two trusted officials, Dägkher and Schnepff, had ordered that Reinbold deserved justice and that Katharina should be arrested and tortured if she did not confess.[11] Sebastian Faber, one of Johannes Kepler's key government contacts, would have been completely preoccupied with the war and could be of little help to the astronomer. After issuing an order of arrest, the Stuttgart governor's men finally tracked down Katharina at her daughter's house. They arrived to fetch her without any warning in the early hours of an August morning. Margaretha herself was dressed only in her long linen smock when the men knocked on the door and a servant woke the family to give them the bad news. The pastor's wife now told Katharina to hide in a closed trunk. In the heat of summer, Katharina slept with only a duvet covering her. This was how the guards searching the house would find her, the old, anxious woman crouching naked in a trunk.

Once Katharina Kepler had dressed herself, armed guards took her first to Stuttgart and later to Leonberg, where Governor Einhorn and the local pastor conducted an initial interrogation on 11 August. Three judges (Severin Stahl, Ludwig Bilfinger, and Hanss Jossen-hanssen) and Werner Feucht, the new civic scribe, acted alongside the governor and a new pastor. Katharina's long-standing legal guardian had just retired. She did not know several of the men in front of her and was very much on her own. The new pastor tested Katharina's understanding of religious doctrine, and she did well. She was honest enough to reveal that in Weil der Stadt, which tolerated Catholics and Lutherans, she had once received the host in a Catholic mass, adding that the priest himself had converted some years later. She rigorously denied any dealings with the devil.

Next, she was confronted with a large group of local witnesses, all of whom accused her. They repeated many of their former allegations, as well as adding new details. Some in the community had clearly avoided her. The butcher said that he had asked Christoph Kepler years ago to make sure his mother was not around when any slaughtering was to be done at Kepler's house. Among the other witnesses, the schoolmaster was carried into the courtroom because he was now completely lame. Was she guilty of causing him such pain?

The old widow told the court that she saw a connection between the butcher's blocked flow of blood, which had made him also lame, and the fact that she knew that he had once cut down a whole green tree. This tree had thus still been full of its own juice of life. His lameness, in other words, seemed like a moral punishment. For her, the butcher's body and actions were connected to a wider moral macrocosm. Such a deep sense of an interdependent human and vegetative nature was integral to a whole world view that did not regard people as individuals in isolation or a tree as a contained specimen. Nature was imbued with the force of life, which was divinely given.

Katharina was happy to admit that she had recommended to the butcher a blessing, and was able to recount it in court. Typically evocative, though also simple and inelegant, the blessing was a mixture of Christian and folkloric elements. It pleaded for God's help to restore well-being:

> God be welcome to me
> On Sun- and sunny days.
> You come riding towards us,
> There stands a human, let yourself be asked,
> God, Father, Son and Holy Ghost,
> And the Holy Trinity,
> Give this person blood and flesh
> As well as good health.[12]

Katharina thought of it more as a prayer and was aware of the Lutheran hostility against superstitious soothsaying. She later claimed to have discussed with three experts on spiritual matters—her son Johannes, the pastor in Linz, and her son-in-law—as to whether or not these words could be offensive. The words were not believed to be automatically efficacious, but were something that might be tried. She remembered using the prayer with her young children when they had been very ill. One of her baby boys had died nonetheless, but she believed that it had benefited her second son Heinrich in his struggle with epilepsy.

But witnesses remembered Heinrich's allegations, and Katharina began to talk more about this difficult child. It turned out that years later she had taken care of one of Heinrich's little daughters at home, and defended the girl against a local boy who had insulted her. Heinrich, as she saw it, had become a 'godless fellow', shaped by his twenty years as a soldier. He had learnt to talk aggressively. They had had an argument about religion. She had told him off for converting to Catholicism, as he sought refuge and care in a monastery. This had made him very angry. Katharina left no doubt that her son's accusations against her were unfair.

Katharina Kepler displayed no mental incapacity or exhaustion as she faced and responded to seventeen witnesses. Despite Johannes's persistent fear about the old woman's imbecility, she spoke clearly, reasoned causally, and was perfectly able to identify natural explanations of what others feared to be magic. Katharina, for instance, explained that some of the drinks she prepared had remained in their jugs overnight or for some days, so that their surface might have developed some skin which might have implied that their properties had changed. Yet 'by her soul's eternity', she emphatically declared, she had never intended to harm anyone. She honestly admitted her angry sarcasm against some in the community who had begun to denigrate her. For instance, she had told a man who called her a witch that she would 'show him' and make bad weather. But these had just been words.

Katharina went through this whole procedure without any legal guardian, responding herself to each allegation in turn. Her memory was perfect—she even remembered having asked someone about accompanying Margaretha to buy socks or garters for a man when she was a young, single woman, years earlier. Katharina had evidently carefully monitored her daughter's courtship and spending, guarding against immorality, and repeatedly endorsing her Lutheran faith. She also was used to controlling herself, despite the fact that her life was at stake. Yet the jury was firmly set against her, and used her self-control as an argument to show that she was emotionally indifferent and dangerous.

Watching her closely, the jury noted that Katharina avoided eye contact with witnesses and, during the whole interrogation, had shown no sign of being moved. She shed not a single tear. When she explained that her husband had repeatedly left to fight in the Netherlands and Hungary, despite the duke's prohibitions, the

scribe noted the jury's suspicion that she had treated her husband so
badly that he could not bear to live with her. Heinrich Kepler in fact
had never said anything to this effect. Yet the jury now empathetically queried whether Heinrich 'for himself' might have 'felt more of
this [being badly treated by his wife] than he had told other people'.
This was judicial partiality.

The report on 11 August ended in a finely calculated fabrication
in order to deepen the ducal chancellors' mistrust. It alleged that
Katharina had known the woman from Eltingen who had been
accused of witchcraft in 1616, but who had not confessed during
torture and been let off. This woman, they added, was a disreputable
peddler, who had met up with Katharina many times as she moved
about. They had also heard that someone had talked to this woman
outside the door of the Leonberg prison tower before she had been
tortured, telling her to 'stay silent and confess nothing'. Now they
suggested that 'for certain' Katharina and the peddler had 'often
come together either in Heumaden or different places and held
their secret talks'.[13]

* * *

Seven days after the report of this interrogation was sent to Stuttgart,
the chancellery told Governor Einhorn to threaten Katharina Kepler
verbally with torture and see whether she was ready to confess
anything. If she still did not confess, Leonberg's governor was to
proceed by accusing her formally as a suspect who needed to be
actually tortured on account of three principal charges: the drinks she
had given to several people that made them sick; her attempt to bribe
the governor; and her wish to have her father's skull dug out to use it
as a drinking cup.[14]

Christoph Kepler's written plea to move his mother and the trial
away from Leonberg arrived one week later. The chancellery decided
to transfer her to a small town called Güglingen, about 60 kilometres

north of Leonberg, near Heilbronn, a place she had never been to before. Johann Ulrich Aulber, Güglingen's experienced governor, in post since 1611, would now be in charge.[15] Einhorn sent his colleague all the files so far, and explained how it was that the civil case mounted by the Keplers against the Reinbolds five years ago had eventually turned into a criminal trial against Katharina. He enclosed the legal document to justify her torture. Einhorn further noted that it was probably unnecessary to repeat any interrogations, since all the witnesses had already testified on oath. Still, he cautiously advised Aulber to confirm this procedure with the ducal chancellery. Einhorn ended his letter with great confidence in the outcome of the case. In his view, he wrote, 'nothing more is needed to find out the truth than Master Jacob in Stuttgart or his successor'.[16] This Stuttgart executioner could be trusted. Einhorn signed piously: 'always recommending ourselves to our dear Lord'.

Aulber was the brother-in-law of Leonberg's advocate Weihenmayer, who had counselled in favour of torturing Margaretha Frisch. Ursula Reinbold knew that Weihenmayer was related to the man who would now help to determine the case, and perhaps her faction, for this reason, had even tried to push for Güglingen as the place of the trial. She asked her lawyer to write to Aulber in Güglingen and ask him to proceed quickly, though, of course, with due respect for orders from the Stuttgart chancellery. Weihenmayer assured Aulber that he would always be happy to help him in turn.[17]

10

KEPLER'S RETURN

W̲ith mounting impatience, Johannes Kepler wrote in the early summer of 1620 to Duke John Frederick, requesting that full transcripts of witness testimonies should be sent to him, at his own cost and using his own messenger. He would then reply to these accounts, especially as he deemed his aged mother to be almost 'devoid of reason'.[1]

On 7 August, his sister, Margaretha, as soon as their mother was imprisoned, alerted Johannes in Linz. He in response sent a furious letter to Duke John Frederick, complaining that Katharina had been 'attacked' in her sleep in the early morning hours at the Heumaden vicarage. The imperial mathematician used the language of filial obligation rather than concern about his own reputation as he announced his intention to take over his mother's defence. Kepler insisted that it was an oldest son's right to know what testimony served as legal basis for such a conviction. He explained that the war made it difficult for him to travel at present. Yet he was planning to pack up his household as soon as possible and stay with his own family in Stuttgart for the duration of the trial. Until his arrival, he hoped that the duke, in his mercy, would give orders that Katharina should be kept in a tolerable prison and supplied with appropriate nourishment. He would, in person, provide her with all his assistance during the trial. This would be the only possible way for him to feel that he had fulfilled the duty he owed to his mother.[2]

As promised, Kepler moved to Württemberg as quickly as he could. He put his entire life on hold, and packed up his household, his books, and his scientific instruments in Linz. He moved his family to a half-way point with him by boat, where they stayed with kind hosts in Regensburg on the Danube. Kepler then rented a horse to ride on to Ulm, stayed with his friend Hebenstreit, and travelled north to Stuttgart. From there, he had to find his way still further north and off the large trade routes, asking for directions to Güglingen, where he knew nobody and few knew of him.

He arrived by the end of September. First Kepler needed to find an inn where he could leave his horse and then make his way to the town hall. He was then led to his old mother in the Güglingen tower. After three weeks' imprisonment, she complained 'bitterly' that she was cold, sad, and lonely, and bereft of comfort. That very month, her daughter Margaretha had moved away. Binder, Margaretha's husband, had taken over his father's tiny parish in Rosswälden, 30 kilometres to the east of Stuttgart on the road via Esslingen to Göppingen. They now lived in the house where he had grown up, right in the centre of the village. The church was more like a chapel, and there was a little school for the couple to run during the winter months. The geographical distance would have made it time-consuming and costly for Margaretha to travel to Güglingen. It also slowed down postal communication. During autumn, moreover, agricultural and household work took every scrap of time. As a wife, Margaretha could not up sticks and move to Güglingen. Georg Binder, too, had become increasingly uneasy about the substantial support he had given to his mother-in-law until she had been taken to prison from his vicarage. Up to the end of Katharina's imprisonment in Güglingen there is no mention that either Margaretha or pastor Binder ever visited her.

Johannes Kepler knew that he was now the only one of Katharina's children who was capable and willing to stand by her. He immediately requested that his mother should be transferred from the grim prison tower to the quarters of the civic guard and be kept in some chamber at her own expense. Costs were to be kept down as much as possible, but given her 'female sex and age' he did not expect his mother to have many needs.[3]

The Stuttgart chancellery responded to this request by having a full discussion among its staff. Nine of the chancellors signed the order that one guard should be employed day and night to watch Katharina.[4] Aulber, Güglingen's district governor, clearly was not pleased. He in turn insisted that Katharina needed to be chained down and watched by at least two guards. Kepler protested that this would be far more costly and unnecessary, as his mother was weak and suffering several impediments of age. Worried about the conditions worsening in the prison in winter, he asked for the trial to continue as quickly as possible.

Kepler also began to take care of his mother's financial arrangements, as her possessions were still under Einhorn's control. He demanded that money should be released to mitigate Katharina's conditions of imprisonment.[5] The civic guard complained that his place was too small to serve as a prison. He had small children. If Katharina stayed, he would go. In the end, it was decided that she should be moved to a room on the upper floor of one of Güglingen's town gates, fastened on an iron chain, and watched by one guard.

By mid-November, Aulber reported that Kepler visited his mother frequently. Aulber also supplied further arguments as to why Katharina needed to be watched by two permanent guards. During one of her meals she had asked the young civic watchman for some water. She then taunted him for not leaving the door open while he had gone to fetch some. 'Oh you are such a bad man, that you do not at all trust me', she lamented. To Aulber's mind, she was trying to manipulate the guard's sympathy in order to prepare her escape. Another time, when the man had brought in her dinner and asked her about what she was doing, Katharina allegedly answered: 'But what am I to do; I am lying here. Dear man, dear man, let me out, I will give you 100 florins in money, and if I don't give you the money I shall give you a letter (of exchange) for 100 florins.' He and the other guards were suspicious and had begun to interrogate her about from where she would get this money. Katharina now apparently denied that she had said anything, only to go on to confess that she had received money from a fellow female prisoner in Leonberg prison before that woman had been executed.[6]

In December, Johannes Kepler understood that Aulber used these extracts from Katharina's 'conversations' with the guards to prove her evil character. Kepler protested that everything such an old woman might say in a clumsy manner was turned against her. Moreover, he complained, the guards used such large amounts of firewood that all her wealth would soon be spent on heating.[7]

Since November, Aulber had been attempting to gain permission from the ducal chancellery for legal support in the accusation by involving Dr Weihenmayer of Leonberg in the trial, who knew the circumstances of the case very well.[8] Aulber had also presented a concise summary of the charges. It rested on one startling premise: a widow, he wrote, was meant to 'be lonely'. Yet, as we have seen, Katharina had never tried to live an isolated life. On the contrary, she had kept travelling, visited other people's houses, and entertained guests. To Aulber's mind, this made her dangerous. He listed everyone Katharina was meant to have harmed, and succinctly presented the case for her torture.[9]

In response Johannes Kepler, following detailed conversations with his imprisoned mother, swiftly prepared a powerful, concise, and clearly structured legal document in her defence. He stressed that she had been forced to be economically active precisely *because* she was widowed. In addition, she had always enjoyed a good name before the Reinbolds had started to defame her on the street and rumours had 'caught on like fire'. This stressed how dangerous and uncontrollable this process had been. The very fact that Katharina had denounced the Reinbolds for abuse signalled her good conscience. On Johannes's last visit to Leonberg in 1609, he had certainly reassured himself of his mother's proper conduct and good reputation. Kepler also mentioned that Katharina had never had to pay a single fine to Leonberg's local court for dishonouring anyone. How could it be just to torture someone like her?[10]

In a curious turn of affairs, the advocate in the Stuttgart chancellery now entrusted with Katharina's case turned out to be pastor Binder's brother. He instantly asked to be relieved of his duties as he also knew Johannes Kepler intimately, trusted him, and had eaten and drunk nearly every day with him in Prague.[11] Even to more distant kin, Kepler, as we have seen, was no lone scholar but honoured family ties.

Even so, the relation with his younger brother Christoph was by now extremely strained. Kepler frankly reported to the duke that the excessive costs of his mother's imprisonment were making the Leonberg pewterer angry. Christoph even alleged that the only reason for Johannes to return to Württemberg and act in his mother's defence was to turn him into a poor man, since each of Katharina's children provided legal surety for any expenses.

Johannes was clearly incensed by these allegations. He, after all, was the one who had had to completely change his life, his career, and uproot his family. By late November, after two months in Württemberg, Johannes already felt that he had lost 'all credit' in his homeland. Desolate, he feared that he might soon have to leave without effecting anything other than 'blame, ridicule and heart-ache'.[12] Had he achieved anything?

On 11 December, before the seasonal 'holidays', Johannes Kepler accompanied his mother to the Güglingen courtroom in the town hall. Governor Aulber read out the charges. He confirmed his intention to conduct the trial quickly. The Keplers repeated their arguments, questioning the legitimacy of a criminal trial. Then Katharina was led back to her room and chained to the floor. This was how she would spend Christmas—imprisoned in a strange town.

* * *

As in Leonberg, Güglingen and its governor had recently executed witches. In 1613, Aulber had presided over the case of a local widow named Maria Mayer. At the time, he had only been in the post for two years. Maria had two children and earned her and her children's living through casual labouring, such as sheep-shearing or mill work. One man had heard her lament to herself about the witches burnt in large numbers by the Catholic prince-bishop of Ellwangen. Was she sympathetic to them? While she was imprisoned, her fifteen-year-old son confessed that he himself had sealed a pact with the devil. A man with an ugly face and eyes, a black beard and goat feet, this devil had taught him how to make rabbits. Mother and son flew on pitchforks to a stable where she rode on a calf and he hit it until it died. The mother had also smeared salve on a baby's mouth to kill it. They had watched the Sabbath, and his sister had joined in as well.

In response to Maria's son's disturbing confessions, Aulber and his local judges had decided to torture her. The executioner they used for this had recently been involved in witchcraft trials in the nearby town of Vaihingen, and brought with him a special instrument of torture for witches who at first refused to confess. Such initiatives to spur on confessions clearly violated the intention of the Imperial Law Code. The instrument was described as a 'rope with buttons', which was tightened around the head. Maria had confessed to nothing in the morning, but in the afternoon was pulled up 'two or three times' on a rope tied to a wheel. Aulber cautiously reported that this had happened 'without particularly martyring her'.

The illegal torturing paid off. Maria soon confessed about two playmates, as well as supplying a long list of crimes against people and livestock, over many years, ever since the devil had visited her when she had been poor and ill. One day, she had felt that the devil was also in her boy's body, just as she could feel that he was in her mouth. They both belonged, with their body and soul, to the devil. He would come to see them in the guise of a citizen, peasant, or black dog. She could hardly stop talking now, and the scribe listed thirty-five points of confession. The only charge she denied was to have attended lively Sabbath entertainments. 'Her whole life', she insisted, she had been 'hostile to dancing'.[13]

On 18 July 1613, the Tübingen lawyers decided that Maria deserved to be burnt as a witch. They tried to make the execution more bearable: a little bag with gunpowder was to be tied to her upper body, so that her heart (as the centre of feeling) should be ripped out at the very first contact with fire.[14]

Only a few months before Katharina arrived, in June 1620, Aulber had investigated another accusation against Anna Hauher, a poor widow. The woman had not wanted to confess anything, and Aulber had not waited to ask the chancellery for instructions but instead, alongside the executioner and two local judges, independently decided to 'handle her a bit more firmly'. The Stuttgart chancellery tolerated such hazy reporting and never asked what exactly had been done. This treatment resulted in Anna confessing to many cases of harm against pigs, calves, horses, oxen, and children over a ten-year period. Sometimes she helped them, she confessed, while at other times she brutally rode them to death. Three other local women assisted her. Anna described the Sabbath, attended by two beautiful young dancing men, at which she herself had mostly just held up the candle for the other women, because she 'was so ugly and old'.

Keen to investigate further, Aulber wrote or talked to anyone, near or far, whom Anna claimed to have harmed. It turned out that many owners of these animals thought that the information was inaccurate—a calf, for example, had died at a different time to that given in Anna's confession. Yet Anna responded by insisting that she had done exactly what she had first confessed. Moreover, she announced that the time of her promised commitment to the devil was about to run out, but that she would not submit to him and rather would fight to renounce her pact. Within less than a month, Anna's file was closed and Aulber sent a final report to the ducal chancellery. He commented on the inconsistencies between her confessions and his findings, but added that she had hinted at yet further deeds and had named five other witches from Güglingen. On 3 July 1620, six of the ducal chancellors and the supreme chancellor ordered Aulber to proceed to the final steps of the trial. Just weeks before Katharina Kepler arrived in Güglingen, therefore, an executioner had stacked up firewood for Anna Hauher to be burnt alive on the stake.

All the same, neither Aulber nor Einhorn were zealous witch-hunters. Aulber informed the duke that of all the five local women Anna had identified as witches, only one was worth investigating. Nobody else had said anything bad about four of them. Yet Kiefferlin's wife, he wrote:

Is an old, bad woman and has always been suspected by everyone for ever, and has recently been publicly accused of attacking a horse, and moreover has been implicated many years ago by several witches who were brought to justice in Storkheim.

This part of the procedure followed the Imperial Law Code and Württemberg practice, according to which a witch's list of companions only merited further investigation if these persons were known to already possess a bad reputation.[15] The chancellery agreed and issued orders to interrogate Kiefferlin's wife, yet no further documentation survives. In all likelihood, the case was either still being investigated as Katharina arrived in Güglingen, or the woman had already been burnt during July.[16]

* * *

Back in Leonberg, rumours were rife throughout the autumn. Some said that Katharina was to be tortured and finally brought to justice. Others reported that the Reinbolds might meet severe punishment. Hence, the glazier Reinbold felt nervous and kept visiting Governor Einhorn and his lawyer, 'Weyhenmeir' [*sic*], to find out any news— so much so that on 17 December, Weihenmayer wrote to Aulber, his brother-in-law. Could he tell him what was happening? He promised to keep any information to himself in a 'manly' manner as well as to repay Aulber 'professionally' for this favour whenever he wished.[17] He promised to cover up any corruption.

Christmas passed and a new year began. On 8 January 1621, Johannes Kepler and Hans Guldenmann, Katharina's cousin and the mayor of her home village, Eltingen, represented Katharina Kepler as witnesses. For the first time they were interrogated as part of a criminal trial, which simultaneously commenced in Leonberg. On 16 January, further witnesses were interrogated in Güglingen, in rooms above a tavern, as the town hall was booked up with other business. Johann Rueff, Güglingen's civic advocate, acted on Katharina's behalf. Christoph Kepler refused to attend either hearing.

The atmosphere was charged. When, in Leonberg, Johannes Kepler wished to discuss what kind of oaths the witnesses would need to swear, he was firmly put in his place, told that the matter could not just go his way. As usual, witnesses were reminded that anyone who lied would lose his or her eternal life. Kepler spoke up again, stressing that 'life and limb', 'honour and sentiment (*Gefiehl*)' were at stake.

Following Kepler's repeated requests, witnesses who testified in the Güglingen hearing raised one arm and three fingers for a properly conducted solemn oath. It was explained to them that they thereby called on the power of God, his son, and the Holy Ghost to let them speak the truth. Otherwise, God and his temporal authorities would, in three terrifying ways, punish those bearing false witness: their fingers or tongue would be cut off in public; they would be excluded from any honourable company; and their life and soul would be damned.

Each witness was then presented with a list of questions that Kepler had drawn up in order to establish that the Reinbolds' accusations had set off an absurd trail of false blame. Kepler had worked on his copy of all previous depositions. His well-trained eye honed in on insufficient evidence. His questions for Beutelspacher, the lame schoolmaster, for instance, were: 'How could he know that the drink had caused his symptoms?' 'Had he not often jumped dangerously and carried as well as lifted heavy loads?'

The mathematician, it seems, used his many conversations with Katharina during her imprisonment to learn about Leonberg people, their stories, and their practices. Kepler now knew that Beutelspacher had only been offered the job of schoolmaster after he had become ill. Before then, he had done much more physical work. Kepler established, moreover, that his mother did the same as many other men and women when she went to the baker's and asked the wife to roast some meat for her in their oven, which was fired up anyway. Katharina had provided him with an astonishing amount of detail.

Johannes Kepler made his own evaluation of his mother's way of showing or concealing emotions. It was her nature, he argued, not to show many facial expressions, no matter whether she was happy or serious, but especially when she argued. She never looked into anyone's eyes when quarrelling, but faced them from the side, as she tried to focus her thoughts. Kepler emphasized that his mother was bold and fearless in her readiness to stand up to anyone challenging her. She typically dealt with unfair comments by warding them off with gestures and words. No one, he summed up, would ever have seen his mother cry.

Johannes Kepler was the only one of Katharina's children old enough to remember all this from watching his parents quarrel as a young boy. More than anyone, he knew intimately Katharina's tough side, which was often on show as she lived through her troubled marriage. While part of him struggled with this aspect of her character, it also made him proud. Ever since he had begun to reflect on their horoscopes, the oldest son had seen aspects of her in himself. The passage about Katharina in his 1619 *Harmony of the World* revealed his urgent need to create emotional distance as he lived with her at home. Now Katharina sat on the stone floor, or perhaps on a single chair, tied down with her iron chain, depending on him alone. As she let him into the details of her daily life, Johannes seems to have found it easier to appreciate his mother. He still identified with the white-haired woman's resilience, her insistence on asserting what she thought was right. It emerged that she had in the past years robustly faced several men on the market square to ask them why they spread rumours that she was a witch and 'beast'. In his own life, he too had defiantly stood up to his opponents.

All the same, Kepler continued to feel profound ambivalence. In writing on her behalf, he once more dwelt on her ageing body as repulsive, '*ungestalt*', and almost inhuman. The guards lent the toothless woman a broken pocket-knife, for her to cut meat into small pieces so that she could swallow without chewing. Right from the beginning of the case, Kepler thought of her physicality as a principal cause of people's fear and rejection, in a battle of the young against the old. He would have read classical literature which dwelt on women's physical decline as grotesque, and also would have met many older women who took care to look after themselves. His own wife was young and fertile, fresh and blooming.

Kepler's feeling of repulsion about an older woman's body was apparently not shared by everyone, or at least not consciously so. Johann Bernhardt Buck, for one, Leonberg's recently appointed pastor, rejected the idea that Katharina's age and appearance had contributed to her accusation. Several old and 'unseemly' people lived in town, the thirty-two-year-old cleric stated, but none of them were suspected of any wrongdoing. The locals, he asserted, judged behaviour, not looks.

Despite the mathematician's standing, in court Buck frankly admitted that he took the Reinbolds' side. To him, they just seemed 'better people'. Ursula was now immobile, and he visited her to administer communion. Every time he reminded her of the need to forgive her enemies before she ate Christ's body and drank his blood, but she kept 'shouting' for God's justice and revenge.[18] Even so, the pastor seemed understanding rather than repulsed. Ursula Reinbold was desperate with chronic pain and managed her helplessness through aggression and pressure on men to help her. She was in a rage and knew how to gain a public voice. One man described how she had shouted out from her window that no one other than Katharina had caused her such pain.[19] The streets were her sounding board and, besides, little that was said loudly in early modern homes was private.

The Imperial Law Code, moreover, attributed legal weight to a victim who kept accusing a person up to his or her own death—and Ursula accordingly seemed to stage her accusations from her bed as if she was close to death. Severin Stahl, one of the three lay judges present at Katharina's last interrogation in Leonberg, was a neighbour of the Reinbolds. The forty-one-year-old often heard Ursula suffer at night and heard her husband's comforting words. Once she furiously begged the glazier to knife her because she could not escape the pain. It was as if she felt imprisoned in her own body. Stahl often talked to the glazier and declared his 'great compassion' for the couple, but did not think this would affect his impartiality in court. He also agreed with Pastor Buck: it was not Katharina's age that raised suspicion, it was her endlessly running about and into people's houses.[20]

Another judge confirmed that Katharina had kept looking down or to the side as she had been faced with witnesses, her eyes moving unsteadily. She had appeared shocked by the charges, but had not shed a single tear. This was seen as uncanny in a culture whose theologians increasingly demanded that hearts needed to be moved. Lutheranism was anything but a rational religion. It created its own emotional drama around the image of a fatherly God. As a Tübingen student of theology, Kepler himself had heard lectures and sermons by Jacob Heerbrand and Johann Georg Sigwart, who proclaimed that natural disasters were controlled by an angry God who wanted his children to cry for mercy. This relentlessly punitive God wanted to see 'hot tears', as Heerbrand once put it, 'which spring from contrite and penitent hearts and run down the cheeks'.[21] Sorrow made you human and civil.

Tears were also taken as a sign of a mother's care for her children. The Swiss doctor and well-known humanist writer Thomas Platter, for example, commented on how he and his brothers had once taken their leave from their peasant mother: 'Except one time when we said good-bye to her, I never saw my mother cry; she was a courageous, manly woman, but rough.' Platter and his brothers repeatedly roamed about in Germany, before making good and settling down. Their mother married three times and then remained a widow with small children. 'She has worked like a man', Platter said:

> [S]o that she can better educate her last children. She hoes, threshes and does other work which belongs more to men than to women, she has also herself buried three children who died during a big plague, because to employ a grave-digger during a plague is very expensive.

Platter remembered once returning home after five years. All his mother asked was: 'Did the devil bring you?' He stayed a few days, leaving her to hoe and thresh, and yet never connected her roughness and his longing for affection to a widow's obvious need for more help from her mature sons.[22]

Katharina did not want to comply with men's idea of when and how she should express emotion. Although she was addressed by the judge as 'Cathy' (*Cätherlin*), and the judge finally spoke to her in more familiar terms, saying 'if you have a pious drop of blood in yourself, then let your eyes flow', Katharina replied: 'I have cried so much, that now I cannot cry any more.' Next, she promised to shout for revenge at the Day of Judgement.[23] She felt angry, not sad. She would not break down. Refusing to cry, in all likelihood, was her way of retaining dignity and strength to live through the rest of the trial.

11

THE DEFENCE

———— ⊂⊃⊃⊂⊃ ————

J ust before Johannes Kepler packed up his household, books,
instruments, and papers in the summer of 1620 in Linz, he
asked Johannes Gringallet, his research assistant, to paint a portrait
of him in oil. Once finished, Gringallet dispatched it to Matthias
Bernegger, Kepler's most trusted friend, who taught political
thought to inspire new political practices in Strasbourg and had
encouraged Kepler to compose an autobiography. The portrait,
Kepler explained in a hastily written note to his friend, was to
stand in for that larger project until he found time to write.[1]
Today, it presents us with our only clue as to what Kepler looked
like as he entered his fifties, lived through the final phase of his
mother's trial, and travelled across lands ridden by war, disease, and
destitution. It is the only representation of the mature Kepler, apart
from a small, crude engraving on the frontispiece of the 1627
Rudolphine Tables. The latter hints at a worn-out, badly paid astronomer working long hours in candle-light for his emperors, wearing a
sloppy nightgown and nightcap.

The Linz painting, by contrast, displays Kepler as a black-haired
and elegantly bearded, dark-eyed man with a youthful air of cheerful
confidence (Figure 34). Kepler once said that by temperament he

Figure 34 Johannes Kepler as portrayed by Gringallet for Bernegger in 1620. © The British Library

offset the effort behind his labours through a cheerful writing style—
a vision of himself he liked because it pointed to a positive person-
ality. For the Linz portrait he was carefully dressed, as if ready to
receive high-ranking men. Indeed, the poet and chaplain John
Donne had passed by in 1619 to meet him as a member of James
I's substantial, costly embassy to end hostilities in Bohemia, led by
Viscount Doncaster. Kepler was taken seriously in his striving
towards confessional peace. Sir Henry Wotton, who served King
James I as diplomat, had met Kepler even more recently in Linz.
Wotton enthusiastically wrote to the aged Francis Bacon about
Kepler's ingenious perspective machine, a 'curiosity' designed to
survey the land more precisely. Kepler had related 'with a smile'
that he had invented it, and explained every detail of how it would
enable rulers to better measure and tax their land.[2]

The Linz portrait depicted him exactly as this kind of man, at ease
to converse about his latest experiments designed to benefit civil
concerns. A tightly cut black velvet gown and breeches perfectly set
off a plain white ruff and cuffs with intricately laced edges. His belt
displayed a precious ruby set in the middle of golden wings. With
his right hand assertively placed on one hip, the imperial mathematician in midlife exuded distinction, intellectual alertness, and an
engaging personality. If Kepler somewhat obsessively thought of his
mother as defaced by age, as *ungestalt*, then this painting showed
Kepler as impressive *Gestalt*, a man at the height of his powers.
Posing for a relative amateur, Kepler would have had to stand still
for hours.

It was worth the effort. For this was a time in which every detail of
appearances—physiognomy, youthfulness or age, gestures, postures,
dress, hair, accessories—was carefully observed and related to others.
As in geometry, proportions meant attractiveness. In Kepler's world,
looks therefore certainly mattered, which explains why he thought
they mattered equally in Leonberg. High-ranking men endlessly

judged appearances in order to gauge who was angling for better positions and whether they were driven by rivalry, self-interest, or by piety and commitment to further the common good. Wotton himself was a master of observation, commenting on Archduke Leopold, for instance, that he was a 'prince of good stature, of fair complexion, inclining to fullness: His face, the very best, as they tell me, of the House of Austria, and better indeed than his fashion', which he thought lacked any 'curiosity' but was matched by a commendable absence of affectation.[3] By October 1620, it was rumoured that Kepler had accepted Wotton's invitation to take up a position at the court of the English king.[4]

Given such scrutiny, Kepler was annoyed to learn that his friend Bernegger had commissioned the Flemish artist Jacob van der Heyden to produce an inferior engraving after the Linz portrait, which his friends ridiculed.[5] It made Kepler look vacant, sad, even unworldly, and possibly preoccupied with obscure thoughts. Kepler's failure to acquire a university post underlined his failure to fit into established Christian norms.[6] As recently as the summer of 1619, the Württemberg church council had reiterated that Kepler was to be excluded from receiving Holy Communion unless he conformed to the meaning of this ritual in an orthodox Lutheran manner. Hafenreffer, his Tübingen teacher and former supporter, in a final letter reprimanded Kepler that he suffered from a 'confused spirit'. He needed to abandon reason and believe in God's secret through simple faith. Reason was blind. If Kepler kept to his views, the old theologian threatened, the astronomer might be surrendered to a 'depraved spirit'.[7] Could the devil attack him?

* * *

Despite Kepler's attempt to conduct himself in public as a civilized man of reason, in April 1621 he once more struggled to control his fury about Katharina's criminal trial. Kepler knew that he had to convince the Tübingen professors of law that, above all, his family had become victims of failed governance. They would decide whether or not his mother should be tortured. He was ready to speak out in protest.

The occasion was perfect. Johann Leonhard Breitschwert (a young disciple of his friend Besold) had invited Kepler to join in the celebrations for his Tübingen doctorate in law.[8] He asked the mathematician to write a poem in his honour. Breitschwert had already been appointed to a position in the ducal council and had recently married a senior colleague's daughter. Office-holding elites were typically protected by such marriages and these alliances made consensus more likely in early modern councils. Breitschwert's father-in-law was the ducal chancellor Ulrich Broll, and had been among those authorizing the torture of Lena Stüblerin in Leonberg in 1620. Broll frequently dealt with witchcraft trials. He was related to a pastor called Jacob Broll, who in turn was a distant relative of Kepler.

A Tübingen doctorate in law was a prerequisite for a university chair in law. It propelled many others to leading positions in government. Yet it was principally a paid ritual which redistributed wealth from elite families to academics and ended in jolly festivities. Precise accounts survive for one typical Tübingen graduate, Constantin Varnbühler. Having just returned from a two-year trip to various Italian cities and universities, he took August and September 1607 to prepare for his degree. Varnbühler first took care to buy linen, silk, fancy buttons, a hat, and two pairs of shoes, as well as taffeta, to properly attire himself and two servants. He visited the barber and commissioned a new piece of jewellery. His rapier, sword, and the small fork he would carry with him to eat, needed polishing. Next on the list of expenses were fees, gifts, and celebrations. Instead of leather gloves, which the academic senate customarily received in most Renaissance universities when a degree was conferred, the young man invoiced his father for the six florins he paid in coin. His doctoral supervisor received a length of superior Italian velvet, costing four florins, as well as the same amount in cash. The man who rang the bells of the *Stiftskirche* was paid, as well as the janitor who lit two 'doctoral torches', and musicians, including a trumpeter who played on the tower. The pastor was presented with wine. Added to this was a small fee for the poor chest, while a full thirty-one florins and thirty kreuzer went to 'Hans Baumann, the inn-keeper at the "Crown", for the usual doctoral meal'. Finally, Varnbühler printed some doctoral theses for a little over two florins and paid a quarter of a florin to the bookbinder for binding and stitching 'several disputations and programmes'. This investment in circulating their modest intellectual content was an irrelevance compared to the enormous sum of 200 florins he paid overall.[9]

Kepler was clearly not looking forward to Breitschwert's pseudo-academic show. Instead, he decided to provoke the newly appointed ducal chancellor and his guests by contributing a long Latin diatribe against Württemberg's jurisdiction. He pointedly wrote of Austria as his fatherland, his *patria*—a deeply emotional term. For in Württemberg, Kepler harshly declaimed, he was 'skinned', like a dead animal. Therefore, he felt like a sad man among those happily celebrating. Why had he been invited at all? Was it because of his well-known ancestor, his grandfather Sebald and former Weil der Stadt mayor? Or had he perhaps been invited because of his own 'art'?

If this were the case, he could only say the following: while astronomy could unintentionally produce some wrong predictions, he had seen the law operated maliciously and in a self-interested way. Legal hearings had been moved, orders carelessly dealt with, and corruption tolerated. Kepler next developed an implicit analogy between Leonberg's governor as 'the moon' and Duke John Frederick and his ducal council as 'the sun'. As the moon had constantly become smaller, it had begun to reflect the sun's rays only weakly and had then completely disappeared. Finally, it had covered the sun with darkness to fully eclipse good government. These legal failings were matters manifest in LEONENSIS, Leonberg.[10]

This extraordinary poetical diatribe hit on the key weakness of centralized territorial governance. Ideally, the duke resided in the capital. Governors represented him in districts. It was often difficult to detect whether they bent the law or were biased.[11] If the duke could not ensure legal fairness for subjects by controlling his governors, Kepler argued, then his rule gave way to darkness and abuse. This was a particularly alarming charge at a time when John Frederick had become so absorbed in foreign policy. From August to late November 1620, the duke had led soldiers into battle. His dynasty's 'heroic blood', John Frederick declared, obliged him to act as 'befitted a loyal, keen patriot'.[12] The estates and his councillors had been desperate to call him back to attend to government affairs. Kepler was right: most Württemberg witchcraft trials and the majority of those which ended in a death sentence were prosecuted during John Frederick's reign (1608–28), which suggests that he insufficiently controlled his governors.[13]

* * *

Kepler's deliberately shocking outburst in April 1621 is easy to understand: he was at the end of his tether. From December 1620 and into summer 1621, Katharina remained imprisoned in Güglingen, although the interrogation of witnesses was concluded on 16 January 1621. Kepler had resided mainly in Güglingen during October and November 1620, and his friend Wilhelm Schickard knew that letters would reach Kepler there. Johann Hebenstreit, another trusted correspondent, was less sure where to find the astronomer. He wrote to 'Johannes Kepler, Mathematician, to be personally handed [this letter] in Leonberg or Güglingen or where he is sure to be found'.[14] By late November, Kepler had left the Stuttgart region and returned to the city of Regensburg, where he had stationed his pregnant wife, their toddler Sebald, and his two teenage children from his first marriage, Ludwig and Susanna.

He considered Wotton's invitation to work for James I, but felt no inclination to accept. First, there was the dangerous passage to England, 'over the sea . . . to the narrow confines of an island'. He also worried about his older children's prospects. Ludwig was aged thirteen and was his father's great academic hope. He wanted him to go to university, but by obtaining a Tübingen scholarship. What was he meant to do in England? At the same time, Kepler felt unsure about his family's future in Linz, now occupied by Catholic Bavarians who were extracting contributions for its army from the populace.[15]

Susanna was nineteen and would need to marry. Despite the war, she bravely travelled back from Regensburg to Linz to collect copies of Book IV of the *Epitome*, her father's pioneering textbook for scholars based on Copernicus rather than Ptolemy, which had been printed locally and in haste before the family had left. Since May 1619, Book I stood on the Roman Inquisition's *Index of Prohibited Books*. Kepler had packed only seventeen copies of the following volumes, and these still lacked a frontispiece or prologue. In November and December, Kepler had fruitlessly negotiated with printers in Tübingen and Ulm to publish Books V to VII.[16]

He managed to finish the manuscript during the next months, benefiting from conversations with Michael Mästlin, his Tübingen professor, who had taught him about a caring, merciful, perfect God as creator of all good things, who watched over every baby's growth in its mother's womb. God could be understood through the book of nature. Beyond scripture lay the heavens. Its principles could be learned through those versed in mathematics and physics as God had created their minds in his own image.[17] Like other natural philosophers, Mästlin had been a pastor before his appointment, and, like Kepler, had been a scholarship boy. He signed letters with four Ms, a most impressive monogram for 'Michael Mästlin Master Mathematician', and made his own observations of the moon. Still, ducal advisers had in 1609 already thought of Mästlin as becoming 'rather old'. For the gallery of Tübingen professors he was portrayed with hollow eyes and a thinning grey beard. Only a few years younger than Kepler's mother, Mästlin nonetheless held on to the Tübingen chair of astronomy, blocking Wilhelm Schickard's promotion to his post until he died in 1631 aged eighty-one. Kepler, who early on in his career had fought hard for his teacher's continued attention and affection, by 1626 referred to Mästlin as a 'grumpy' and 'senex' old man, one year later joking that he remained 'the sole father of all Tübingen academics'. Already in 1620, Mästlin was the last of Kepler's most important living teachers—even the theologian Hafenreffer (who began to refer to himself as 'old boy' in his late fifties) and Sigwart had recently perished. Mästlin apart, a new generation took over (Figure 35).[18]

Alongside completing the *Epitome*, Kepler now urgently needed to put together his mother's legal defence. After his daughter Cordula was born in January 1621, he once more left his family. By April, Hebenstreit addressed a letter to Kepler to be delivered to the Tübingen pharmacy.[19] On 21 May, Kepler sent a note to Bernegger to say that he had stayed in Tübingen on his 'urban plunders for the court-trial', to obtain further legal advice. The letter asked for the friend's help in sending him an astronomical book published eighty-one years earlier, in 1540.[20] From late May, Kepler wrote from Stuttgart. In August, he included no location next to the date on a letter which survives and wrote to Bernegger about his 'roaming year'. His best friend had recently been upset by a malicious rumour that Kepler had been to Strasbourg without calling on him. Yet the mathematician had not ventured further south than Tübingen.

Figure 35 Michael Mästlin depicted as an old man for the gallery of Tübingen professors in 1619 (compare Figure 23): Mästlin was a contemporary of Katharina Kepler. © University archive Tübingen

In early May, Kepler handed Güglingen's governor, Aulber, a formal document in defence of his mother. By mid-May, Aulber told Kepler that the whole file still remained in the ducal chancellery, and Kepler desperately addressed the chancellery's advocate, Hieronymus Gabelkhover, to prevail on the ducal officials to continue with the trial. His mother, Kepler wrote, had now been imprisoned for ten months. She was seventy-four years old and on the brink of losing her reason and spirit, her property, and her health.[21] By June, Aulber himself reported that Katharina Kepler had become extremely impatient and kept saying that she feared that her affairs were being held up on purpose, pleading to speed things up so that they would 'once come to an end'.[22]

Not much of Kepler's correspondence survives from the final period of the trial. Kepler would have felt cut off from the world of international correspondence, which even in Linz marked his life with reasonable rhythms of regularity. He had to borrow books from Schickard's library, when he himself had been used to lending other people books from his wide-ranging collection, now in storage. He even tried to get hold of key international works by providing astrological services, about which he felt deeply ambivalent. When Julius Friedrich of Württemberg, one of the duke's younger brothers, took astrological counsel on how he might 'make it into chronicles' to increase his descendants' honour, Kepler asked in return to be sent the works of the confined Italian visionary writer Tommaso Campanella. One of his correspondents reported that they contained similar thoughts to the *Harmony*. Kepler kept up his relations with the court by dedicating a treatise on the eclipse of October 1605 to John Frederick, and was rewarded with a silver-and-gold gilt cup worth twenty-three florins.[23]

While the trial languished during the summer of 1621, Kepler travelled to Frankfurt in order to have the completed *Epitome* printed there. He carried the manuscript with him as well as Schickard's unusual, alluring wood-blocks, which skilfully illustrated 'Fumes around the Sun' or the 'Refutation of Brunian infinitism'.[24] A scientific milestone, the *Epitome* counts as the first 'systematic complete presentation of astronomy' which introduced the idea of 'modern celestial mechanics'. To its author's mind, it did no less than finally explain the 'very Book of Nature, in which God the Creator manifested and represented in part and by a kind of writing without words his essence and will towards mankind'.[25]

* * *

Kepler's extraordinary confidence was supported by his very special network of Tübingen friends. We need to remind ourselves of who these men were, in order to understand how, despite all the constraints imposed on him, Kepler felt part of a discussion about new types of knowledge and social reforms. This intellectual world was not provincial, but at the cutting edge of what was possible in Europe at the time.

Wilhelm Schickard (1592–1635) was the son of a carpenter and woodcutter and a nephew of the great Württemberg architect. His uncle had built Württemberg's architectural ideal city: *Joytown*, or Freudenstadt. This now hailed as a haven for religious exiles from the Austrian lands and was built in the shape of a square, like the heavenly Jerusalem. Wilhelm had studied in Tübingen and had become a Lutheran clergyman in the small town of Nürtingen, but meanwhile passionately nurtured his own expertise in inventive constructions, drawing, engraving, astronomy, and Hebrew. Since 1593, Nürtingen's castle housed Ursula von Württemberg, who had been aged only twenty-one when her husband, Duke Ludwig, died. Ursula was active in making medicines for the local poor and employed distinguished women to help her. She also greatly encouraged Schickard to write down as well as draw his astronomical observations, and told Duke John Frederick about this talented young man. As a result, Schickard dedicated an extraordinarily beautifully illustrated, hand-coloured description of the comet in 1618 and detailed history of comets in Württemberg to the duke, which included a drawing of him with his ingenious observational instrument. Comets, he reiterated, demonstrated God's almighty power.[26] As Schickard had just taken up a badly paid Tübingen chair in Hebrew, the duke duly promised him an eventual salary increase. Schickard, meanwhile, earned extra money through private tuition in a range of languages he mastered in addition to skills ranging from hydraulics to fortifications, architecture, and scenography. Kepler praised him as a man who philosophized with 'his mind and hand' rather than only with his brain.[27] He embodied a new way of generating knowledge (Figure 36).

Apart from this young friend, Kepler relied most on Christoph Besold (b.1577), the astonishingly prolific and far wealthier Tübingen law professor, appointed to his chair in 1610 (Figure 37). Both middle-aged men formed part of an intellectual circle that was deeply critical of the fact that Protestants and Catholics spent most of the time engaged in controversial, hair-splitting doctrinal debates as well as obsessively policing heterodoxy. As they saw it, this debate lost sight of the more important question of how to live faith truthfully and foster ecumenical thinking through a return to early Christian principles. Besold had built up one of the most significant private scholarly libraries of his time. Its nearly 4,000 manuscripts and volumes were usually sourced from Tübingen's book-seller and printer Eberhard Wild, a man who was himself at the node of an international network distributing prohibited spiritualist writings, for which he faced prosecution in 1622. By 1625, Besold stated that the law of nature was to believe what one wanted with a free conscience.[28]

Besold's library was encyclopaedic and up-to-date, with hundreds of books on astronomy, mathematics, medicine, history, politics,

Figure 36 Kepler's younger and most inspiring friend and collaborator during the time of the trial, the multi-talented Wilhelm Schickard, who 'philosophized with his hands', holding an astronomical instrument with a symbol of a benevolent sun which he also used for woodcuts in Kepler's works (see Figure 4). © University archive Tübingen

Figure 37 The lawyer Christoph Besold, as depicted by his friend Wilhelm Schickard in 1618, which incorporates positive maternal imagery through an allegory of generosity on the left. © University archive Tübingen

geography, theology, oriental languages, and modern literature, with a focus on French, Spanish, and Italian works. He inscribed books with his name and the device 'I renounce you, Satan—I unite my self with you, Christ', as if these words could spiritually charge every volume. This impressive collection must have completely filled the rooms of Besold's Tübingen town-house, which probably stood in a street called Münzgasse. There, Tübingen's most reputable professors lived, lined up in prime position next to the chancellor and close to the River Neckar in high, elegant, five-storey, timber-framed constructions. This home library enabled Besold to publish prolifically on political science and historical themes as well as edit medieval theologians ranging from Johannes Tauler to Girolamo Savonarola. He read Hebrew and published on the divine right in the Old Testament to criticize contemporary absolutism. In 1618, Besold asked Kepler for comments on his forthcoming pamphlet on the new world and the origins of its inhabitants, *De novo orbe conjectanae*, which he in turn dedicated to the mathematician.[29] In addition, of course, he wrote about civil law.

Besold's wife, a distant relative of Kepler, complemented her husband's spiritual interests. She herself was closely connected to the book-seller Wild, and was esteemed as a lover of the flourishing culture of German poetry. The Besolds' house was open to students wishing to learn modern languages who wanted to discuss ideas with like-minded people. At their heart was the burning question of how to reform society and faith in a 'dangerous age'.[30]

One of the couple's frequent visitors was the much younger Johann Valentin Andreae (b.1586), son of the pharmacist Maria and the alchemist pastor Jacob Osiander, ever keen to discuss his influential prophetic ideas.[31] Andreae, for many years, had energetically endorsed the value of 'new' discoveries, as he intended to create a fraternity of those keen to disseminate knowledge of 'new plants, new fruit, animals', and to find 'new axioms'. This was to improve the church and moral philosophy in a 'new solid castle or house' to create harmony on earth and fight any dissonance brought by the devil.[32] He expected every schoolchild to know thousands of plant names and characteristics to appreciate the 'spectacle of nature'.

These ideas had just culminated in Andreae's 1619 Lutheran utopia of a Christian Republic. One of the most significant utopias written in the period, the book was published before Campanella's better known *City of Sun*, which, however, circulated as manuscript in Tübingen from 1613.[33] Andreae's *Reipublicae Christianopolitanae Descriptio* set out an ideal Christian community without money, poverty, dense social hierarchies, and thus without a noble class. As in Freudenstadt, burgher-houses were arranged around a square, each of them with its own garden. Communities were led by wise men distinguished by true piety, judicial reasoning, and scholarship. Learning was most highly esteemed and underpinned by deep respect for craftspeople whose knowledge was generated from making rather than reading. Its natural philosophers tried to understand the properties of minerals and metals through 'real, genuine chemistry' carried out in seven workshops and confidently held that: 'If you do not settle disputes by means of experiments, if you do not make use of suitable instruments to improve the sciences and make them more comprehensive, you are worthless.'[34]

A keen mechanic and builder of clocks and automata, pastor Andreae presented one of the earliest visions of how ongoing scientific research into and detailed sensate awareness of God's creation could be the very foundation of a new society for the benefit of mankind. Andrea's progressive Christian city-state was to contain a splendid church with an impressive organ, an extensive public library, a laboratory, a pharmacy, an anatomy research centre, a museum of natural history and one of astronomy, a showroom for optical and astronomical instruments, as well as an arts and drawing workshop, suited for technical as much as narrative visual crafting.

His pedagogy took a clear position in the contemporary debate about whether senior schools should continue a humanist emphasis on perfecting classical languages or integrate scientific learning and things to see, feel, smell, and understand. A correspondingly ambitious curriculum would be taught in a boarding school open to every boy and girl. It would also rigorously regulate hygiene, manners, and religious instruction.[35]

Andreae, who thought of Kepler as part of a new Christian fraternity of likeminded intellectuals, believed gardens were a key source of pleasure, offering 'sweet aromas, improvement of the air, honey, medicines, birdsong, instruction' as well as ingenious water and acoustic features. Above all, plants rooted everyone in an enjoyment of beauty in relation to a prospect of regeneration. Human beauty, Andreae wrote, is like the 'flowers gathered in a single year: we are born we grow up, bloom, fade and whither. From our death comes further birth and multiplication.' Age did not make anything superfluous or corrupting, it bore no threat. This vision explains Andreae's corresponding utopia that the elderly of 'both sexes' in Christianopolis would be cheered up, treated with honour, and asked for advice. Although old age seemed like an illness, the elderly were to be honoured as experienced practitioners of life. Their opinions were far more useful than anything that a 'subtle theory' might provide.[36]

In 1620, Andreae felt excited about putting some of his ideas into practice as he took on a major position in Calw. This was a Black Forest town on the south-western fringes of Württemberg, marked by a booming proto-industrial production of technologically inventive light woollen cloths dyed in vibrant colours that were distributed as far as Italy and Poland. The pastor vigorously started social experiments. Merchants and other citizens were recruited to join a Christian foundation, which, among other projects, paid to create a public library, pay poor children's school fees, and support ill people.[37] To extend his Christian society beyond the community, Andreae recruited Besold, Kepler, Bernegger, and Wilhelm Schickard.[38] Here there was no sense of defeated ideals, despite the considerable burdens of the time. These men were driven by an interest in the new field of political science and by their faith. All of Kepler's and his fellow students' Tübingen professors of theology had perished: most recently Johannes Georg Sigwart, in 1618, and Matthias Hafenreffer, in 1619. The voices of Kepler's generation grew louder.

* * *

It must have been all the more frustrating for Kepler to have to busy himself with a trial. Schickard's friendship as well as Besold's expertise and access to his specialized library made Kepler decide to base himself in Tübingen while carefully composing the defence for his mother. Besold would later claim eight florins for advice, while an unspecified Tübingen advocate, perhaps Besold himself, received the significant sum of forty florins in lieu of the 'documents'. It remains unclear to what extent Besold or another lawyer involved themselves in the defence.[39] As Kepler put his mind fully to the task of acting as his mother's advocate, he was doubtless engulfed by an intense sense of anger, evident in his extraordinary poetic attack—reminding government lawyers of their duty to prevent abuse that wrecked the accused and their family's livelihood. How could the centre of government allow darkness to take over?

Kepler regarded proper rule as rooted in music, geometry, and arithmetical progressions which encapsulated divine understandings of harmony and order.[40] He had recently dealt at length with the insufficient mathematical foundations of Jean Bodin's famous *Republic*. He questioned the French intellectual's attempt to define justice through intermediates between geometrical and arithmetic principles which were then linked to the realm of politics and society. In this Aristotelian tradition, the relative amount of power of a ruler, the nobility, and the populace was derived from numerical patterns. Yet only a non-mathematician, Kepler sharply commented in Book III of his *Harmony*, could think that 2 stood in the same proportion to 4 as 6 to 8 (as 2 is half of 4, but 6 more than half of 8). This discussion led him to advise that a supreme regent could either be a king, the aristocracy, or the whole populace. It was most important to reign with 'subtle harmony rather than static, mathematical laws', for the sake of the public good. Kepler concluded:

> I should recommend harmonic proportions, with no reference to a geometric relationship, no reference to arithmetic equality, but reference simply to the *accords*; and I should demand those subtle analogies are less important than *harmonic accords*, and similarly that inflexible administration of both kinds of justice yields place to the supreme rule and welfare of the state.[41]

This emphasis on accords, which had to be sensed in different situations, underlined Kepler's idea of harmonic rule. It was a special craft linked to intuition, tacit knowledge gained through experience, a gift to apprehend complexity and an ability to act in the interest of 'general well-being, according to the circumstances of the time and without much pomp'.[42] This craft evidently was difficult to systematize and not just linked to reason, but neither did it have anything in common with reverence for the arcane.

Kepler in turn lent no support to Bodin's idea that power should ideally be vested in a hereditary monarch, but pointed out that the number of able rulers was always very small. He thus argued against Bodin's representation of the monarch, nobility, and populace through the numbers 4, 6, and 7. Rather, Kepler held that the populace needed to be represented through the number 9 (so that the initial gap of 2 increases by 1 at every step and the further progression from 9 would be 13), to replace dissonance with political harmony, in which the nobility could perfectly mediate. At the same time, Kepler did not idealize the aristocracy, but affirmed the importance of a political science, led by lawyers, in which the 'decisions of judges which are the most just and according to the yardsticks of the laws and of justice should be turned inside out and subjected to the most detailed examination by those learned in the law'.[43] Only institutionalized legal scrutiny ensured fairness—and Kepler must have had Besold in mind, who argued that territorial princes should be checked in their power by imperial law courts and their estates. The outcome of this outline of politics was a world away from Bodin's call for order in a troubled world through obedient subjects (in his *Republic*) and his spectacular plea for the burning of witches as politics in action to save the land (in his treatise on witchcraft, the *Démonomanie*).[44] Kepler even explicitly warned about provincial governors who might play 'the role of a little king', not hesitating to deviate from laws. He alluded to Leonberg's governor, Einhorn.[45]

Men like Kepler took matters of justice as reflecting on a government's legitimacy. He concluded Book III of his *Harmony* with the prophetic sentence 'I myself indeed ... shall in the following books declare the works of the Lord.'[46] Kepler ended his Tübingen poem for the freshly appointed ducal councillor Breitschwert by wishing him God's 'spirit and power' to walk on the path of his profession 'towards eternal life'.[47] He thus left no doubt that the particulars of his mother's case possessed general significance for the state of Württemberg and could inform concepts of political authority as such. They also had lasting consequences for God's judgement of judges and rulers, as his instruments on earth to serve mankind.

12

THE TRIAL ENDS

⎯⎯⎯∞∞∞⎯⎯⎯

Witchcraft and its legal treatment had never been alien to Kepler's intellectual sphere. Kepler's friend and godfather to his son Ludwig, for instance, was Johann Georg Gödelmann (1559–1611), a lawyer who had grown up in Württemberg, to become the 'greatest' of the 'early Protestant legal experts of witchcraft'. As a Saxon diplomat, Gödelmann regularly visited Prague.[1] As soon as the witch trials multiplied in the 1580s, he had insisted that regular legal procedures must be obeyed, as the Imperial Law Code prescribed. Witchcraft could not be treated as exceptional crime. The charge needed to be well established and two reliable witnesses were required before any suspect could be tortured. Gödelmann repeated the Lutheran position that it was up to God to separate the wheat from the chaff. It troubled him to see the 'populace' shouting 'To the stake!' Many suspects were so fragile that torture terrorized them into confession. Legal experts had to be consulted at all costs.[2] Gödelmann's 1591 treatise on magic, sorcery, and witches was immediately translated into German in 1592 and republished several times. In it, he argued that Sabbath meetings, weather-making, or physical transformations were impossible. It followed, therefore, that these activities could not be subject to legal questioning. There was not an army of witches that needed to be fought against. Only some individual witches did real harm, because the devil had special powers over 'worn-out, stupid, ignorant old women' who were poorly instructed in Christian faith. Gödelmann thus distinguished between suspects who suffered from self-delusion and deserved medical treatment, those who made a pact without causing any harm and, in his view, deserved no capital punishment, and finally a small group of serious offenders who entered a demonic pact, committed real *maleficium* with the devil's help and deserved to die.[3] In 1610, Gödelmann wrote to Kepler from Dresden in order to borrow his copy of Martin Del Rio's *Investigations into Magic*, and a letter from Kepler to James I reveals that he and Gödelmann had discussed the English king's surprising arguments that witchcraft could reliably be proven by submitting suspects to the ordeal of floating on water. James I had published his *Daemonologie* in 1597 and asserted that witches raged more ferociously as the world was coming to an end. The king adhered to the Calvinist idea that all but the elect bore the image of the Devil rather than the Creator. Women were unlikely to be among the elect. Just as Eve had been deceived by the Serpent, so women had proven to be a frailer sex, which neatly explained why there was only one man among every twenty witches. James contested that floating was a perfect test, because the 'water shall refuse to receive them in her bosom, that have shaken off them the sacred Water of Baptisme'.[4]

Kepler read about, and in all likelihood discussed, these controversial subjects with other friends who had to deal with them as an urgent practical issue. Most notably, Johann Georg Herwart von Hohenburg (1553–1626), a lawyer, committed Catholic, keen astronomer, classical philologist, historian, mathematician, and Kepler's patron for many years, was appointed Bavarian Supreme Chancellor in 1590. Hohenburg consistently supported the anti-witch-hunting party at the Bavarian Court Council. For decades, protagonists of rigorous witch-hunting and their opponents had argued bitterly. Between 1601 and 1604, they created an international forum for debates at the Munich court and Ingolstadt's university.[5] The question of whether or not witchcraft trials should be conducted according to the strict demands of the Imperial Law Code remained at the heart of these heated discussions. Those in favour of relentless persecution argued that God might punish lenient judges and rulers. They insisted that one witch's denunciation of others should count as reliable evidence and justified torture of these suspects.[6] In the end, the moderate party won, and implemented the policy that the Bavarian trial procedures must follow the Imperial Law Code's cautionary rules. Adam Tanner, a Jesuit and one of the moderates' key protagonists, developed this idea of legal justice in witchcraft cases for many years, until he finally published it as part of his moral theology in 1627.[7]

* * *

In 1621, when Kepler was assembling his defence in Tübingen, many of these early critical voices could not yet be referred to through book citations. Kepler could nonetheless insist on a particular trial procedure—the *Formular*-procedure developed in Roman Law, which demanded that all documents had to be presented in writing. This was a stroke of genius—it fully informed the defence about the evidence and allowed Kepler to work with his usual tools of textual scrutiny. So detailed had the interrogations become that Kepler could no longer provide a crisp analysis of the case. His 1617 supplication had identified three interlinked general causes for his mother's persecution: (1) enmity against his mother due to her social situation as a widow; (2) pervasive cultural fears against old women; and (3) a new governor, ready to act. To present an effective defence, Kepler now needed to discredit every single witness through legal reasoning. He used particular facts derived from a close investigation of the evidence.

Such a fact-orientated inquiry of 'things themselves' was increasingly championed in all intellectual fields.[8] Kepler's education had nurtured his patience for puzzling over specifics. No trial documentation would bore him. He had closely combed through literary and scholarly texts all his life, encouraged by the humanist devotion to meticulous philological analysis as well as a new Mannerist delight in keeping the mind flexible through enigmas, riddles, hidden jokes, intricate conceits, and allegorical word play. Galileo, for instance, loved jumbling up letters or composing anagrams to encode new discoveries. In 1610, he had kept astronomers brooding over Smaismrmilmepoetaleumibunenugttaurias—to relate that he had observed the highest planet (*altissimum planetam*) triple-shaped (*tergeminum observavi*), as Saturn did not seem a single star but made up of three stars which were very close to each other.[9]

This had trained Kepler to attend to details and contradictions in the testimonies, a skill he had also honed in refuting scholarly opponents. The new taste for experiments and observations taught him how to assess *who* was doing the thinking, with what kind of authority and intentions, in a *particular* case, to produce what kind of data. If history and philology were needed to evaluate data presented by ancient writers, sociological context was needed to evaluate contemporary scientific arguments about singular natural phenomena, such as comets.

These intellectual habits explain why Kepler rigorously interrogated testimonies to establish which might be reliable. It mattered to any natural philosopher whether someone who observed, say, orbits, was male or female, socially marginal, self-interested and known for major moral shortcomings, or, by contrast, possessed a solid social status and was long experienced in particular areas of knowledge. Such insights from the human sciences and legal hermeneutics forged in antiquity had become just as important in natural history, and explain why leading minds took care to appear authoritative in the impression they made on others through observing etiquette and decorum. How they spoke, dressed, wrote, collaborated, and got themselves into print generated trust in their just and moral behaviour, their intellectual content, and supported their claims for originality.

In their actual writing, good natural philosophers then drew on legal methods to argue persuasively about who deserved to be trusted. They tried to end fruitless controversies about what was true or not in tricky matters by reaching a consensus about reasonable conclusions. These methods 'bound science to scholarship and mathematics to letters'.[10] This was why Kepler not only read the documentation in his mother's case but also listened attentively to Katharina in the Güglingen prison, as she described how it was normal to act in her world, how a Leonberg widow did widow-like things. Kepler did not descend from an elevated life of the mind to dirty details of a criminal trial. Years of arguing his case in science had prepared him to mount an exceptionally effective defence.

* * *

Kepler's lengthy legal defence first attacked the ability of many witnesses who had been interrogated in January to testify reliably; they were simply too young to rely on anything other than hearsay about his mother's reputation. It was a strong legal requirement that a bad reputation needed to be well established before an accusation could be made. Kepler sarcastically commented that Leonberg's new pastor, Buck, had displayed such 'vehemence, as if he had served as Inquisitor for many years'.[11] Was Lutheran justice, he asked, really different from a Catholic tribunal? The young pastor's partiality seemed evident. He had refused to offer Katharina Kepler communion, but had visited Ursula Reinbold at home to give her the sacrament, even though the latter was bursting with hatred. Christian faith demanded that you forgave your enemies. Like Buck, other witnesses were partial, filled with envy and hate, and thus unreliable in their testimony.

Kepler went on to present Ursula Reinbold as a superstitious, irresponsible, factious, self-interested woman who had misinterpreted natural causes and, by implication, had no right to speak in a properly conducted inquiry. She had taken the wrong medicines, but ascribed her symptoms to 'the imagined witches'. Next, she had used her powerful network by spreading rumours among high-ranking friends as well as the lowest kinds of people. Katharina's civil defamation charge had thus turned into a criminal trial in which Katharina now stood accused and faced torture on the basis of vague suspicions. She had never confessed to any crime. These matters of life and death needed to be handled with complete legal rigour and in consideration of the fact that even 'the most reasonable men' might err. Three prominent legal commentators were cited in Latin to argue that only sufficient evidence justified torture. In addition, Kepler argued that the Imperial Law Code demanded two impartial witnesses for such capital crimes, and, according to legal experts, these and all other witnesses would have to be men, as women were more credulous, superstitious, and changeable.[12]

This was not a general defence of women, then, but an argument that created hierarchies between 'good' and 'bad' women based on their alleged sexual morality—and, characteristically for Kepler, affirmed that a woman's mind was in general inferior to a man's. To establish factual evidence for his defence from superior male witnesses, Kepler had read the depositions closely and now referred to testimony from old Hans Beutelspacher and the saddler Michael Stahl, both of whom had been reputable members of the court and old enough to have known Katharina for most of her life. (Stahl, in fact, now lived in the house on the market square which Katharina and Heinrich had moved into when they had first come to Leonberg.)[13] They had never thought of her as a bad woman. This supported Kepler's argument that only Reinbold's rumours had caused other people to blame Katharina for their misfortunes, and that this process had gathered further momentum only once the legal hearings had started. This explained why Katharina had then been accused of causing people's symptoms through sorcery when she passed by someone or visited their house. Kepler once again relied on several legal commentators who argued that these accusations could not be seen to constitute reliable evidence, and that a majority of local people needed to think of a person as a witch *before* rumours by one party had spread.[14]

The mathematician stuck closely to the Imperial Law Code. He pointed out that none of the women who had been locally condemned had indicated Katharina as a fellow witch, despite the fact that several of them had been severely tortured. According to the Law Code, such denunciations from witches would have been strong evidence.[15] He moved on to an important critique of illegal torture. Kepler made clear that he had acquired information about how these female suspects had been treated with extreme violence: 'everything they knew about themselves and others was pressed out of them with *intolerable* pain and martyrdom'. One of them, he shockingly revealed, had lost her thumb in the thumbscrews through 'barbarous torturing'. The most common legally sanctioned practice in Württemberg at that time was to stretch a woman by pulling her up on a wheel rather than to use thumbscrews. Kepler also claimed that this woman had then been questioned illegally about whether Katharina was a witch. Had Kepler obtained information about Margaretha Frisch, the old woman from Leonberg, and was her barbarous torture the reason why she died in prison so quickly in January 1620 after her final interrogation?

Further, Johannes Kepler argued, it was one thing to run into people's houses (as his mother did), and another thing to be a witch. Any association between these two would make any old, garrulous, and frequently disliked woman vulnerable to this far-fetched accusation. This insistence that any general unease about a woman's behaviour had to match with specific reasons for suspecting her of *sorcery* was a key legal argument for caution.

Kepler next set out why it was paramount to distinguish between natural and unnatural illnesses, and went into considerable medical detail to make his statement as authoritative as possible. Its ingenious noting of details which could then conclusively be dismissed made this one of his rhetorical masterpieces. All these magical mystery diseases, Kepler argued, could be explained through medical knowledge and common sense:

> ... that Beitelspacher has lame limbs, Bastian Mayer's wife has perished, the tile-maker woman has an open thigh, that the bathing-master's apprentice felt unwell in his stomach for several hours and threw up, that Stoffel Frick had pain in his thigh for a day or two, that the deceased pastor's daughter in Gebersheim has a bad foot, that Daniel Schneider's children died, that Haller's daughter felt pain on one arm, that Jerg Beltzen lost one sow, Oswald Zangen one calf, that Michael Stahl's cow became restless and ill, but soon recovered . . . from these stories and facts . . . no specific deeds of witchcraft will be derived, for many mentally ill women [*phreneticae mulieres*] can be found, and many who suppress their monthly bleeding . . . which looks for another exit through evaporation, and often causes great trouble in the head and strong pain. Many women, who have much blood during their youth, and bleed like horses, find with time, when they remain infertile (like the Reinbold woman), that the excessive bleeding or gall inflames the spiritus epatici, which causes terrible illnesses in their head. Many entail vitium uteri, which is part of Reinbold's sterility . . . and likewise causes chronic illness and head pain. Every day, many men and women die of lung disease and even more children of other illnesses. One finds many hunched, lame people. Among people who often lift or carry heavily or jump it is not uncommon that their spine is dislocated.

This, Kepler explained, in turn dried the lower limbs and could take men's potency.[16] Kepler did not rule out that sorcery might inflict harm. But in these cases, the pain was immediate and severe from the start, rather than increasing gradually. In Reinbold's case, moreover, there was certain evidence that she had taken strong medicines that might have harmed her. Perhaps, Kepler suggested, she herself had just taken the wrong jug when visiting Katharina, who had always drunk from her own mixture of healing herbs without any side effects whatsoever. Other witnesses admitted frankly that they had already suffered symptoms before they had encountered his mother. It was unnecessary to remind judges that cows and pigs perished of natural causes every day. In fact, the baker's cow had died during a time when many places had experienced a decimation of their cattle (see Figure 38).

Next, Kepler needed to tackle his brother's damaging accusations. He admitted his unease, recounting how Heinrich had run away from the family aged sixteen, without even finishing his apprenticeship. He had 'grown up in warfare', and had come home more bad than good when he had returned to his mother fifteen years later. Heinrich had not behaved as a good child by appreciating his mother's sacrifices, but—as one witness had reliably testified—had blamed his mother for leaving him hungry. This had led him to be angry and insult her as a witch. But this presented no legal evidence for her *being* a witch, and Heinrich of course had never been interrogated about his abuse. In addition, Katharina had shown herself to be a good Lutheran by reprimanding her son about converting to Catholicism.[17]

Every element of seemingly damning testimony was therefore addressed and explained in its wider context—of natural disease, a person's bias, family quarrelling, or simple mishaps. Katharina, her oldest son conjectured, had cried out ten years earlier that she wished she were a witch—in front of a young seamstress who was staying with her—only because she had burnt herself on a frying pan. A witch would have felt nothing! Over and over again, a passage ended with quotations from the few available legal commentaries to

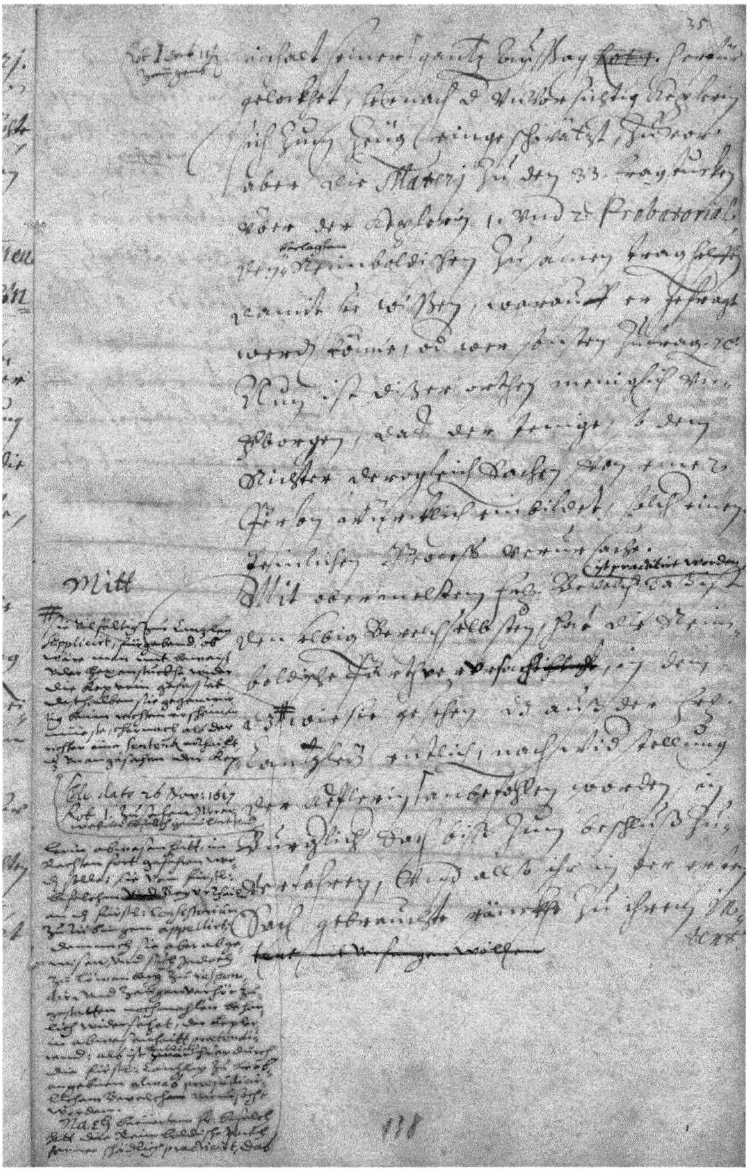

Figure 38 A page from Kepler's concluding defence for his mother, with his marginalia. HStASt A 209, Bü.1056, 183r. © Stuttgart, Hauptstaatsarchiv

warn that no propositions advanced by dubious witnesses or under dubious circumstances justified torture. This, then, was a pioneering defence, because it stayed so close to the legal arguments mounted by moderates in the debate about the persecution of witches, working through them in every detail.

* * *

A further skill that Kepler used was to establish the historical context of any accusation in relation to the age of the witness. Thus, he calculated that if Severin Stahl's deceased wife had seen Katharina touch a pig twenty-five years ago, she would have been only seven years old at the time and hence would not have been able to testify reliably in court.[18] The tile-maker's girl, Kepler independently established, had been baptized on 8 November 1604 and hence had only been eleven years old when she provided her testimony.[19] Similarly, he picked up on any inconsistent detail, as when witnesses first alleged that Katharina had touched the left leg of the pig and later testified that it had been the right.

Allied to such arguments was Kepler's astonishing attempt to make the case that his mother was an honourable lay medic. Kepler did not deny that his mother had provided medical advice, but he underlined that expertise in such matters often formed part of a woman's experience and family tradition. He had changed his tune about his mother, because he understood this was the only way to defend her reputation and his own. Rather than decrying Katharina's apparent interest in her mother-in-law's medical practices, as he had startlingly suggested in Book IV of his *Harmony of the World* in 1619, Kepler now referred to the fact that his mother had gathered expertise in dealing with a painful skin disease (*Erysipel*) affecting the face and lower thighs. She had treated her husband, and talked about the symptoms with Barbara, her daughter-in-law, when visiting the Keplers in Prague. Next, she had embarked on a series of experiments based partly on the knowledge she had received from Barbara, who suffered from the condition, as well as her mother-in-law, whom Kepler now described as 'an honest and well known good doctor'. This was the carefully gathered and validated experience she had offered when advising the tile-maker's wife.[20]

Kepler therefore used the defence to argue that a woman's experience, observation, and experiment over a long period of time and in dialogue with older insights constituted a basis for reputable and probable, if not certain knowledge. Exactly the same claim was used to prove any natural philosopher's credibility. His strategy, in sum, was to create a different sense of his mother as a person—not as an old, marginal, illiterate, and superstitious woman, but as a pious citizen who passed on and developed medical knowledge reliably and had carefully used herbs for her own health. This construction was only plausible because of well-known role models, such as the duchess Sibylle and Maria Andreae, who were admired for their remedies and pious medical practice. Most of these female pharmaceutics experts were Lutheran. Their medical knowledge had begun to be published, further championing the idea that natural knowledge was acquired through experience, laudable as long as it was guided by piety and virtue. Just like these women, Katharina Kepler, even though her illiteracy clearly distinguished her from them, never charged for her medical advice or treatment, and thus was not self-interested. These experimenting females had carved out a new social role for women as respected healers, and Kepler now strategically tried to make his mother's practices resemble their pioneering attempts.[21] Kepler had even asked his mother about the mixture she drank every day, and established that it was wine with vermouth and *Carda benedictus* or blessed thistle, sometimes with a pinch of hyssop, which is known to purify the blood and stimulate urine. None of this was dangerous. On the basis of this specific detail, Kepler once more cited precise evidence to deconstruct the accusation: the bath-keeper 'had only disliked some of the drink, and never claimed that all of it had made him ill'.

In order to underline that his mother was pious and charitable rather than a superstitious, selfish, and financially greedy woman like Reinbold, Kepler further referred to Katharina's healing verse as a 'prayer' rather than a blessing. He insisted that it included no unchristian words. If it entailed any superstition, he finally conceded, this resulted from old papist traditions rather than any connection with sorcery.[22] Here was his repeated insistence that utterances needed to be interpreted in their correct historical or social context to provide proof of anything.

* * *

A severe challenge for Kepler in constructing his skilful defence nonetheless remained: how could he persuasively contextualize the fact that his mother had asked for her father's skull to be dug out of its grave? Was this not a clear sign that she had tried to obtain a tool of magical sorcery? He had evidently asked her further questions in prison about the incident, and now related the following story. Katharina had only gone to the graveyard to take care of the wreath on the grave of a grandchild who had recently died, so that it would not be destroyed when another grave was being dug out. This clearly supported the impression that she generally conducted herself in a caring, empathetic, and Christian manner.

As she had seen the gravedigger working next to her deceased father's grave, it had innocently occurred to his mother that she might have his head set in silver. Kepler explained why she had thought of this as normal. Many sermons reminded her of mortality and she had heard that a drinking cup from a parent's head might be suitable to further such contemplation. She had seen actual examples of this and heard about several populations throughout the world which used such heads in joyous celebrations. No father's skull had ever been used for sorcery. She had a completely different context for its use. Hence her request did not make her sufficiently suspect to justify torture. Moreover, she had asked in broad daylight and accepted the gravedigger's refusal. In fact, the gravedigger himself had testified that he was surprised how much had been made out of this exchange during the trial.[23]

Finally, Kepler needed to explain why his mother had offered Einhorn the wretched silver cup as a bribe. He completed his portrayal of an aged, extremely fearful but pious woman, who had wanted to end the defamation as quickly as possible by influencing a governor who had been hostile to her all along. Kepler argued that she had offered him the cup not in order to silence the dispute, but to speed up her civil defamation charge—and thus to further a proper legal inquiry.[24] To account for her inability to cry, the mathematician insisted that tears sometimes naturally dried up in people, especially when old, and their lack could not be taken to prove anyone's guilt.[25]

Then followed Kepler's grand concluding argument on ethical grounds: Katharina now was a very old, weak, mentally impaired woman who had experienced much in her life and raised those of her children who had followed her guidance honourably. Her family background was honourable, and she had never been punished for any bad behaviour in her life. Her long imprisonment since 7 August 1620 had made her suffer more than enough through its squalor, the pain of being enchained, and the threat of violence. None of the evidence justified that she, a human being created 'as the noblest creature' and in God's likeness, should undergo torture.[26] The book of Genesis remained the benchmark of all appeals for legal equality and justice in this age. God had created each human in his own image and likeness.

* * *

It took until 20 August in the summer of 1621 for the next court session to take place in Güglingen. Governor Aulber presented the judges with a written copy of the Keplers' defence alongside its cool confutation by Hieronymus Gabelkhover, the ducal court's advocate. Katharina and Johannes Kepler appeared together in court, and Kepler demanded at once to be able to skim through the final accusation. This came as a shock. Tightly argued and referencing Latin legal as well as theological commentators, Gabelkhover left no doubt that Katharina had to be tortured. She was held responsible for several acts of harm against people and animals as well as for attempting to bribe the Leonberg governor in order to avoid any hearings before she escaped the country. Kepler's defence was refuted for diluting clear evidence, for instance that she had promised Einhorn the silver cup. She had been a suspect person present at places where harm had happened. Moreover, she had practised soothsaying, had a bad reputation, and a son who said that she had driven his father away. Her testimony was inconsistent, and Jean Bodin, among others, clearly regarded this as reason enough to justify torture. Added to this was Katharina's inability to meet any of her opponents' eyes. Following Bodin, her incapacity to shed tears strengthened the case for torture. This was regarded as a physical as much as a mental sign of inhumanity.

Gabelkhover defended Ursula Reinbold's reputation—there was no evidence that she had been in prison for illegitimate sex with the coppersmith Jerg Zieher before her second marriage, twenty-three years ago. It was difficult to identify witnesses of sorcery, but unlikely that young people or women maliciously imagined things they had not seen. Gabelkhover engaged, to some extent, with Kepler's discussions of particulars, only to demonstrate that he had a response to each of them. Then he declared that the evidence far outweighed Kepler's variously 'dyed' and hence dubiously colourful 'excuses'. There was no reason to doubt the judges' opinion so far. The case clearly needed to be moved on through torture.[27]

Kepler might have thought that he had mastered the art of convincing factual argument, but now stood accused of making up much of his contexts, histories, and proofs.

* * *

Barely any time remained for Kepler to compose his concluding defence. A legal ultimatum had been set, and he had to submit it within three or four days. He had been able to plan for it in outline since May, but now needed to respond to the specific points of emphasis and particular arguments in Gabelkhover's surprisingly severe accusation. Why had the chancellery entrusted Gabelkhover with the task? Kepler's influence on government officials now pre-occupied with war had clearly waned. Like the defence, this final text was mostly written down by Johann Rueff, his mother's appointed Güglingen advocate. Two other local scribes simultaneously helped to copy Kepler's furiously written draft into sixty-four neat pages. Kepler carefully went over this version, completing it with marginal glosses, additions, and corrections. Desperate to end the case, he handed it in before time, on 22 August 1621.[28]

He began by objecting to Aulber's unclear handling of the trial procedure, and then tackled Gabelkhover's list. Nothing prevented anyone from offering any official a gift, and the fact that his mother had done so certainly provided no evidence for witchcraft, especially as she had already been to see Einhorn twice before, who was refusing to take her defamation charge further. He once more detailed Einhorn's shortcomings—how the governor had moved dates for hearings and delayed the case. Next followed another discussion of how reliable the witnesses were, replete with remarks which clearly betrayed Kepler's deep irritation and growing impatience. Losing his grip on polite communication, Kepler called one of them 'a fable-woman', and Beittelspacher a 'fable-man', 'idiot' and 'little girl's schoolmaster', in whose brain one would not expect to find much.[29] He once more argued that his mother's imprisonment needed to be recognized as punishment in itself. The cause of this misfortune had been a systematic campaign conducted by Reinbold, who had known how to exploit an atmosphere of fear that had swept across the land after witches had been burned in nearby Sindelfingen—where a new governor had in fact instigated nineteen witchcraft trials between May 1615 and October 1616.

Much of Kepler's discussion was detailed and repeated the defence. But its middle section contained bravura elements of rhetorical persuasion which demonstrated the absurdity of the accusers' claims. During the past months, Kepler had prepared to list all the conflicting evidence of when exactly Reinbold was meant to have received the fatal drink. He presented this factually, so as to demonstrate that Gabelkhover's horridly patched-up account fell apart under close scrutiny. It made Katharina Kepler 'a witch' for '8, 9, 10, 18, 20, 25 years', a numerical progression which any trained mathematician could only dismiss as completely random and unruly.[30]

Kepler used medical facts to back up his depiction of Reinbold as a fundamentally immoral and by now mentally deranged person: illegitimate sex easily caused illnesses which were treated with mercury. This in turn affected the brain. It seems as if Kepler had also used the past months to gather further information about Ursula Reinbold's youth in the Franconian town of Ansbach. He now alleged that she had been impregnated by a local pharmacist's apprentice, who had in turn given her medicines to terminate the pregnancy. These had made her sterile.[31] This once more effectively dramatized the attack by a malicious, infertile woman on an honourable mother. He established Katharina as good and Reinbold as evil by pointing to their behaviour. Katharina had guarded her attractive daughter Margaretha vigilantly against young lads who had sometimes 'pushed in the door of her house [to gain access to] the daughter'.[32] If anything, Kepler suggested, Reinbold had mental and physical attributes usually associated with witches, while Katharina had proved herself a moral Christian and had by now borne the hardships of widowed motherhood for thirty-two years. He sarcastically commented that there would be bloody tears to cry if the family's civil defamation against the Reinbolds were ever allowed to continue.[33]

Kepler had also prepared a pointed attack on the argument that Katharina was casting charms. He clearly had received information that Gabelkhover himself had put the accusation together. Indeed, Kepler pointed out that such prayers were commonly used for healing, so much so that a number of them had been printed in none other than Dr Osswalt Gabelkhover's well-regarded publication on *Württemberg German Medicine*. His opponent's older relative had been a court medic under Duke Frederick since 1598, and his 'boock of physicke' had even been translated into English. His patronage, up to his death in 1616, had obviously helped Hieronymus's own career.[34] In Kepler's view, Katharina's prayer contained poetic sentences (he quoted the greeting of the Sun, 'salve Sol', as an example) and appealed to the Holy Trinity, rather than any diabolic powers. Gabelkhover's accusation had absurdly referenced Peter Binsfeld, the Catholic doctor and fervent demonologist of Trier, in order to argue that superstitious soothsaying was a common practice of witches rather than normal women.[35]

Kepler also dismissed Bodin and other demonologists of his ilk who recommended 'quick procedures'. It had been shown many times how dangerous it was to threaten humans created in God's likeness with torture on charges of occult crimes. He repeated the moderate contention that these were matters in which even the most learned easily erred. In Katharina's case, problems of evidence and procedure were particularly marked. Württemberg had always, therefore, advocated caution in witchcraft trials. Among legal commentators, Kepler referenced Johann Zanger in particular, a Lutheran lawyer and professor in Wittenberg, who had published his work *De quaestionibus seu torturis reorum* in 1593 in which he insisted that humans had been created in God's image and torture was a 'fragile and dangerous matter'.[36] This brilliantly underlined that he and his mother, who themselves stood accused of heterodoxy, in fact followed more orthodox Lutheran views than some prominent government officials.

On 22 August, all the documents were sent at once to the Tübingen law faculty, for its professors to now decide whether or not Katharina Kepler was to meet the torturer. In the same month, Reinbold, the glazier, once again accused the Kepler family of delaying the trial in the hope that Katharina would die. He therefore demanded an upfront payment of 300 florins to compensate his wife before any sentence was passed.[37]

* * *

In the event, Tübingen's six professors of law worked quickly. Advice on civil and criminal cases occupied most of their time, aside from teaching. Tübingen was the duchy's university, and its appointments and activities had been closely controlled by the Lutheran church and government since 1601. Orthodox beliefs and complete loyalty to any ruler were a condition of holding a chair. Protestantism in no way encouraged independent thought. Rather, the law faculty functioned as an agency of efficient state government. Every new appointment needed to be confirmed by the duke, and there were annual visitations by a mixed body of high-ranking government and church officials. From 1644 onwards, every sentence in a Württemberg criminal trial would need to be first agreed by the Tübingen professors of law. Before then, they were mostly consulted in difficult cases and to license torture. The professors drew on several major European writers on criminal law, although by 1621 this literature was still very limited in scope. The same quotes from the same books served them to work through their case-load. Katharina's trial was one of 2,460 civil and criminal cases which landed on their desks between 1602 and 1648. Only 28 cases (5.4 per cent) dealt with witchcraft. One of the six colleagues would present a judgement for discussion and a vote. The others usually agreed. A scribe neatly copied the resulting letter into a bound, indexed volume before sending out the original letter to the Stuttgart chancellery and relevant district governor. This institutional framework encouraged law by precedent.[38]

The Tübingen lawyers followed Tübingen theologians in treating witchcraft cases cautiously. They prohibited torture in almost half the cases and instructed the executioner to pull an offender up on a wheel in less than one-third (30.7 per cent) of those trials where they did permit torture. They agreed completely that a woman's inability to cry was no evidence for her crime (although their first discussion of this issue dates only from 1627).[39] They insisted on proper procedures throughout Württemberg's localities. Only witnesses who had made their depositions under oath could be considered. Everything needed to be properly documented. Enemies, dishonourable people, strangers, and children were usually excluded from testimony. Vague rumours bore no weight.[40]

Besold, surprisingly, positioned himself amongst the strictest voices in the Tübingen team. He was adamant that even those witches who confessed to the spiritual crime of being a witch, but without harming anyone, should be sentenced to death. This underlined his deeply religious view of how dangerous it was for a godly society to include people who worshipped the devil. Like most contemporaries, moreover, Besold believed that witches could actually cause harm, despite the fact that Tübingen preachers repeated for decades that they only imagined their ability to do so. At the same time, Besold joined his colleague's advocacy of procedural caution in line with the Imperial Law Code. He rigorously defended the view that only proper, proven evidence and accusations from at least two reputable witnesses justified any degree of torture.[41]

In Katharina's case, everything hinged on how the Tübingen lawyers assessed the evidence. On 10 September 1621, Besold and his five other colleagues sent Aulber a characteristically brief and diplomatic one-page document, fully in line with precedent. They held that much of the evidence was not sufficiently supported, and, given her old age, did not justify proper torture. Yet the woman could not simply be absolved either. A final attempt to 'frighten the truth out of her' was needed. Katharina was to be led to the usual place of torture, to face the executioner. He was to show his instruments and threaten to use them, although he was not allowed to actually touch or torture her.[42]

This would be Katharina Kepler's final ordeal.

13

KEPLER'S DREAM

Unsurprisingly, governor Aulber was not pleased with the decision from Tübingen. He did not expect Katharina Kepler to confess anything under such circumstances and was concerned about the useless expenditure on documents and messengers. With the grape-harvest about to begin and other 'autumn affairs' to see to, he reported that he was as busy in his fields and vineyards as he was in the office. The best solution seemed not to prolong matters that appeared to have a foregone conclusion. So when Johannes Kepler put pressure on Aulber to let them know in advance the day on which his mother would meet the executioner, the governor gave in.

Aulber next needed to find a man to undertake the job. The task was complicated, as there was an ongoing quarrel in Güglingen about who had the right to torture, hang, burn, or behead. The Stuttgart executioner was up against a nearby knacker who buried dead and diseased animals, but also did some torturing and executing 'on the side'. Aulber urged this *Wasenmeister* from Vaihingen to come and help end the case quickly. Instead of arriving at seven o'clock in the morning, however, the man turned up at midday, so that the session needed to be moved to the next morning.

The skills of any executioner with a brief to formally apply 'verbal torture' (*Verbaltortur*) included pretending that they would go on to use their instruments. This put enormous strain on women's nerves, especially as they needed all their energy to appear emotionally engaged and devout in order to create the best possible impression and avoid a legal appeal for proper torture.[1]

It is more than likely, though, that Kepler knew from his Tübingen friends that what would now follow was a pretence, and that he would have let Katharina know. He could prepare his mother for encountering a third-rate occasional executioner—the psychological pressure would therefore be low. In Nuremberg, prisoners during the same period would be tightly bound on the rack or a chair to see the legendary executioner Franz Schmidt describe his instruments of torture in the most terrifying manner, boasting of how he had used them to extract the truth from the most obstinate villains. Yet Katharina probably knew that she would not suffer any further pain if only she kept on denying her guilt.[2]

In the early morning of 28 September, Katharina was escorted from the tower gate to the town hall. There is no doubt that she felt this to be a dramatic moment. Aulber's subsequent report was based on detailed minutes taken down by the scribe. Turned into direct speech, this is what Katharina said: 'I do not want to confess or admit anything at all. Even if you treat me whatever way you want, and tear one vein after the next out of my body, I would not know what to admit to.'

They could not ignore this voice: I do not want to confess, I do not know. She now acted out her innocence through displaying sincere piety. She could never be a heretic, and saw herself only as being on God's side. Only he was a fair judge. Katharina fell down on her knees to say the Lord's Prayer. She exclaimed that God should now send a sign in case she was a witch or beast and had ever had anything to do with witchcraft. 'I will die for this', she asserted,

'God will reveal the truth'. She continued: 'He will not take his Holy Ghost from me, but stand by me. I have not done any harm to the glazier's wife, the schoolmaster or anyone else who accused me.' Katharina concluded forcefully by appealing to her conscience: 'If I would be forced by pain and martyrdom to admit anything it will not be the truth. I would have to lie about myself.'

This performance was typical of those women strong enough to resist in this situation. All of them confidently appealed to their Christian faith. They drew on their knowledge, drummed into them by Lutheran pastors, that God never made mistakes in his Last Judgement, but that humans frequently failed in their judgements. Yet not all women persuaded their questioners: one Württemberg woman who had resorted to this argument in 1618 was sharply reprimanded not to 'simulate being so pious and nice'. In despair, she later hanged herself with a bedsheet in prison, after someone told her that the executioner would now stretch her.[3] Terror of torture was intense. In the same year, another woman, Maria Hohenstein, fared better. Tears ran down her cheeks as she swore not to have done anything to a baby she was accused of bewitching. She asked whether some might not dig up its corpse and put it in her arms. God would send a sign if she were guilty. He was not absent, she had said, but ready to communicate his messages. 'As much as God has suffered and died for me', she asserted, 'I hope that my sighing will not end until I face the Lord.' This performance of religious contrition through crying and sighing was crucial to proving credibility. At the same time, Maria had showed determination to name injustice and declaimed that 'as long as she breathed in and out she wanted to lament the violence and injustice they had done to her', in order never to bring shame onto her family or dead ancestors 'below the earth'. Religion empowered women to resist extraordinary strain, so as to preserve the honour of their past and future families.[4]

Katharina Kepler still refused to cry, even when threatened with torture. She conceded that she had sometimes given herbs to people, but never thought they might affect people adversely. She had not caused any serious illness—the glazier's wife had already been suffering from symptoms when she arrived in Leonberg and the schoolmaster had previously suffered an accident by jumping over a ditch. Katharina repeated her request that God should send a sign of her innocence. Like Maria and other women, Katharina asserted that God would punish those who had brought her into such trouble. The governor, judges, and executioner kept on threatening and reminding her of her deeds for some time, but she remained constant and entirely coherent. Finally, Aulber ordered the guards to take Katharina back to her cell, where an anxious Johannes presumably awaited her.[5] Six days later, his mother was unlocked from her iron chain and set free, after fourteen months of incarceration under the severest conditions.

* * *

Leonberg's governor, Einhorn, received the news by letter a few days afterwards, in early October: Katharina Kepler was absolved, and Leonberg was ordered to bear part of the considerable costs of her trial and imprisonment. He instantly protested to the Stuttgart chancellery. This would 'forever' leave its shameful mark on his own reputation and be used by the Keplers to abuse him gravely. Moreover, how was the district meant to pay? Its population was worn down by the duke's demand for war contributions. Katharina still owned her meadows and fields. If she returned, people undoubtedly would want to kill her in revenge. She was ill-famed in the whole region. Einhorn and others remained adamant that she had made people incurably ill for a long time. There was a seventeen-year-old youth, he explained, who was about to perish due to Katharina's malice. It was frightful to listen to her older victims daily lamenting their excruciating pain. He and his obedient subjects, Einhorn evocatively ended his plea, were willing to serve the duke with their life, property, and blood in any emergency—but Katharina Kepler could not return to live among them.[6]

The Kepler siblings managed to obtain a copy of this shrewd letter. They quoted it as they petitioned the duke to allow their defamation charge against the Reinbolds to be taken up again (but not under Einhorn's biased governance). In this, they calibrated their appeal to show that the duke's reliance on popular loyalty during the war had to be reciprocated by responding to requests of this kind. On 12 April 1622, the chancellery ordered Einhorn to send copies of the complete documentation relating to the defamation to a civic court in either Cannstatt or Tübingen.[7] The documentation never arrived.

Just as Einhorn received this order, Katharina Kepler died, aged seventy-five, on 13 April. No evidence survives about the final six months of Katharina's life after her imprisonment and how it affected her, nor do we know the circumstances of her burial or the location of her grave. It seems that her remarkable resources of resilience had been stretched too far. In early October, Johannes or probably his sister Margaretha, would then have brought their mother to the small village of Rosswälden by foot, or perhaps they had paid for a bumpy ride on a cart. She had stayed with her daughter and the pastor Binder in another new place, their village vicarage. Binder would have buried her. A trip to Linz would have been even more demanding for Katharina, and it would have required secrecy about the trial, as Johannes Kepler had never told anyone there the reason as to why he had temporarily moved back to Württemberg.

* * *

For Kepler there were now the money matters to sort out. Like looking for patronage and support, this was something he had had to do all his life. Used to tight finances, periodically worried about poverty, and continuously fighting for the actual payment of his full salary as imperial mathematician ever since he had begun to serve Rudolph II, Kepler could never afford to regard money matters as too mundane for his concern. He courted financial gifts in return for offering his books, counted pennies, noted every expense, chose his first wife not least because she was well-off and his second wife because she was frugal. He claimed back any expense he possibly could and carefully listed debts. With more than a hint of wishful thinking, the frontispiece of his *Rudolphine Tables* would eventually depict the imperial eagle dropping down valuable florins (*Thaler*) from its beak.[8]

Katharina's legal inheritors were her living children, as well as her deceased son Heinrich's two orphan girls—Anna Maria and Anna. Johannes had chosen Wilhelm Bidenbach, the upper chancellery lawyer, to represent his interests in relation to his siblings. Here were Kepler's claims: he had not received his salary of 400 florins during his absence from Linz, and in addition he had spent 300 florins on travel and subsistence.[9] This was a vast sum to compensate. Yet Christoph Kepler was entirely prepared to admit his part in increasing expenditures by moving the trial away from Leonberg. Although he had still tried to manipulate Katharina's inheritance in his favour in March 1621, while his mother was imprisoned, he now withdrew from any claims on the inheritance. Christoph Kepler thus made his peace with his siblings.[10] The pewterer estimated that they had inherited 1,000 florins from their father, and the rest of the inheritance should have amounted to 3,000 florins. He would be happy if the costs of his mother's nourishment in prison could be covered, as well as the family's legal costs, the expenses Margaretha had incurred through looking after Katharina at home, and Johannes, through travelling. Johannes duly received all of Katharina's immovable wealth—five fields, which he would own until 1628, when he still paid the community his share for the night watch.[11] Then there was a quarter of meadowland, which Margaretha took over to cover her expenses on her mother's behalf, but not without recording that she would be happy at any time to leave it to Johannes should he wish her to do so. In the end, Christoph Kepler's total inheritance amounted to a pitiful thirteen florins.[12]

Instead of further dividing the family, these arrangements had brought it closer together again. They acknowledged who owed what to whom, emotionally as much as materially.[13] High inflation during the war made it complicated to arrange for the family's share of payments for Katharina's imprisonment. In 1624, Johannes still liaised with his brother-in-law Binder to settle final payments that the family owed to Governor Aulber in hard coin, as well as to set aside a small charitable sum for the orphaned nieces. He also decided to lease his lands to Christoph, who had to pay annual dues to Margaretha, who in turn handed them on to Kepler's son Ludwig once he studied in Tübingen. Kepler remained watchful, though, and instructed his Tübingen friend Wilhelm Schickard to strictly tell Ludwig in advance that he should never directly ask his uncle for money. Kepler feared that Christoph only waited for the chance to generously provide assets in order to then push his older brother out of his property rights.[14]

* * *

Meanwhile, Kepler's return to a normal life in Austrian Linz with his family had proved difficult. Württemberg foreign politics shifted back to neutrality in the autumn of 1621. The duke and the majority of his councillors returned to the idea that the empire could only be preserved if religious polarization was avoided. The Bohemian crown had been lost, and Lutheran Württemberg would not go into battle to preserve the Palatinate for Frederick as Calvinist ruler. A stress on moderation, unity, and concord guided foreign policy once again.[15]

Yet in Linz, Bavarian troops continued to occupy the land and oversaw the rigorous implementation of counter-Reformation measures. During the first months after Kepler's return, he could imagine that friends and acquaintances, as well as Tübingen enemies, might comment upon the end of the trial, as they surely did. Schickard, for instance, wrote to Bernegger that many had not expected Kepler's mother to be absolved.[16] In November 1621, Kepler needed to respond urgently to unpleasant accusations from Tycho Brahe's family that he had wrongly taken the Danish astronomer's invaluable observations and instruments with him to Württemberg. As he clarified, he had carefully locked these in a special chest and left them securely in the building of the Upper Austrian Estates.[17] It came as a considerable relief when, in December, Emperor Ferdinand II confirmed Kepler's ongoing post as imperial mathematician. And despite the Catholic occupation, Kepler was not expelled from his post at the local Protestant convent school.

Little correspondence survives from this period. By March 1622, Kepler received worrying news that two Tübingen professors were under attack for their heterodox Protestant views. One of them was Besold. It was only by the end of spring 1622, after his mother's death, that Kepler started to gradually slot back into his old routines of scholarly exchanges. He discussed arguments in writings which were sent to him and wrote reference letters for promising international scholars—such as the Egyptian Joseph Abudakan, a professor of Arabic and Hebrew. Kepler's wife Susanna was pregnant again. In May he very belatedly sent a letter of thanks to the Regensburg doctor, Oberndorffer, and his wife—whom he had known since their time together in Graz—for accommodating his family. He posted money to cover some remaining debts at the local pharmacy. Apart from this, Kepler appears to have kept to himself far more than before the trial, even in relation to his most intimate friends. No letter to Bernegger was sent before August 1623. In April 1623,

Wilhelm Schickard cheerfully announced from Tübingen that he would continue his linguistic accomplishments by moving on from Arabic to Ethiopian, but remarked that he had not heard from Kepler for some time and would like to be in touch again. Ever creative and busy devising substantial new projects, Schickard would soon send him a design for one of the world's first calculating machines.[18] As late as 1624, Kepler wrote a letter defying rumours about his absence from Linz. He had never explicitly told friends, the Austrian estates, or his assistant Gringallet why he had been away, but maintained that he had spent one year fighting 'against an enemy of his family'.[19]

Meanwhile, Kepler had started writing a book on calculating logarithms, a mathematical problem he loved. He also knew he was under pressure to finally finish his monumental work on the *Rudolphine Tables*. He needed to find ways to finance and arrange for the complicated printing of these comprehensive calculations of planetary orbits, although the book-trade had just entered a serious crisis due to the instabilities of war and inflation.[20] In order to start working, Kepler took out all his manuscripts, endless columns of data, and papers from their various places of storage in Linz. As he did so, the mathematician was pulled towards one of the strangest works he had ever written. Penned years earlier, it had never been printed. Its title read *Dream or Astronomy of the Moon*, in Latin: *Somnium*.

* * *

The central idea went back to his student days. He had begun to toy with the thought of composing a small, imaginative treatise on what the lunar region as well as the revolving earth and other planets looked like when seen from the moon. In 1593, he took his quill to pen a draft. A few years later, Kepler read Plutarch's *The Faces of the Moon* as well as Lucian's *True Story*, which includes a stopover on the moon.

Kepler next continued conversations with friends in Prague about how to develop his creative idea, as he tried out telescopes and supported Galileo's new observations of craters and mountains rather than a perfectly smooth moonscape. Finally, in 1609, Kepler took up his quill to write up properly this story about a universe in motion, stimulated not only by the scientific discoveries of his age but also its taste for the occult, literary play, and informed speculation. 'Hermeticism, magic and demonology', one commentator summarizes, frame 'his defence of the Copernican revolution'.[21]

As Kepler stood at his desk he decided to introduce a 'scientific' part through a narrative preface. This merged real and imagined elements, a device which served to re-create the experience of dreaming:

Its first person narrator is an astronomer living in contemporary Prague, just like Kepler. He reads a book about Bohemian history, which tells the story of an old female ruler and skilled magician, who faces an uprising. One night, the narrator falls asleep. He dreams that he is now reading a book from the Frankfurt book fair. It tells the story of a man from Iceland. He is Duracotus and has been fathered by an astonishingly potent local fisherman aged 147, who died when Duracotus was aged three. His mother is a witch, who has recently died. This allows Duracotus to write about their relationship and an extraordinary mutual adventure. Once, they obtain a wise demon's astonishingly factual account of how one can travel to the moon as well as what the region and its population are like. The narrator's dream abruptly finishes as he is woken up by wind and rattling rain in Prague. Water wipes out the end of the book in the dream.[22]

This narrative plot sets out the unusual relationship between Duracotus, who is growing up in Iceland, and his mother, Fiolxhilde, who raised him on her own, in captivating detail. This is what we are told about them:

Fiolxhilde earns a living by selling little white goatskin bags filled with herbs and embroidered amulets to fishermen. She takes her small son with her when gathering herbs in special places and at special times with magical rituals. Yet she never reveals what goes into the bags.

As he becomes older, Duracotus is so curious about the ingredients that once takes a knife to cut a bag open. When Fiolxhilde sees this, she is so incensed that she will be unable to sell it to her fisherman client that she sells her son to him instead. Duracotus boards a boat which sails to the island of Hven, to deliver a letter to the Danish astronomer Tycho Brahe.

Duracotus stays on the island, learns Danish, astronomical observation, how to use instruments and how Brahe and his many students do collaborative work. After five years, he returns to Iceland, where his mother has lived full of remorse about her angry decision, but now is delighted to see that Duracotus has become an astronomer. As it is too dark and cold for Fiolxhilde to gather herbs during winter, she accompanies him as he looks for patrons and in their conversations keeps comparing what she knows to what he has learnt about the heavens. She is proud of her knowledge as 'the only thing she possesses'. She becomes emotional as she announces that she can now die, because she has passed this knowledge on to her son. Just as the witch wants to know everything about what Duracotus has been taught, so her mature son, with his enduring curiosity for knowledge, begins to question his mother about her teachers and arts.

Fiolxhilde tells Duracotus that there exist spirits who particularly love the shadowy light of Iceland in winter. She especially relates to one of them. He is very gentle and either takes her to any place she wishes to, or teaches her in detail about distant places she is too afraid to visit herself. Fiolxhilde says that she would very much like to go to one of these places accompanied by her son. Duracotus excitedly agrees and asks her to summon the spirit so that they can take off at once. Spring has arrived. Fiolxhilde goes to a crossroad to shout for the spirit, whom they must silently await. As they cover their heads with clothing, a strange, rasping voice tells them about Levania, an island fifty thousand German miles up in the ether.

The spirit just keeps talking, rather than taking them on the four-hour journey. For the rest of the treatise, the spirit's words bear out what Fiolxhilde has implied by saying that he provides her with information as *valid as that which her son obtains from book-reading and observation. The spirit first explains that there are strict regulations about who is allowed on the trip: very few people altogether, who must be completely devoted to the spirits, and never any German men, as they will invariably be either too fat or too tender. Dried up old women who have spent a life-time riding he-goats at night or forked sticks are approved of as perfect travellers; so are Spanish men and others with trim, firm bodies from constant horse-riding or sailing to the New World on a diet of dried codfish, garlic, and other unappealing foodstuff. These travellers will discover the moon as a place with high mountains, deep and wide valleys, as well as caves and grottoes in which rapidly growing, short-lived inhabitants roam about in crowds and protect themselves from extreme temperatures.*

* * *

Kepler's story recast notions of the witch as evil by portraying a woman who made a living from selling magical herbal mixtures to benefit sailors, was thirsty for knowledge about the heavens, and had gained the trust of a good spirit. She was an emotionally connected woman, who deeply loved her son and felt sorry after punishing him once. Kepler seems to have shared his story and even the manuscript with friends in Prague. In 1611, the baron of Volkersdorf, a teenage aristocrat travelling with his tutors, took a copy to Tübingen.

Back in Linz, as Kepler reflected on this in the light of his mother's trial, he decided that he needed to prepare the manuscript for print. He angrily told his imagined readers what he thought had happened with that Tübingen copy of the manuscript in the 1610s: 'Would you believe':

> that in the barber shops (especially if there were any people to whom the name of my Fiolxhilde is ominous on account of her occupation) there was chatter about this story of mine? Indeed, from that very city and house there emanated malicious gossip about me in the immediately ensuing years.

Kepler specifically had 'his friends' in mind as he wrote this. 'You', he addressed them:

who are familiar with my affairs and with the reason for my last trip to Swabia, especially those of you who have met with the manuscript before, will be of the opinion that this little book and those events were ominous for me and my family.

Kepler clearly felt that this manuscript of *The Dream* had caused lasting damage, for, as he now explained:

when this gossip was taken up by senseless minds, it flared up into defamation, fanned by ignorance and superstition. If I am not mistaken, you will judge that my family could have gotten along without that trouble for six years, and I without last year's journey, had I not violated the precepts of this Fiolxhilde in the dream.

This played intriguingly with the suggestion that his literary creation might have some real power and presence. Kepler then announced what made him want to publish *The Dream*: 'I therefore decided to avenge this dream of mine for the affair just cited, by publishing the book, which will be another punishment for my adversaries.' It would prove them wrong.[23]

Having arrived back in Linz, settling back into his normal life, Kepler felt strangely guilty for unintentionally causing all of his mother's and family's trouble. At the same time, he was extremely angry with anyone who might have stupidly or maliciously drawn analogies between him and Katharina, and Duracotus and Fiolxhilde the witch.

He imagined that the 'barber' who had picked up and passed on the gossip was Urban Kräutlin, Ursula Reinbold's now deceased brother. At the time, Kräutlin had practised as a Tübingen barber-surgeon as well as acting as personal barber to Prince Frederick Achilles.[24] In making all these connections about how his manuscript had circulated, Kepler in Linz convinced himself that Kräutlin had implanted the idea that Katharina might be a witch after hearing about *The Dream*. Kräutlin had then lodged it in Ursula's mind, in the Leonberg community, and perhaps even some court circles. In the dedication of the delayed Book V of the *Epitome* Kepler suggestively lamented 'the cruelty of a private enemy of mine'.[25] He had known the force of enmity ever since he had gone to boarding school, and a list of 'enemies' formed a subcategory in his account of his life aged twenty-seven as much as it did in the astrologer Cardano's biography. Rivalrous enmity made sense of conflicts, but in this case he had never even met the man. So what could have produced such a random attack, he wondered, and had his *Dream* manuscript set it all off?

It is possible that Kepler's initial worry that he himself might be accused of practising forbidden arts, and that his reputation as a natural philosopher might thereby be blown apart, originated from that same fear. Yet before returning to Linz, Kepler had never once referred to *The Dream* as a causal factor for the trial.[26]

His intense feelings of guilt and anger after his mother's death are therefore more likely to have been a psychological reaction after the immense emotional strain he had endured during the past six years. In the *Harmony* he had written about his mother as a 'woman who is the cause of all her troubles', and then he had vigorously taken over his mother's defence, secured her release, and returned to Linz, only to hear shortly afterwards that she was dead. In the aftermath of her death, and suffering from exhaustion, he seems to have felt, in contrast to what he had claimed in 1619, that she had *not* been the 'cause of all her troubles'. Rather it had been he, Johannes, her son.

* * *

Kepler had felt guilty remorse and anger of this kind before, at the end of the difficult relationship with Barbara, his first wife, in which heartfelt love and growing admiration for her virtuousness, beauty, and cheerfulness had often combined with immense frustration. After Barbara had died, Kepler in 1612 composed an extraordinary letter to a woman whom he believed to be among a whole group of Prague people who thought he had troubled his wife psychologically. Had he exposed her to his high-minded thoughts and unorthodox religious reflections or pressured her to assist his astronomical labours, he wrote? In the same year, Württemberg theologians had once more reprimanded him for his 'many curious questions' and dangerous subtleties. Whether he really sent this letter to anyone is unclear, but Kepler wrote there about his marriage and feelings in unusually intimate and characteristically self-scrutinizing terms.[27]

He justified himself by asserting that he had always been sexually faithful and really loved the woman. Yet their marriage had been troubled by the emperor's chronic failure to pay Kepler's salary. As he had no independent wealth, he had asked Barbara to draw on hers. In addition to these pressures, she had in her final years become chronically ill and melancholic. This had obscured her memory. She had often been angry, too, and not willing to accept any of his decisions, even if they had been sensible. Kepler criticized himself with remarkable honesty, for sometimes insisting too rigidly on his own point of view and thus failing to understand the conflicts they were undergoing. He described their marriage as a process of emotional learning: when he had seen that her feelings were seriously hurt, and that she was sad rather than furious, he had stopped insulting her. He had become more patient, but also suffered from her abuse of him. Barbara had complained in front of an acquaintance that Johannes was 'disgusting' for getting involved in her affairs. Why, for instance, did he worry about her not spending enough on dressing well? He should stick to his books.

Kepler's letter continued with other recollections of these emotionally fraught years that haunted him, but then expressed the same mixture of anxious fantasies, guilt, and anger against enemies that he would again experience after his mother's death: 'But I believe by our true God that the devil wants to prepare a different game for me and wants to bring me under suspicion that *I killed her* with high religious matters or even Calvinist errors about God's providence by making her melancholic and worried in her thoughts.' He imagined that others accused him of driving Barbara into madness.

Writing was Kepler's way of communing harmoniously with God as well as combating his worst fantasies. His ability to admit to anger in words balanced his traumatic fears. With his quill, this middle-aged scholar with his 'sapless' body felt like a soldier, or like the valiant reformer Martin Luther toppling the pope by penning his thesis. Kepler was not only a scholar who wanted to further harmony, but took part in a culture of scholarly writing which was partly motivated by the fantasy that words could do things—act, damage, and harm people. At the very least, words *vexed* opponents, in a favourite expression scholars used at the time. Sharpening one's pen had a literal meaning. During the following ten years, working on *The Dream*'s edition would become Kepler's way to imagine himself powerfully enacting revenge, even though Kräutlin had long died and Ursula Reinbold would eventually perish in 1628, aged sixty.[28]

* * *

Punishing his enemies, for Kepler, took the peculiar form of appending a large number of endnotes to the old manuscript, which would eventually be printed four years after his own death, in 1634. Unusually, every sentence was peppered with footnotes to account for the correct source of each and any of his literary ideas back in 1609. The ostensible purpose was to show that his plot about Duracotus and Fiolxhilde had had absolutely nothing to do with himself and his mother, but related to books he had read or things he had done in Prague. No other footnoted apologia of this kind had ever been printed before. These notes constituted their own text, as the world's first hyper-text, to demonstrate the absurdity of having to prove what had informed his writing in Prague (Figure 39).

He needed to be precise in tracking what had inspired him. Kepler had actually drawn on characteristically diverse genres ranging from

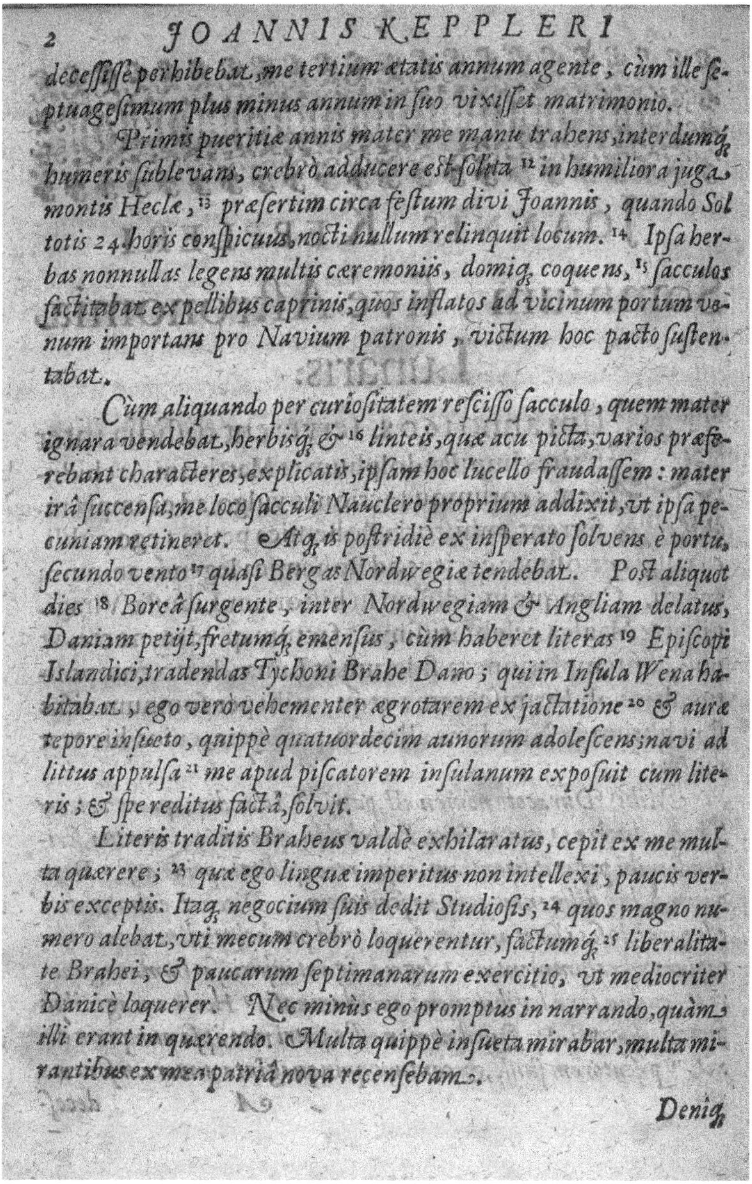

deceßiße perhibebat, me tertium ætatis annum agente, cùm ille fe-
ptuagefimum plus minus annum in fuo vixißet matrimonio.

Primis pueritiæ annis mater me manu trahens, interdumq́;
humeris fublevans, crebrò adducere eſt folita [12] in humiliora juga_
montis Heclæ, [13] præfertim circa feſtum divi Joannis, quando Sol
totis 24 horis confpicuus, nocti nullum relinquit locum. [14] Ipfa her-
bas nonnullas legens multis cæremoniis, domiq́; coquens, [15] facculos
factitabat ex pellibus caprinis, quos inflatos ad vicinum portum ve-
num importans pro Navium patronis, victum hoc pacto fuſten-
tabat.

Cùm aliquando per curiofitatem refciffo facculo, quem mater
ignara vendebat, herbisq́; & [16] linteis, quæ acu picta, varios præfe-
rebant characteres, explicatis, ipfam hoc lucello fraudaffem: mater
irâ fuccenfa, me loco facculi Nauclero proprium addixit, vt ipfa pe-
cuniam retineret. Atq́; is poſtridiè ex infperato folvens è portu,
fecundo vento [17] quafi Bergas Nordwegiæ tendebat. Poſt aliquot
dies [18] Boreâ furgente, inter Nordwegiam & Angliam delatus,
Daniam petijt, fretumq́; emenfus, cùm haberet literas [19] Epifcopi
Islandici, tradendas Tychoni Brahe Dano; qui in Infula Wena ha-
bitabat; ego verò vehementer ægrotarem ex jactatione [20] & auræ
tepore infueto, quippè quatuordecim annorum adolefcens; navi ad
littus appulfâ [21] me apud pifcatorem infulanum expofuit cum literis; & fpe reditus factâ, folvit.

Literis traditis Braheus valdè exhilaratus, cepit ex me multa quærere; [22] quæ ego linguæ imperitus non intellexi, paucis ver-
bis exceptis. Itaq́; negocium fuis dedit Studiofis, [24] quos magno nu-
mero alebat, vti mecum crebrò loquerentur, factumq́; [25] liberalita-
te Brahei, & paucarum feptimanarum exercitio, vt mediocriter
Danicè loquerer. Nec minus ego promptus in narrando, quàm_
illi erant in quærendo. Multa quippe infueta mirabar, multa mi-
rantibus ex mea patriâ nova recenfebam.

Deniq́;

Figure 39 A page from Kepler's *The Dream*, with footnotes 12–25. © The British
Library Board, 531.k.13(9), p. 3

ancient philosophy to contemporary travel writing and ethnographies which accumulated tantalizing information about remote countries. From Linz, he was in no position to double-check every reference. For instance, he footnoted that his idea about the superpotent Icelandic father was taken from George Buchanan's *History of Scotland* and the Orkney Islands. It mentions 'a fisherman who at the age of 150 became the father of several children by a young wife'. In fact, Buchanan tantalized his readers with the tale of a man who married aged 100 and was still going out on a boat aged 140.[29]

Despite such small infelicities, this apparatus of references displayed that Kepler's literary creation had been fed by a rich diet of reading as well as plenty of oral communication. Kepler did not attempt to hide the way that the Prague milieu almost expected him to perform in a way which played with occult fascination. For decades, many people in courtly intellectual circles had been attracted to cabbalistic investigations that attributed mystical significance to numbers and Hebrew letters—Rudolph II even corresponded with Frederick of Württemberg about a Hebrew book he reportedly possessed. Kepler himself knew Hebrew. Around 1600, Jewish intellectual life in Prague with its ghetto, influential financiers, and internationally connected merchants flourished under the chief rabbi Judah Loew ben Bezalel's cultural leadership. Loew knew of Tycho's investigations and was an extremely learned man striving for harmony and universal education. He died in 1609, just when Kepler was intensely studying the Jesuit Martin Del Rio's treatise on magic and composing *The Dream*.[30] Its term for the moon was 'Lebana', as 'Hebrew words, being less familiar to our ears, inspire greater awe and are recommended in the occult arts'.[31] In 1608, Kepler even confessed to having started a small project on the 'geometric cabbala', although he instantly added that in his natural philosophy such symbols never served to reveal anything secret and he never forgot that he merely played.[32] At Rudolph's court and in

Prague's high society, occult interests led to a similar fascination with an ancient Scandinavian spirit world.

* * *

The most evocative passage in the introduction to *The Dream* describes how Fiolxhilde, the witch, sits at the crossroad to summon the gentle daemon of science:

> *My mother went away from me to the nearest crossroad. Raising a shout, she pronounced just a few words in which she couched her request. Having completed the ceremonies, she returned. With the outstretched palm of her right hand she commanded silence, and sat down beside me. Hardly had we covered our heads with our clothing (in accordance with our covenant) when the rasping of an indistinct and unclear voice became audible.*

Kepler used no less than seven endnotes to comment on this short passage. Astronomy, he explained, possessed features corresponding to a magical ceremony. It was certainly not a spontaneous exercise, but required a dramatic process of 'repose, recollection of ideas, and set words'. To further contextualize this passage, Kepler related that during his Prague years he often 'carried out a special procedure in connection with a certain observation'. Men or women would come to watch him perform in a house. He would first hide from them inside in a corner, block out daylight, next construct 'a tiny window out of a very small opening', and then hang a 'white sheet on the wall'. Only at this point would he invite in his audience to see the pinhole-camera work. 'These were my ceremonies', he now declared, 'these my rites.' Kepler disclosed his optical demonstrations as a magical game. He challenged his readers:

> Do you want characters too? In capital letters I wrote with chalk on a black board what I thought suited the spectators. The shape of the letters was backwards (behold the magic rite), as Hebrew is written. I hung this board with the letters upside down in the open air outside in the

sunshine. As a result, what I had written was projected right side up on the white wall within. If a breeze disturbed the board outside, the letters inside wiggled to and fro on the wall in an irregular motion.[33]

Light could be manipulated to make Hebrew legible—and sight, he knew, is characterized by its distortion of vision.

Kepler went on to admit that even his idea that the witch would stretch out the palm of her right hand to command silence after completing the incantation of the demonic spirit was likewise inspired by his own practice in Prague: 'I used to tack on these very games too, which the spectators enjoyed all the more for realizing that they were games.'

The astronomer ended his commentary by taunting readers as he glossed his idea that mother and son should have covered their heads as they witnessed the spirit unfold his insights: 'With this very fine rite (*ha, how magically magical!*), shortly before I conceived the plan of this book, we had observed a solar eclipse on October 2/12, 1605.' He and envoys from the Count Palatine of Neuburg had been on the balcony of the pavilion in Rudolph's garden, taking off their coats so as to block out daylight.[34] This, in other words, had not been a magical ceremony, but just a practical device. It was all show.

Scientific results needed to be demonstrated to audiences in order to secure patronage. These audiences had their own expectations, which he—like anyone else in his position—had been happy to satisfy. Kepler's taunt turned out to be that magical practices could not be defined as a realm radically distinct from the higher planes of natural philosophy.

Of course there was more to magic than mere games. For another footnote asserted that a science of the heavens could only be gained by allowing the mind to go through the 'earth's shadow', in which evil spirits dwelt. In this respect, it was vital to observe solar as well as lunar eclipses, even though this implied exposing oneself directly to a phenomenon that evidently brought much misfortune to mankind, bearing out the principle that darkness encouraged the bad spirits to attack earth.[35]

* * *

Kepler took these bad spirits to be real, just like the good spirits, who never practised harmful magic but furthered knowledge. Footnoting Olaus Magnus's influential *History of the Northern People*, which had shown that magic was common in Scandinavia, Kepler added that 'the dim light and unbroken nights' in those lands were likewise conducive to good spirits. Shorter working hours encouraged leisurely philosophizing, so much so that Julius Frederick of Württemberg had been most impressed on more recent travels to find 'remarkably learned' people in the north, ready to 'impart their philosophy to strangers'.[36]

Kepler now introduced the spirits that his mother conversed with as an allegory of empirical knowledge. They were the sciences disclosing the causes of phenomena. He had named them demons after the Greek word *Daemon*. This term, Kepler explained learnedly and based on Plato, itself derived from *daiein*, meaning to know.[37] This allusion exemplified exactly the kind of philologically clever wittiness which, in the intellectually high-pressured milieu of Rudolph II's Prague court, had divided those who understood it from those who did not. The further implication was that only a Tübingen barber would be unable to see beyond the literal meaning of the term.

Other endnotes in this extraordinary reworking of his old manuscript were ironic or jocular rather than factually historical or philological. They belong to a lost mental world in which one compendium of jokes, published in 1603, could distinguish between amusing jokes, witty aphorisms, biting jests, memorable pleasantries, funny stories, apposite verses, rural riddles, absurdities, and scurrilous jokes. Every rhetorical textbook of the time cultivated an ability to use such witty display to make an impression at dinner parties or

work.[38] Kepler thus used one footnote to explicate a scurrilous joke
about his teacher Mästlin's fat physique as opposed to his delicate
mind: 'The lighter the weight a man carries on his delicate bones,
The swifter he flies to the heavenly homes.' So as Mästlin was heavy,
he stuck to earth and to his Tübingen position into old age.[39] On
another occassion, Kepler wrote a poem for a medical doctoral
student, imagining him as a fading skeleton.

Although this mindset may be so alien to us that we fail to grasp
what was so funny about these jokes, they clearly encouraged mental
agility, fanciful risk-taking, derisive opposition to authorities, and
playful speculation in the intellectual culture of the time. All humanists
were trained in composing verse and epigrams to give such sentiments
expression. They were an aesthetic commentary on, as much as
testimony to, the human condition. Kepler commented on the fact
that Fiolxhilde thought that she had passed on all her knowledge to her
son with a little verse to suggest that this merely bore testimony to the
effects of wishful thinking and delusion, which typically left humans
confused about the boundaries between the real and unreal:

> A charioteer dreams about a carriage,
> A judge about a legal fight.
> The wealth you seek by day,
> You acquire at night.[40]

In other notes, Kepler openly acknowledged that he could not now
remember why he had written a particular something while in
Prague. He explored plausible hypotheses as to why, back then, he
might have thought of something, or criticized his own style.[41] This
undermined any idealized notion of scholarly genius or science as
only rooted in objective thought that could be finite. A natural
philosopher's reflection, he had previously argued, needed to be
honest about uncertainties and mistakes. This characterized intellectual activity as a developing skill throughout anyone's life. It was

linked to environments and memory rather than as anything objective and controlled. Kepler's characteristic self-scrutiny and ability to place himself in history hence enabled him to present *The Dream* as 'the product of a specific time, place, and experience'.[42]

Kepler's notes kept insisting on how his ideas had evolved in relation to audiences as recipients of ideas, in a process of communication that anticipated their responses. True to this principle, the endnotes also implied different readers, several times using direct speech, as if he imagined himself actually speaking to past and present collaborators: 'I have a very old document, which you, most illustrious Christoph Besold, wrote with your own hand . . . in the year 1593, on the basis of my essays . . .'—this was when they had studied at Tübingen; or by calling on the spirits of those who had witnessed something with him: 'You remember, oh envoys.' He attacked the ignorance of those at universities and elsewhere who still blinded themselves to Copernicus's, Galileo's, as well as his own discoveries—all of which were based on *reasonable* testimony drawn from empirical observations and critical reading.

* * *

Kepler thereby affirmed his distinct approach to how we can know anything. Rather than defending a mechanistic, purely analytical mindset based on mathematical certainties, he advocated speculating and imagining as part of logically causal explanations. *The Dream* illustrated that all taken-for-granted knowledge corresponded to the limited imagination of earth dwellers: 'Hence, if we transfer the imagination to another sphere, everything must be understood in an altered form.'[43] Informed empirical observation depended on this carefully constructed sense of reliability—God, Kepler had affirmed in 1604, had placed humans on a rotating earth so that their perception changed all the time.[44] To read and contextualize past and present knowledge critically was just as important. All results needed to be discussed in a gentle spirit for the benefit of mankind and praise of God. Yet human nature was rooted in needs that were always difficult to classify neatly as either 'religious' or 'magical'. This led Kepler to question any 'mythical autonomy of science'—by pointing out, as we have seen, that natural philosophers demonstrated their results to convince a public by means that might be called magical rather than analytical and 'pure'.[45] Even more radically, he would insist that 'science had sprung from superstition in the first place', as astronomy had grown from a belief in divination and human need to foretell the future. Knowledge about nature responded to human questions about life—it could never be wholly removed from emotions.[46]

The Dream summed up Kepler's own fears of being misread. It also expressed the possibility that his thoughts expressed in printed letters might jump off the page to shape reality. Bad spirits had taken his words to harm himself and his family. Yet all he had wanted to achieve through his scholarship was peace and a playful enjoyment of God's creation for mankind, as well as, admittedly, personal recognition and more pay.[47]

* * *

Alongside his work on footnoting *The Dream* edition, Kepler would spend the following years trying to finally complete and print his *Rudolphine Tables*. In 1625, he travelled back to Swabia and Tübingen for the first time since the trial. By 1626, in the wake of ever-tightening Catholic controls in Linz, Kepler's access to his books was severely restricted. He left the city with his family in November, to live in Ulm, where the *Tables* were eventually printed. Despite all the difficulties, this filled him with zeal—'It's now or never', he wrote to Schickard in April 1627. By September 1627, the work was done.

That winter, however, he was honoured in Prague, promised large sums on paper, and told that he could return to Prague as imperial mathematician if he converted to Catholicism. He also met Albrecht von Wallenstein, the triumphant imperial military commander and aggressive war financier, who had just been given the tiny Lower Silesian duchy of Sagan. Wallenstein had been in the forefront of escalating the conflicts that underlay the Thirty Years War. It was he who devised the politics of using occupied areas to feed troops, which prolonged the entire conflict. Kepler had twice worked out Wallenstein's horoscope and knew his problematic character well. Yet when the commander offered to host him as a scholar in Sagan, to pay the remaining salary the emperor owed him, and to pay a respectable annual salary as well, Kepler accepted the deal. All his life, his major ups and downs had been related to whether or not he got paid. In addition, Sagan lay in Silesia, which remained relatively tolerant in matters of religion.

Kepler and his family moved to Sagan in July 1628, where Wallenstein soon implemented counter-Reformation measures and Kepler once more needed to negotiate special conditions due to his religious beliefs.[48] His foremost project in this isolated place was to set up a printing press, which arrived in 1630, and he promptly printed *The Dream*. Ludwig, his oldest son, was still studying medicine in the best Protestant universities. In March, Susanna, his oldest daughter, married a greatly talented and pleasant mathematician called Bartsch, who could help Kepler as an assistant. Bernegger helped to organize their wedding feast in Strasbourg which was attended by both of Kepler's siblings—Margaretha and Christoph. It was a splendid day, as reported by Bernegger in his usual generous way in a letter, and a great celebration of Kepler's own name. This would have been an opportunity for all the family to meet up again for the first time after Katharina had died—except that Kepler himself did not undertake the long trip from Silesia. In April, another baby daughter was born and Kepler, now aged fifty-nine, was busy helping his wife and organizing the baptism.

When the emperor temporarily dismissed Wallenstein in September, Kepler once more worried about his family's financial security.

There were debts to be paid to printers, and not much cash left. Kepler took the money and an old mare to track down Wallenstein and present him with the major work he had produced under his patronage. He dressed in his sturdy travelling clothes—a black woollen coat and gown, a cap with rough lining, brown stockings, a felt hat, an old leather belt, boots, spurs, a pistol, and powder-flask—to arrive in Catholic Regensburg by early winter. Yet the strain was too much. Ill with high fever, Johannes Kepler perished in November 1630. Within days, he was buried in the Lutheran graveyard outside the city walls, to 'measure earthly shadows', while his mind was 'raised to heaven', as read the famous lines he composed in advance of his death.

The family kept on fighting for money and printing his work, including *The Dream*. By 1634, Kepler's impoverished widow, Susanna, stood at the Frankfurt fair, trying to sell the small Latin treatise she did not understand. Its title-page was extremely simple. The prologue about Duracotus and Fiolxhilde took up four pages in tiny, compressed italic letters. This was not a work like any other, for, bizarrely, fifty footnotes jostled for space at every turn. The Daemon's science-fiction tale about the moon was printed in larger type. Like a dream itself, the whole publication looked strange and other-worldly, a curio, despite the fact that Kepler's son Ludwig had contributed a prologue and dedication to the Landgrave of Hesse. Few copies survive.[49] Susanna would have to bury two more sons before her own death in 1638, leaving her two daughters orphaned. Kepler's grown-up children from his first marriage, Ludwig and Susanna, lived long lives and had many children. Ludwig would safely hold on to his father's thousands of sheets filled with signs, words, drawings, and calculations.

* * *

What happened to the other men and women we have encountered in this book? Ursula Reinbold's husband, the glazier, remarried within eight months of her death, and in 1655, he died aged eighty-five.[50] Governor Lutherus Einhorn remained in office until 1629. He would still cooperate with Christoph Kepler, who became one of Leonberg's criminal court judges in 1625, without even having to serve in the town magistracy, despite the fact that he was not rich, had no family connections to other judges, and had not been trained as a scribe. This was a special honour. At last the pewterer achieved his goal of gaining the highest respect in his local community as well as preserving order. Christoph Kepler retained this office up to one year before he died in 1633, aged forty-six—his only son, Sebald, born in 1621, would follow him in his craft and also became a local mayor.[51]

Württemberg suffered severe outbreaks of plague and was devastated in the aftermath of the Battle of Nördlingen in summer 1634. The duke fled into exile. General Matthias Gallas, the imperial military commander, now occupied Leonberg's castle, where Sibylle and Maria had once mixed their medicines to help the needy. By 1635, half of Leonberg's population was killed by plague. In Rosswälden, Georg Binder perished in 1634 after marauding soldiers violently assaulted him.

Of all those who had been involved in Katharina's trial, Margaretha Kepler was the one who lived the longest and whose life, despite all the hardship of the times, took the most interesting turn. She still corresponded with her brother Johannes in Sagan up to a year before his death, and was keen to help his older daughter meet and marry the right kind of man.[52] When Binder died, Margaretha herself moved back to the vicinity of Stuttgart to marry Georg Conrad Maickler, another Lutheran pastor and one of Württemberg's most distinguished spiritual poets.

Maickler (1574–1647) had studied theology in Tübingen and faithfully served his parish in Fellbach, which he joined in 1610. He baptized 1,583 children, celebrated 580 weddings, and

painstakingly noted down 2,566 deaths in his church books, lamenting the horrendous toll taken by the plague among the community
during the Thirty Years War. Maickler had begun to compose major
spiritual poems in Latin as a schoolboy, was honoured as poet
laureate later in life, and rewarded with his own coat of arms. His
collected works were published just before he married Margaretha,
and during their marriage he would continue adding new
poems. He died aged seventy-three, a well-known and respected
man. An epitaph which hangs in his Fellbach church today depicts
him with a row of four pious wives, Margaretha being the last of
them.

Margaretha composed her own heartfelt German poem in his
memory, dense in spiritual feeling, to describe how harp music raised
her courage to carry on after her husband's death and to anticipate
the future joy of paradise. Whereas Katharina looked forward to
eternity in order to finally gain justice, her daughter connected the
prospect of death to a language of sentiment, strength, and belong-
ing. In contrast to her mother's generation, who usually remained
illiterate, Margaretha had used all her life the educational opportunities that Württemberg's schooling had offered. Now in her sixties,
she signed herself 'Margaretha Maicklerin, née Kepplerin', proud of
her family name.[53]

* * *

The Thirty Years War would remain the only serious challenge to
that 'remarkable mindset' engendered by the German Reformations:
general religious tolerance for Lutherans, Calvinists, and Catholics in
the empire, and tolerance for only one of these confessions in every
particular principality. In 1648, the Peace of Westphalia restored a
complex polity which was at last capable of regulating tensions and
sustaining devolved governments. Polemical warfare continued, but
Germany never again conducted a religious war amongst its states.[54]

Germany's larger territories increasingly controlled local officials, requiring them to report on legal procedures and maintain vigilence. Suspects resisted. This situates their experience at the core of German history and accounts about the struggle for justice in past worlds.

EPILOGUE

───⦿⦿⦿───

Nothing quite prepared me for the moment when I first got off the bus at Eltingen, the village in which Katharina Kepler was born. Looking at rows of beautifully restored half-timbered houses with their pots of bright red geraniums outside, I recognized the village well. Then I spotted the monument for Katharina, which I knew about from a local history of the trial. The statue (Figure 40) depicts a young, slender, female reaper. It is a work by Jakob Fehrle (1884–1974), professor of art at Schwäbisch Gmünd from 1928, passionate about sculpting elongated gothic girls. Fehrle held his post throughout the Third Reich and took on several Nazi commissions for public art, while at the same time some of his previous work was removed by the Nazis from collections as degenerate. Seeing the sculpture made me appreciate even more strongly its oddity in relation to what we know about the woman it represents.

This village street prides itself on being the prettiest in south Germany. Further along is the Leonberg archive, exactly opposite the house in which Katharina Kepler was born and raised. As I sat down in the archive to start my research, I immediately asked whether there had been any newspaper reports on the sculpture's

Figure 40 The Eltingen monument for Katharina Kepler. © Photograph: Ulinka
Rublack

unveiling. Some hours later, the archivist placed a local newspaper article on my desk, dated 25 October 1937, which recorded the speech of Eltingen's mayor Carl Schmincke. Schmincke held office from 1934 to 1938, and the street is to this day named after him.[1] It was his project to demonstrate the 'new spirit' of the Nazi takeover in what had been an overwhelmingly Communist community. Two rundown houses and a barn had been demolished to create a more beautiful and wider street that allowed for better traffic flow.

A small space was created for Katharina Kepler's monument to serve as a symbol of this community of 'peasants and workers', a 'symbol of work and industriousness', as Schmincke explained, 'upright, proud and strong'. The mayor's speech claimed the whole street as a site of memory, which had witnessed much hardship during many years of plague and war. The reaper was to commemorate one woman's fateful story. Schmincke praised Katharina's combative nature, her strength, her unique character, and love of truth. He even argued that her steadfast denial of the witchcraft charge had paved the way to end persecutions in Germany as a whole.[2] 'People of Eltingen, be proud of this work, your village well, the landmark of your community,' Schmincke emphatically exclaimed before unveiling the figure.[3]

* * *

The Third Reich was fascinated by witches. Many publications turned their persecutions into a highly emotional topic. They used these emotions to attack the Catholic church, to re-establish Nordic religion, and avenge past German 'sisters', whom they imagined as blonde and blue-eyed protectors of the German race, rituals, and wisdom. In 1935, Heinrich Himmler even set up a special force to analyse witchcraft files gathered from archives which operated until 1944. Against this vision of witches as heroines, another strand within Nazism claimed that these women had been degenerate and deluded outsiders, who had rightfully been hunted down by ruthless Germanic men.[4]

Current views of Katharina Kepler remain oddly divided. In the tradition of the very first study based on the trial records, studies in Germany usually empathetically regard her as a largely innocent victim of the Reinbolds' campaign. Most recently, a popular German writer has portrayed her as a heroic herbal medic.[5] An American historian, by contrast, characterizes her as a difficult, bizarre, and half-crazed old crone.[6] This is part of a growing trend, which began with the writer Arthur Koestler's account that Katherina had become a 'hideous little woman' whose evil tongue and 'suspect background predestined her as victim'. She was, Koestler writes, 'an inn-keeper's daughter, brought up by an aunt who was said to have perished at the stake, and her husband had been a mercenary who vanished after barely escaping the gallows'.[7] Anglo-American writing increasingly implies that there was every reason to see Katharina Kepler as a witch. The writer Kitty Ferguson refers to Johannes Kepler's early description of her as 'not a pleasant woman' and sums up: 'Her acquaintances regarded her as an evil-tongued shrew. She had been raised by an aunt who was burned at the stake as a witch.'[8] Several publications present the myth that Katharina's aunt was burnt as a witch as historical fact. Yet this charge was only invented by the Reinbolds, and never repeated in the official accusation by the governors in the criminal trial. We only have records for three witchcraft executions in Weil before 1616, and there is no evidence that one of these women in 1559 or 1595 might have been related to Katharina.[9] In this way, the Reinbold party's malicious slander lives on.

More perplexing still, even the editor of the witchcraft case employed by the Kepler commission in Munich has recently decided to characterize Katharina Kepler as a witch-like woman. In contrast to the previous edition of Kepler's collected works, which presented all the trial records and thus allowed readers to form their own

opinion of the evidence, the commission has decided to print only
Kepler's brief concluding defence in its new edition of the scientist's
complete works. The editor confidently asserts: 'Fiolxhilde indeed is
the Ur-image of Kepler's mother. Katharina's impetuous, fierce
nature may have found expression in the event of Fiolxhilde's
decision to expel her son Duracotus.'[10] Thus, even the idea that
Katharina inspired Kepler's literary creation of a witch lives on—
despite the fact that the key reason Johannes Kepler wrote endnotes
to the *The Dream* was to deny that his mother was anything to do
with Fiolxhilde.

The most influential treatment of Katharina for an English-
speaking audience remains John Banville's prize-winning novel
Kepler. This fictionalization from the 1980s portrays Katharina as a
crude old woman who continues to live in Weil der Stadt and makes
a dangerous business of healing by boiling potions in a black pot. She
meets with old hags in a kitchen infested with cat smells. Outside in
her garden lies a dead rat. Kepler desperately tries to hide his
mother's magical arts from his wife as they visit; and Katharina
searches for a bag filled with bat-wings. Katharina Kepler is emotionally disconnected and three grey hairs sprout on her chin.
During her trial, this rough woman enjoys having 'attention lavished
on her'. There is a final scene in which both Kepler and Einhorn are
imagined to be present when Katharina is tortured. Christoph's
repudiation of Katharina is foregrounded, and so is Johannes
Kepler's fear of his reputation. Their mother is portrayed as horrendous, scary, disgusting, and she might well be a witch.[11]

* * *

My book has tried to piece together all facets of genuine historical
evidence to see things from different points of view and distinguish
the voices in these documents, as in a libretto. When Linz was voted
the cultural capital of Europe in 2009 and commissioned Philip

Glass and the librettist Martina Winkel to write an opera about Johannes Kepler, the idea was to centre on the astronomer's science and faith, his self-image as a young man, and the destructions of war. His family life and friends, his connections, and, of course, his life with Katharina in Linz and the witchcraft trial are excluded from this story. This may have been partly so as to distinguish it from Paul Hindemith's opera about Kepler, *The Harmony of the World*. Hindemith worked on it from 1940 to 1957 and the opera includes an interpretation of Katharina's trial. He integrated the sources to some extent, but rather oddly presents Katharina Kepler as a conjuring woman who has tried to make Johannes drink from the grandfather's skull so as to magically enlist him for a utopian project which she will mastermind: she wants to use alchemical laboratories to alleviate mankind from poverty and sickness. Katharina completely wants to possess her son, who refuses her ideas and thus ruins her life's dream even as the trial ends in her release. She is deluded; whereas her son remains a hero 'lifted far above the way of men'.

Yet, as we have seen, Kepler did not work 'autonomously' and constantly dealt with constraints. When his friend Matthäus Wacker, for instance, shouted down the news from his coach in the street outside Kepler's house in Prague that Galileo had discovered the moons of Jupiter with his telescope, this led to an intense outburst of feelings, ranging from exhilaration and joy to shame and confusion, as well as envy and anger as Kepler first gained access to Galileo's book. Kepler and Wacker overcame this conflict over cooperation and competition; and Kepler's *Harmony* even defined love as an affect made stronger by working through dissonance.[12]

My book has therefore attempted to show that entering into Johannes Kepler's real voice reveals aspects of human experience which are often not spoken about or seen in relation to men of science. Emotions, ranging from fears to fascinations, all played their part in his world. Kepler held contradictory ideas about femininity. He could value the female as life-giving force, and held that mothers particularly shaped their offspring. The earth itself was female and active. As astrology did not accommodate notions of gender, he came close to working towards a notion of social psychology to explain his mother's behaviour. This was pioneering for his time.

One of the benefits of seeing Kepler in relation to others rather than regarding him as a dispassionate mind is that he becomes a far less overwhelmingly torn and tragic figure. This customary portrayal is partly to do with posthumous artistic depictions of Kepler (which he would have hated). They frame him as a troubled man in a troubled time. To many commentators, he has appeared as a man who, against this background, sought refuge by escaping to an imagined harmonic world of the heavens in a finite universe. His key biographer regarded him as 'un-political'.[13] Yet Kepler saw many aspects of his period in positive and hopeful terms, and was full of excitement about ongoing creation on earth as much as in the heavens. The absence of future religious wars in Germany would have been exactly what he anticipated, as it represented harmony after an interval of strong dissonances: God's way, he affirmed, was to finish quarrels with a happy ending. Discussions about political sciences were central to his circles and he included his reflections on politics in the *Harmony*. In Sagan he felt happy that his publications had stimulated people's striving for knowledge, which in turn acted on the spirits in heaven and reflected back on societies by improving their manners. The portrait his assistant executed of him in midlife reveals how much he could be at ease in his intellectual position, as he communicated with intimate friends and passing international diplomats. In part, we can see Johannes Kepler as a man with a smile, proud of his cheerful style.

Kepler's family life was always busy, as each child and baptism brought with it godparents and social networks and knitted him into society. He shared the pain of seeing children die, but also had the privilege of seeing two of his children mature into successful adults who remained connected to him. Kepler was respected socially as well as intellectually, and was a man who always found new positions. The mathematician tirelessly worked to achieve what he wanted. Despite all the constraints, the *Harmony, Rudolphine Tables,* and many other major works were eventually published. He was excited because his work seemed to considerably advance everything the ancients had known. The *Tables*, Kepler thought, ushered in astronomy's maturity. That is why we remember him.

Of course, every son has a mother, and the mother–son bond is psychologically rich. Galileo's mother, who came from a well-off family, brought her son before the Inquisition for calling her a whore and crone, or 'Gabrina', which was also the name given to the nasty, ugly old witch in Ariosto's famous poem *Orlando Furioso*. She demanded Galileo's attention when she found him absorbed in his work during visits, and employed a spy to check on whether he went to mass or to his mistress. Once she even got someone to steal lenses out of his house 'to see great distances'. She died in 1620, aged eighty-two, in Florence. One year earlier, Galileo's brother, a court musician in Munich, commented in a letter that it surprised him little to hear that she behaved dreadfully. He consoled Galileo: 'But she is much aged, and soon there will be an end to all this quarrelling.' Frictions between Galileo's mother and her sons are all that the biographies of *his* life tell us about. On the basis of four surviving letters, one biographer even condemns Galileo's mother for the fact that the astronomer was emotionally withdrawn and suggests that her 'bullying', 'devious' nature might have discouraged him from marrying. No one has taken the trouble to research her life and point of view to avoid such obvious bias.[14] Yet, as we have seen, men in this period had choices of how to relate to their mothers, and this fundamentally mattered to how they envisaged the world. Johann

Figure 41 This statue shows how some men in this period were exceptionally able to publicly express respect and love for an elderly mother without idealizing her physical features, to turn their creative work into a moving record of their relationship. Rudolf Sirigatti, bust for his mother Cassandra, with the tribute: 'Ridolfo, whom I bore, sculpted this as a tribute of love', 1578. Marble, 206 cm × 65.7 cm. © Victoria and Albert Museum, London

Valentin Andreae, who admired his mother's ethos and botanical knowledge, imagined an ongoing social role for old people in his pioneering utopian vision. They would be valued for their experience (see Figure 41).

Kepler typically felt ambivalent towards his mother, not least because he identified so strongly with some of her physical and mental characteristics. We have seen that at various points in his life he could be just as fraught with mixed feelings in relation to himself or his first wife. Still, he regularly kept up relations with his mother, just as he would continue to be in touch with his much younger sister all his life. Kepler had no doubt that his mother had always been Christian in her views; after all, she had financially supported him to become a pastor. Katharina Kepler brought up and supported this exceptionally gifted and emotionally intense boy, she visited him and for periods lived with her grown-up son. He respected her achievements as an illiterate widow with little family help in bringing up two young children. In particular, he valued Katharina's achievement in seeking a respectable marriage for her daughter to a Lutheran pastor. Because of her age, he regarded her as someone who needed protection. At the same time, Kepler's more conservative views of women led him to fear Katharina's inconsistency, talkativeness, argumentativeness, and weakness far more than appears justified.

To further capture this society's often contradictory voices and emotional experiences, I wanted to understand what it must have been like for a woman such as Katharina to live through her marriage and pregnancies, raise her children, and look after her old father. It says much that this father, in his will, praised her as loving and caring—she was clearly emotionally capable of extending love and care to a father who completely depended on her. It also says much that she never once appeared in front of the town courts for quarrelling, unlike so many others, including Christoph Kepler, her (apparently reputable) artisan son. None of the witnesses saw her as someone who involved herself in insults. We know that she supported three of her children as best she could, and there is no trace of her quarrelling with any of them before the trial. None of this makes her a heroine. Yet why should we wish to turn her into one?

Instead of censoring her anger as meaningless 'quarrelsomeness' it is important to understand what might have made her angry and who in that society passed judgements on whether a woman's anger was legitimate or not. We can ask what made her tough at times and whether this related to what support her society offered a widow who still raised children and had a disruptive son, Heinrich the Younger, whom everyone knew could easily get out of control. Who cared for her? There was little concern for her ordinary human emotional needs, her feelings of worry, sadness, or abandonment; of being excluded or unfairly treated; or her wanting to enjoy some pleasure and laughter. There were needs she had to silence. What did it mean to live in a society that valued women mostly as those who emotionally cared for others? This made women 'good', but at the same time this idealized capacity was devalued in relation to men who were thought to possess a superior mind and 'reason', so much so that their emotional carelessness was acceptable. How *did* women cope with being regarded as less attractive and even potentially uncanny humans as their fertility declined?[15]

My account has discussed the trial in this broader context of a society's values and rules of how emotions could be expressed during a time of social change. This must give anyone pause before turning a woman such as Katharina Kepler into a purely negative figure. Women like Katharina resisted saying that they were witches—and this meant resisting a false authority that told them they were of less value, or were morally weak. They usually evoked God as the highest authority to support them, as someone who would understand them as they spoke truth to power. Self-silencing, not being able to resist, and feeling denigrated, can lead to destructive behaviour and psychological torment. Katharina, despite her vulnerability as a very old, imprisoned, woman, did not just give up.

During the last decades, historians have begun to reconstruct the lives of ordinary people like Katharina Kepler in communities across the world. Bertrande Rols and Martin Guerre as well as Menocchio, a Friuli miller before the Inquisition, remain the best known of these 'micro-histories'.[16] *The Astronomer and the Witch* is designed to complement our sense of this period by taking us into a Lutheran world as the Reformation came of age, celebrated its first centenary in 1617, and moved into the Thirty Years War. Such history 'from the ground up' is the craft of restoring nuance to our account of past lives and respect for different voices from a wide social spectrum through the use of local archives. Sceptics of this approach raise an important question: how can the story of exceptional individuals and trials tell us anything of 'universal import' about a 'silent majority'?[17] The answer is obvious: by setting them in a broad enough context. I have written this book not just as an attempt to gain a better understanding of individuals, but also of families, a community, and an age.

Notes

PROLOGUE

1. On the frequently cited case of Agrippa von Nettesheim's alleged defence of a woman in 1520 see Vera Hoorens and Hans Renders, 'Heinrich Cornelius Agrippa and Witchcraft: A Reappraisal', *Sixteenth Century Journal*, 43/1 (2012), 3–18.

2. Friedrich von Spee, *Cautio criminalis, or, A book on witch trials*, trans. Marcus Hellyer (Charlottesville: University of Virginia Press, 2003). On witchcraft figures see Wolfgang Behringer, *Witches and Witch-Hunts: A Global History* (Cambridge: Polity, 2004), 149–58; William Monter, 'Witch Trials in Continental Europe 1500–1600', in B. Ankerloo, S. Clark, and W. Monter, eds, *The Period of the Witch Trials* (London: Athlone Press, 2002), 1–52; and Brian Levack, *The Witch-Hunt in Early Modern Europe*, 3rd edn (Harlow: Pearson Longman, 2006), 21.

3. Patrick J. Boner, *Kepler's Cosmological Synthesis: Astrology, Mechanism and the Soul* (Leiden: Brill, 2013), 171.

4. Frisch, *Opera*, 364.

INTRODUCTION

1. *KGW*, vol. 13, 20; Max Caspar and Walther von Dyck, eds, *Johannes Kepler in seinen Briefen* (Munich: Oldenburg, 1930), vol. 1, 16, to Mästlin, 18.1.1595.

2. Lyndal Roper, *Witch-Craze: Terror and Fantasy in Baroque Germany* (New Haven: Yale University Press, 2004), esp. ch. 7; Charles Zika, *Appearances*

of Witchcraft: Visual Culture and Print in Sixteenth-Century Europe (London: Routledge, 2005), ch. 3.

3. The territory was called Wiesensteig. Sceptics renewed and further developed previous objections. The Strasbourg preacher Geiler von Kaysersberg had set out in 1508 that witches thought their dreams were true, Source no. 71 in: Wolfgang Behringer ed., *Hexen und Hexenprozesse in Deutschland* (Munich: Deutscher Taschenbuch Verlag, 1988), 113–14.

4. See especially H. C. Erik Midelfort, 'Johann Weyer in medizinischer, theologischer und rechtsgeschichtlicher Sicht', in Hartmut Lehmann and Otto Ulbricht, eds, *Vom Unfug des Hexen-Processes: Gegner der Hexenverfolgung von Johann Weyer bis Friedrich Spee* (Wiesbaden: Harrassowitz, 1992), 53–64.

5. *Tractatus de confessionibus maleficiorum et sagarum*, Trier 1589, translated as *Bekantnuß der Zauberer und Hexen: Ob und wie viel derselben zu glauben* (Trier: Bock, 1590), 180, 'Der fünffte Beschluß'.

6. Bodin's 1580 treatise *De la démonomanie des sorciers* was translated into German six years later and became a particular influence on German magistrates. For this and the following see the magisterial discussion by Stuart Clark, *Thinking with Demons: The Idea of Witchcraft in Early Modern Europe* (Oxford: Oxford University Press, 1997), final chapter, 668–82, as well as Jean Bodin, *La démonomanie des sorciers*, 4th edn. (Lyon: Antoine de Harsy, 1598), and Claudia Opitz-Belakhal, *Das Universum des Jean Bodin: Staatsbildung, Macht und Geschlecht im 16. Jahrhundert* (Frankfurt am Main: Campus, 2006).

7. Robin Briggs, *The Witches of Lorraine* (Oxford: Oxford University Press, 2007), 51 and graph.2.1; Nicolas Rémy, *Demonolatry*, trans. Montague Summers (London: J. Rodker, 1930, first published in 1595).

8. Martin Del Rio, *Investigations into Magic*, ed. and trans. P. G. Maxwell-Stuart (Manchester: Manchester University Press, 2000), 252 and, on judges, 276.

9. Wolfgang Behringer, *Witchcraft Persecutions in Bavaria: Popular Magic, Religious Zealotry and Reason of State in Early Modern Europe* (Cambridge: Cambridge University Press, 1997), 195.

10. Johann Georg Sigwart, *Ein Predigt vom Hagel und Ungewitter…* (Tübingen: J. A. Cellio, 1613), 10–16, 18–21, 27; H. C. Erik Midelfort, *Witch Hunting in Southwestern Germany 1562–1684: The Social and Intellectual*

Foundations (Stanford: Stanford University Press, 1972), ch. 3; Sabine Holtz, *Theologie und Alltag: Leben und Lehre in den Predigten der Tübinger Theologen 1550–1750* (Tübingen: Mohr Siebeck 1993), 281–2; sermons by Johann Georg Sigwart are representative of the genre. Kepler followed this teaching on providence, which at the University of Tübingen was reinforced by his professor, Jacob Heerbrand, see Charlotte Methuen, *Kepler's Tübingen: Stimulus to a Theological Mathematics* (Aldershot: Ashgate, 1998), 57.

11. Midelfort, *Witch Hunting*, 36–53; Sönke Lorenz, 'Einführung und Forschungsstand: Die Hexenverfolgung in den südwestdeutschen Territorien', in S. Lorenz and J. M. Schmidt, eds, *Wider alle Hexerei und Teufelswerk: Die europäische Hexenverfolgung und ihre Auswirkungen auf Südwestdeutschland* (Sigmaringen: Thorbecke, 2004), 195–212; and figures for Württemberg from 1497 to 1750 in Anita Raith, 'Herzogtum Württemberg', in Lorenz and Schmidt, *Hexerei*, 225.

12. They fell victim to a counter-reformation prince-provost, soon to be promoted to a prince-bishop, who zealously believed in his fight against evil. Some of the accused confessed to demonic pacts just to escape torture; for a list of accused men and women see source no. 166 in: Wolfgang Behringer ed., *Hexen und Hexenprozesse in Deutschland* (Munich: Deutscher Taschenbuch Verlag, 1988), 252.

13. Max Caspar, *Kepler*, ed. and trans. C. D. Hellman (New York: Dover, 1959), 255, talks about a mania, but was written before serious research on the persecution of witchcraft started in the 1970s; the seriously problematic publication is the only book in English which claims to be a treatment of the trial; James A. Connor, *Kepler's Witch: An Astronomer's Discovery of Cosmic Order Amidst Religious War, Political Intrigue, and the Heresy Trial of his Mother* (San Francisco: HarperCollins, 2004), for the quote see 17. This book lacks a real engagement with the literature on witchcraft and gender in Germany and the author relied on a translator to comprehend the trial documents.

14. In 1605, Kepler thus remarked that he rejected the common saying 'I hate common folk and keep them away from me' as much as many alchemists' arrogant claim that their exclusive learning was 'reserved for wisdom's children', *KGW*, vol. 15, 182; Caspar and von Dyck, *Kepler in seinen Briefen*, to Herwart, 28.3.1605, 225; even though his relationship to common people in reality was more ambivalent.

15. *KGW*, vol. 15, 235; Caspar and von Dyck, *Kepler in seinen Briefen*, to Heydonus in London, October 1605, 249.

16. Boner, *Cosmographical Synthesis*, 2; this related to his prolonged interest in Aristotle's writing *On Generation* and the Belgian sixteenth-century natural philosopher Cornelius Gemma, see Caspar and von Dyck, *Kepler in seinen Briefen*, 11.10.1605, 250; *KGW*, vol. 15, 258; for an emphasis on Kepler's views of an ensouled earth see also Siegfried Wollgast, *Philosophie in Deutschland zwischen Reformation und Aufklärung 1550–1650* (Berlin: Akademie Verlag, 1988), 221–63; Volker Bialas, *Johannes Kepler* (Munich: Beck, 2004), 99–119; on witches as intelligible see Clark, *Thinking with Demons*, 321–4.

17. *KGW*, vol. 14, 422; Caspar and von Dyck, *Kepler in seinen Briefen*, to Fabricius 4.7.1603, 189.

18. This vision of human aliveness is beautifully expressed in a letter to the Styrian estates, 1.5.1596, this letter appears not to have been edited in the *KGW*, vol. 13; Caspar and von Dyck, *Kepler in seinen Briefen*, 35; see also his letter to Herwart 28.3.1605, Caspar and von Dyck, *Kepler in seinen Briefen*, 233; *KGW*, vol. 15, 187.

19. On his inspiration to think about irregular regularity through sublunary nature and mechanical movement see Caspar and von Dyck, *Kepler in seinen Briefen*, vol. 2, 67, in marginal notes to a letter from Mästlin, 1.10.1616; on the ellipse vol. 1, to Fabricius, 1.8.1607, 290; *KGW*, vol. 16, 14.

20. Nicholas Jardine, *The Birth of History and Philosophy of Science: Kepler's Defence of Tycho against Ursus, with Essays on its Provenance and Significance* (Cambridge: Cambridge University Press, 1984), 278; for an extended commentary see *KGW*, vol. 1, 446–8; the whole passage is on pages 329–32, with a commentary on 459–61. For Kepler's commentary on possible decline through the invasion of barbarians and a decline through effeminate morals see *KGW*, vol. 1, 208; his chronological table praised Rudolph II as first emperor under these special constellations after Charlemagne, to whom the whole treatise was dedicated, 183. On discussions of the Nova see also Patrick J. Boner, ed., *Change and Continuity in Early Modern Cosmology* (Dordrecht: Springer, 2011).

21. In 1604; Johannes Kepler, *Schriften zur Optik 1604–1611*, ed. Rolf Riekher (Frankfort am Main: Harri Deutsch, 2008), 79, in the dedication to Rudolph II.

22. 'Did it ever happen under the Roman Empire that a Sarmatian or German fleet, sailing from the Mediterranean land and [*sic*] brought corn, thus bringing down the high price of grain?', Jardine, *Birth of History*, 278.

23. Kepler applauded the Dutch as much as the Spanish; and even though his account particularly stressed the importance of Gutenberg's invention of printing, Kepler did not describe this advance in patriotic terms, as so many other Germans did. On the assumption of German patriotic leadership by Protestants in 1619 through the reform of learning see Bruce T. Moran, *The Alchemical World of the German Court: Occult Philosophy and Chemical Medicine in the Circle of Moritz of Hessen (1572–1632)* (Stuttgart: Steiner, 1991), 107–9.

24. Thomas Kaufmann, '1600—Deutungen der Jahrhundertwende im deutschen Luthertum', in Kaufmann, *Konfession und Kultur: lutherischer Protestantismus in der zweiten Hälfte des Reformationsjahrhunderts* (Tübingen: Mohr Siebeck, 2006), 420–3. On the following see also A.-C. Trepp in L. Daston and M. Stolleis eds, *Natural Law and Laws of Nature in Early Modern Europe* (Aldershot: Ashgate, 2008), 129–31; Volker Leppin, *Antichrist und Jüngster Tag: Das Profil apokalyptischer Flugschriftenpublizistik im deutschen Luthertum 1548–1618* (Gütersloh: Mohn, 1992). On the pluralism of Lutheranism in the seventeenth century see Thomas Kaufmann, *Dreißigjähriger Krieg und Westfälischer Friede. Kirchengeschichtliche Studien zur lutherischen Konfessionskultur* (Tübingen: Mohr Siebeck, 1998), esp. 149.

25. Frances Yates began this exploration of ideas in her *Rosicrucian Enlightenment* (London: A R, 1986).

26. Joachim Whaley, *Germany and the Holy Roman Empire*, vol. 2 (Oxford: Oxford University Press, 2012), 330–44.

27. For a Württemberg example with an image of the genealogical chart going back to executions in 1619 see Anita Raith, 'Herzogtum Württemberg', in S. Lorenz and J. M. Schmidt, *Wider alle Hexerei und Teufelswerk* (Ostfildern, 2004), 235.

28. This paraphrases Marshall Sahlins's and Eduardo Viveiros de Castro's definition of kinship in Marshall Sahlins, *What Kinship Is—and Is Not* (Chicago: Chicago University Press, 2013), 1.

CHAPTER I

1. The best account remains Walter Grube, *Der Stuttgarter Landtag 1457–1957: Von den Landständen zum demokratischen Parlament* (Stuttgart: Ernst Klett, 1957).

2. For this and the following information on family matters see the detailed and archivally verified information in Gerd Wunder, 'Die Ahnen und Verwandten von Johannes Kepler', in *Genealogisches Jahrbuch*, vol. 19, 1 (1979), 121–46, here 138. I believe that Katharina Kepler was right, for in 1547 Habsburg-Spanish troops led by the Duke of Alba had occupied Leonberg for three weeks.

3. Sabine Holtz, *Theologie und Alltag. Leben und Lehre in den Predigten der Tübinger Theologen 1550–1750* (Tübingen: Mohr, 1993)—these theologians in turn trained the entire pastorate of the duchy.

4. In 1554, her father still had children from his first marriage and he remarried in 1585—it is most unlikely that as mayor and innkeeper he would have remained unmarried for a long period after the death of his first wife: see Wunder, 'Die Ahnen'.

5. *KGW*, vol. 19, 313–14.

6. Wunder, 'Die Ahnen', 122.

7. Historians have also considered the possibility that Heinrich and Katharina had sex illicitly before their marriage and were forced to marry because she was pregnant. But signs of pregnancy were usually only recognized later on at this time, as losing a period was interpreted in a different way. Katharina always spoke of Johannes being premature, which supported her honour, but his physical weakness throughout his life would appear to support this claim.

8. Sheilagh Ogilvie explores this in depth for Württemberg in *A Bitter Living: Women, Markets, and Social Capital in Early Modern Germany* (Oxford: Oxford University Press, 2003).

9. David Parrott, *The Business of War: Military Enterprise and Military Revolution in Early Modern Europe* (Cambridge: Cambridge University Press, 2012), 89–91.

10. Helmut Breimesser, ed., *Schwäbische Landsknechte: 'Lebensbeschreibung des Schärtlin von Burtenbach' und 'Burkhard Stickels Tagebuch'* (Heidenheim: Verlagsanstalt, 1972), 117–44, quote 131.

11. Volker Trugenberger, *Zwischen Schloss und Vorstadt: Sozialgeschichte der Stadt Leonberg im 16. Jahrhundert* (Vaihingen: Melchior Verlag, 1984), No.167, calculated from 1 morgen as 0.3316 hectares.

12. HStASt, A 309, Blutbücher.

13. These StALs were registered in 1630, Trugenberger, *Zwischen Schloss*, 23.

14. Trugenberger, *Zwischen Schloss*, 160.

15. Anneliese Seeliger-Zeiss and Volker Trugenberger, *'ein seliges end und fröhliche ufferstehung'. Die Leonberger Grabmäler des Bildhauers Jeremias Schwartz in ihrer sozial- und kunstgeschichtlichen Bedeutung* (Leonberg: StAL, 1998), 46.

16. Every Christian was to work diligently and joyously, regularly attend church and enjoy temporal goods in appropriate ways, rather than to increase profits or hoard wealth, Sabine Holtz, *Theologie und Alltag: Lehre und Leben in den Predigten der Tübinger Theologen 1550–1750* (Tübingen: J.C.B. Mohr, 1993), 225–9.

17. Seeliger-Zeiss and Trugenberger, *'ein seliges'*, 80, in 1607; and on the marble effect, 101–2; on preaching against real marble see Holtz, *Theologie*, 151, on Heerbrand.

18. StAL, Stadt-und Amtsrechnung 1579/80, Gerlingen and Heimertingen, 100 *Scheffel* of spelt each.

19. See reference in Frisch, *Opera*, 417.

20. Paul Warde, *Ecology, Economy and State Formation in Early Modern Germany* (Cambridge: Cambridge University Press, 2006), 68.

21. Trugenberger, *Zwischen Schloss*, 57.

22. Warde, *Ecology*, 81f., and R. Johanna Regnath, *Das Schwein im Wald. Vormoderne Schweinehaltung zwischen Herrschaftsstrukturen, ständischer Ordnung und Subsistenzökonomie* (Sigmaringen: Thorbecke, 2008), esp. 270.

23. Warde, *Ecology*, 74, 126—at least half of all households had cows, a third pigs, a quarter sheep, and possibly two-fifths none of these animals.

24. StAL, *Gerichtprotokollum*, October 1600, Meister Jerg Christoff.

25. StAL, *Armenkastenrechnung* 1620; *Vogt-und Rüggerichtsprotokolle* 1619/20.

26. Heinrich Theurer and B. Weißhaupt, see Trugenberger, *Zwischen Schloss*, Übersicht 20.

27. Trans. Caspar, *Kepler*, 174, to Herwart, 10.12.1604, in Caspar and von Dyck, *Kepler in seinen Briefen*, 208; *KGW*, vol. 15, 69; on the context of men's responsibilities see Ulinka Rublack, 'Pregnancy, Childbirth and

the Female Body in Early Modern Germany', *Past & Present* (1996), 84–110.

28. StAL, Stadt-und Amtrechnungen, 1579/80, with thanks to Bernadette Gramm for identifying this source; on the previous information see Wunder, 'Die Ahnen', 123, based on archival evidence.

29. Fernand Hallyn, *The Poetic Structure of the World: Copernicus and Kepler* (New York: Zone, 1990), 129–31; Kepler quote to Herwart 28.3.1605, Caspar and von Dyck, *Kepler in seinen Briefen*, 234; *KGW*, vol. 15, 187.

30. Heide Wunder, *'He is the Sun, She is the Moon': Women in Early Modern Germany*, trans. T. Dunlap (Cambridge, MA: Harvard University Press, 1998), 205.

31. StAL, *Gerichts Protocollum* vol. 5, n.p., 1584 v. Bernhart Siglin; vol. 6, 12.1.1587 v. Linhart Holltzing.

32. Johannes Kepler, *Selbstzeugnisse*, trans. E. Hammer and ed. F. Hammer (Stuttgart: Frommann, 1971), 27.

33. *KGW*, vol. 19, 315.

34. For fees and details see Trugenberger, *Zwischen Schloss*, 144, 183; on letters to a Tübingen student see Walther Ludwig, ed., *Vater und Sohn im 16. Jahrhundert: der Briefwechsel des Wolfgang Reichart genannt Rychardus mit seinem Sohn Zeno (1520–1543)* (Hildesheim: Weidmann, 1999); Kepler's letter in relation to his scholarship is printed in Caspar and von Dyck, *Kepler in seinen Briefen*, vol. 1, 3–6.

35. StAL, *Testamentum*, 274–6.

36. Wunder, 'Die Ahnen', 139.

37. *KGW*, vol. 16, 97, 422.

38. *KGW*, vol. 15, 315; Caspar and von Dyck, *Kepler in seinen Briefen*, to Mästlin, 31.3.1606, 262.

39. Biographical details for Binder are in Christian Sigel, *Das evangelische Württemberg*. II. Hauptteil, vol. 2, 1931 (typescript), 353–4; in 1606 there had been some suspicion of him being involved in a theft, but this was not substantiated and obviously did not hinder his career.

40. StAL, *Steuerliste* 1614, Katharina Kepler, 195. On the overall number see Trugenberger, *Zwischen Schloss*, 210; on the situation of women see Ogilvie, *A Bitter Living*; and for widows and the increasing Protestant emphasis on their support see Gesa Ingendahl, *Witwen in der Frühen Neuzeit: eine kulturhistorische Studie* (Frankfurt am Main: Campus, 2006).

CHAPTER 2

1. The correspondence is preserved in HStASt G 60, Bü.8; Paul Sauer, *Herzog Friedrich I von Württemberg 1557–1608: Ungestümer Reformer und weltgewandter Autokrat* (Frankfurt: Deutsche Verlagsan Stadtarchiv Leonberg, 2003), 164–72; on the increasing assertiveness of ruling women as widows to still demand power and recognition see Nina Johansson, '*die grenzen der Witwen wird er feste machen . . .*': *Konstruktionen von Weiblichkeit im lyrischen und didaktischen Werk der Herzogin Elisabeth von Braunschweig-Lüneburg (1510–1558)* (Stockholm: Klett Verlag Stockholm University Press, 2007).

2. W. Grube, *Der Stuttgarter Landtag 1457–1957* (Stuttgart: Klett Verlag 1957), 262, 'weil der mensch nach dem ebenbild Gottes erschaffen'.

3. Grube, *Landtag*, 263.

4. On Paludanus's collection see Harold Cook, *Matters of Exchange: Commerce, Medicine, and Science in the Dutch Golden Age* (New Haven: Yale University Press, 2007), 116–30.

5. For a summary see J. A. Vann, *The Making of a State: Württemberg, 1593–1793* (Ithaca: Cornell University Press, 1984), 28–9; Ulrike Weber-Karge, '*–einem irdischen Paradeiss zu vergleichen–*': *das neue Lusthaus in Stuttgart: Untersuchungen zu einer Bauaufgabe der Renaissance* (Sigmaringen: Thorbecke, 1989); Sauer, *Herzog Friedrich I von Württemberg*, 129.

6. After an Italian report to the Pope in 1591, see Daniel Jütte, *Das Zeitalter des Geheimnisses: Juden, Christen und die Ökonomie des Geheimen (1400–1800)* (Göttingen: Vandenhoeck, 2011), 268.

7. Bruce Moran, *The Alchemical World of the German Court: Occult Philosophy and Chemical Medicine in the Circle of Moritz of Hessen (1572–1632)* (Stuttgart: Steiner, 1991), 8, 11–12.

8. Nettesheim (1486–1535) was widely known for his *De occulta philosophia*, 1531–3, see William R. Newman, 'From Alchemy to "Chymistry"', in L. Daston and K. Park, eds, *The Cambridge History of Science*, vol. 4 (Cambridge: Cambridge University Press, 2006), 502.

9. Tara Nummedal, *Alchemy and Authority in the Holy Roman Empire* (Chicago: Chicago University Press), esp. 115; 127. The famous Mantuan Jew called Colorni was recruited as court alchemist in 1597 and provided with a laboratory, see Jütte, *Geheimnisses*, 297–304; see also Andrea Heck,

ed., Cat. *Von Goldmachern und Schatzsuchern. Alchemie und Aberglaube in Württemberg* (Stuttgart: Hauptstaatsarchiv, 2013).

10. Erhard Cellius, *Wahrhaffte Beschreibung Zweyer Raisen*, Tübingen 1603, Cellische Truckerey, 'Was braucht die Alchymi für Kohl/Die diesem Herrn gefellt sehr wol?/Dardurch man kann alle Metall/Ja die gantz Natur uberall/Also scheiden und resolvirn/Und in vollkommen Esse führn./Das ausser Kupffer würdt gut Goldt/Wie mans aus der Erdt graben solt./Auß Kreuttern ein solch Wasser brennt/Das ein halb Todten wecken könnt./Ein Salz und pulver auch bereit/Die gut weren für all Krankheit./ Und aus dem Leib als durch ein Thür/Was ungesundt treiben herfür. Ja auß Erd Holtz/Erz/oder Stein/Auß Thiern und allem in gemein/Erfewren ein Subtiles Oel/Welches vertreibet manche fähl:/Ja das den Menschen gsundt erhelt/biß zum Termin von Gott bestelt./Und als in solcheer Quantitet/Die einer für ein Wunder het./Das sovil sollte Operirn/Und die Gesundheit promovirn./Solchs alles durch das Fewr geschicht/Und würdt in Brennöfen verricht./Ist das nicht ein herrliche Kunst?/Und würdig grosser Herren Gunst?'.

11. Nummedal, *Alchemy*, 124–5, 129, on universal medicine see Sauer, *Herzog Friedrich I von Württemberg*, 155, in relation to Conrad Schuler in 1605.

12. Nummedal, *Alchemy*, 131.

13. Jütte, *Geheimnisses*, 24; as well as unusual experiments in job retraining, as when one failed alchemist and medic was employed as ducal pastry chef rather than being publicly hanged, see Sauer, *Herzog Friedrich I von Württemberg*, 152.

14. For the general prominence of theologians among natural philosophers and an interpretation see Ann-Charlott Trepp, *Von der Glückseligkeit alles zu wissen. Die Erforschung der Natur als religiöse Praxis in der Frühen Neuzeit* (Frankfurt am Main: Campus, 2009), 467–74.

15. Evans, *Rudolf II*, 283; Ann-Charlott Trepp, 'Religion, Magie und Naturphilosophie: Alchemie im 16. und 17. Jahrhundert', in Lehmann and Trepp, eds, *Im Zeichen der Krise: Religiosität im Europa des 17. Jahrhunderts* (Göttingen: Vandenhoeck & Ruprecht, 1999), 473–94, and Kaspar von Greyerz, 'Alchemie, Hermetismus und Magie', in *Im Zeichen der Krise*, 415–32; on Osiander, Schuler, and Haffner see Moran, *Alchemical World*, 156–7.

16. Moran, *Alchemical World*, 158; 167.

17. Trepp, *Glückseligkeit*, Part I; Johann Arndt was a Lutheran pastor closely following Paracelsian ideas.

18. *In das Wunderbad Fürstl. Würt: Badenfahrt: Welche Chur... Herr Friderich/ Hertzog zu Württemberg und Teck... Sampt deren Edlen Ritterschaft und Officirer/Den 9. May/Anno 1607. angefangen... Und was einem jeden ge-fehlet/oder für ein Krankheit gehabt hab...* Schleyß, Johann (Stuttgart: Grieb, 1607); Sauer, *Herzog Friedrich I von Württemberg*, 229–33; on Protestantism and spas in England see Alexandra Walsham, *The Reformation of the Landscape: Religion, Identity, and Memory in Early Modern Britain and Ireland* (Oxford: Oxford University Press, 2011), 566.

19. This in particular means to argue against Bruce Moran's influential contention that German courts were infused by a culture of doom and depression, which fuelled their interest in alchemy.

20. One example from Württemberg was Helena Rucker, who was the daughter of a prominent Nuremberg physician and first married to the Nuremberg preacher Andreas Osiander, one of the most significant German Lutheran theologians, before entering a second marriage with the prelate of a former monastery in Württemberg. Rucker had corresponded with Paracelsus and was appointed first court pharmacist in Württemberg, Pfeilsticker, *Dienerbuch*, § 352. Alisha Rankin, *Panaceia's Daughters: Noblewomen as Healers in Early Modern Germany* (Chicago: Chicago University Press, 2013).

21. Pfeilsticker, *Dienerbuch*, vol. 1, 363, 'Kräutermänner- und mägde'.

22. WLB, HB XI 41, 157; Sibylle's own medical books are listed in WLB Cod.hist.fol.1069.

23. Gessner, *Von dem Wolff*, CLV.

24. WLB, HB XI 41, 22rv (Herzwasser) and 135; Rankin, *Panaceia's Daughters*, 205–6.

25. Sachiko Kusukawa, *Picturing the Book of Nature: Image, Text, and Argument in Sixteenth-Century Human Anatomy and Medical Botany* (Chicago: Chicago University Press, 2012), 155; William Eamon, 'Markets, Piazzas and Villages', in L. Daston and K. Park, eds, *Cambridge History of Science* (Cambridge: Cambridge University Press, 2006), 210; for a particularly interesting piece of terra sigillata with Arabic characters under its handle and plant decorations see E. Fucikova, ed., *Rudolf II: The Court and the City* (London: Thames & Hudson, 1997), 505.

26. Kusukawa, *Picturing*, esp. 133.

27. Florike Egmond, 'Correspondence and Natural History in the Sixteenth Century: Cultures of Exchange in the Circle of Carolus Clusius', in Francisco Bethencourt and Florike Egmond, eds, *Correspondence and Cultural Exchange in Europe, 1400–1700* (Cambridge: Cambridge University Press, 2007), 115–20.

28. The pioneering study here is Keith Thomas, *Man and the Natural World: Changing Attitudes in England 1500–1800* (Harmondsworth: Penguin, 1983), 226; most recently see Rankin, *Panaceia's Daughters*.

29. The fourth book is dedicated to natural philosophy; on the notion of correspondences see *Johann Arnd's Sechs Bücher vom Wahren Christentum* (Stuttgart: Steinkopf, 1930), 564; see also Trepp, 'Natural Order and Divine Salvation: Protestant Conceptions in Early Modern Germany (1550–1750)', in L. Daston and M. Stolleis, eds, *Natural Law and Laws of Nature in Early Modern Europe* (Farnham: Ashgate, 2008), 129.

30. Ronald Gobiet, ed., *Der Briefwechsel zwischen Philipp Hainhofer und Herzog August d.J. von Braunschweig-Lüneburg* (Munich: Deutscher Kunstverlag, 1984), 362 on Arndt.

31. Theodor Thumm, *Christliche Predigt uber die Leich* (Stuttgart, 1614) 358.

32. Ahnengalerie Schloss Ludwigsburg, Schlossverwaltung Ludwigsburg.

33. Roman Janssen, 'Heinrich Schickhardt im Spiegel seines Buchbesitzes', in Robert Kretzschmar, ed., *Neue Forschungen zu Heinrich Schickardt* (Stuttgart: Kohlhammer, 2002), 7–51.

34. See the description in Erasmus Grüninger, *LeichPredigt* (Stuttgart, 1614) 59.

35. Alfons Elfgang and Ehrenfried Kluckert, *Schickhardts Leonberger Pomeranzengarten und die Gartenbaukunst der Renaissance* (Bierlingen: Kluckert, 1988), 18.

36. Alfons Elfgang, Rosemarie Münzenmayer, '"Medicina", Familie und Repräsentation: Herzogin Sybilla und ihr Pomeranzengarten', in *Schlösser Baden-Württemberg*, 3 (2009), 12–15.

37. Werner Fleischhauer, *Die Geschichte der Kunstkammer der Herzöge von Württemberg in Stuttgart* (Stuttgart: Kohlhammer, 1976), 6.

38. J. V. Andreae, *Christianopolis*, intro. and trans. Edward H. Thompson (Dordrecht: Kluwer, 1999), 273.

39. Johann Valentin Andreae, *Nachrufe, Autobiographische Schriften, Cosmoxenus*, ed. and trans. F. Böhling et al. (Stuttgart: Frommann-holzboog, 1995), 82–5.

40. Roman Janssen and Oliver Auge, eds, *Herrenberger Persönlichkeiten aus acht Jahrhunderten*, Herrenberger Historische Schriften, vol. 6 (Herrenberg, 1999), 203.

41. HStASt Stuttgart, G 60, Herzogin Sibylle, C, Verzaichnus, Was noch weiter in der Hofapotheck so vorgehendem Inventario ist einverleibt. Auffgezeichnet, den 23. February 1615.

42. Thumm, *Christliche Predigt*, 357; *Verzaichnuß/Der Ordnung und Procession*, 515.

CHAPTER 3

1. In Leonberg, the daughter of Jacob Korn, the town scribe, married a man whose inventory survives and perfectly achieved the same look, StAL, *Inventuren und Theilungen*, 29.10.1632, Leyrer.

2. W. Grube, *Der Stuttgarter Landtag 1457–1957* (Stuttgart: Klett, 1957), 280; A. E. Adam, ed., *Württembergische Landtagsakten, Unter Herzog Friedrich 1608–1620* (Stuttgart: Kohlhammer, 1910), 270.

3. Alexander Schmidt, *Vaterlandsliebe und Religionskonflikt: politische Diskurse im Alten Reich (1555–1648)* (Leiden: Brill, 2007), 331–50.

4. Magnus Rüde, *England und Kurpfalz im werdenden Mächteeuropa (1608–1632). Konfession—Dynastie—kulturelle Ausdrucksformen* (Stuttgart: Kohlhammer, 2007), 248, in a Spencerian poem; on the festivities in context see Sara Smart and Mara R. Wade, eds, *The Palatine Wedding of 1613: Protestant Alliance and Courtfestival* (Wiesbaden: Harrassowitz, 2013).

5. On such themes see Peer Schmidt, *Spanische Universalmonarchie oder 'teutsche Libertet': das spanische Imperium in der Propaganda des Dreissigjährigen Kriegs* (Stuttgart: Steiner, 2001).

6. For efforts in Heidelberg see Rüde, *England und Kurpfalz*, 159.

7. L. Krapf and C, Wagenknecht, eds, *Stuttgarter Hoffeste: Texte und Materialien zur höfischen Repräsentation im frühen 17. Jahrhundert* (Tübingen: Niemeyer, 1979), 6, 96.

8. *Stuttgarter Hoffeste*, 100–2. See also Helen Watanabe-O'Kelly, *Triumphall Shews: Tournaments at German-Speaking Courts in their European Context 1560–1730* (Berlin: Gebr. Mann Verlag, 1992), 37–64 on the festivals of the Protestant Union.

9. *Stuttgarter Hoffeste*, 333.

10. Axel Gotthard, *Konfession und Staatsräson: Die Außenpolitik Württembergs unter Herzog Johann Friedrich (1608–1628)* (Stuttgart: Kohlhammer, 1992).

11. Gotthard, *Konfession*, 19–22, 98–9; W. B. Patterson, *King James VI and I and the Reunion of Christendom* (Cambridge: Cambridge University Press, 2000).

12. Fleischhauer, *Renaissance*, 305–15.

13. *Stuttgarter Hoffeste*, 351–4 and Werner Fleischhauer, *Die Geschichte der Kunstkammer der Herzöge von Württemberg in Stuttgart* (Stuttgart: Kohlhammer, 1976), esp. 33–47.

14. *Stuttgarter Hoffeste*, 344.

15. *Stuttgarter Hoffeste*, 348.

16. V. Trugenberger, *Zwischen Schloss und Vorstadt: Sozialgeschichte der Stadt Leonberg im 16. Jahrhundert* (Vaihingen: Melchior, 1984), 26, these were in Stuttgart, Göppingen, Calw, and Bietigheim.

17. StAL, *Armenkastenrechnung* 1620, n.p.

18. Paul Warde, *Ecology, Economy and State Formation in Early Modern Germany* (Cambridge: Cambridge University Press, 2006), 82–4, 208.

19. This is brilliantly worked out for the area in Warde, *Ecology*.

20. StAL, *Stadt-und Amtprotokollum*, 27.1.1615, 3.

21. StAL, *Stadt-und Amtprotokollum*, 24.1.1615.

22. StAL, *Stadt-und Amtprotokollum*, 26.1.1615.

23. Trugenberger, *Zwischen Schloss*, Tabl.1, 20.

24. StAL, *Stadt-und Amtprotokollum*, 23.1.1615.

25. HStASt G60, Bü.5, Anstellungsvertrag, November 1613, 2: 'So solle er allwegen zuvor mit der fürst. fraw wittib oder ihren fürst. gd. hofmaistern auß der sachen conferirn und ihre mainung und gedanckhen darüber vernemmen und seinen Berichten einverleiben', esp. 5, 9–12. Abschrift Bernadette Gramm.

26. The fate of the fourth suspect remains unclear. The most reliable data are provided by Bernadette Gramm at the Leonberg civic archive, see also HStASt, *Blutbücher*, which do not specify the crimes though, only names and sentences.

27. There are none recorded in HStASt A 209 or 309, and only noted in the Straf-und Urteilsbuch, which is preserved in HStASt, A.

28. Anita Binder, 'mit dem feuer vom leben zum tod...: Hexenverfolgung in Sindelfingen', in *Sindelfingen und seine Altstadt—ein verborgener Schatz*, Sindelfingen 2013, 427–46, here 441–2, these specific sources have remained in the local archive.

29. Trugenberger, *Zwischen Schloss*, Nr. 259 and Nr. 152; as early in 1624, when Ursula turned fifty-seven, the Reinbolds were both admitted to the local home for sick and old people, the *Spital*.

30. StAL, *Gerichtsprotokollum*, Bd.6, Summer 1597, n.p.

31. Pfeilsticker, *Dienerbuch*, 317.

32. Warde, *Ecology*, 215; 330 for figures on theft.

33. StAL, *Gerichtsprotocollum Eltingen*, 12.10.1615.

34. The original files are preserved in HStASt, A 209, Bü.1055 (up to 13.2.1621) and Bü.1056. I have checked these against the Frisch edition, which is referenced throughout this book, *Opera*, 365–6.

35. Frisch, *Opera*, 366.

36. Frisch, *Opera*, 367.

CHAPTER 4

1. He kept reflecting on this and, later, thought that stones could cause storms, Boner, *Cosmological Synthesis*, 150, and on the relevance of weather more generally 151; *KGW*, vol. 14, 330; Caspar and von Dyck, *Kepler in seinen Briefen*, to Fabricius, 2.12.1602, 177–8.

2. Kepler, *Harmony of the World*, 363–4; Caspar translates farts as *Winde*, *Weltharmonik*, 259.

3. *KGW*, vol. 19, 57.

4. *KGW*, vol. 19, 8; for a translation of Kepler's later letter to the estates on 15.5.1596, see Caspar and von Dyck, *Kepler in seinen Briefen*, 35–7.

5. *KGW*, vol. 13, 74f., late March 1596; for the contemporary number of dinners see Jütte, *Geheimnisses*, 300, drawing on the alchemist Colorni's letters, who arrived in 1597.

6. *KGW*, vol. 13, 50–4.

7. *KGW*, vol. 19, 324; vol. 13, 83; 220.

8. *KGW*, vol. 1, 26/27; an appreciation of the elegance of this publication is best gained through looking at the plates in an original edition rather than

the available translation: Johannes Kepler, *Mysterium Cosmographicum: The Secret of the Universe*, trans. A. M. Duncan (New York: Abaris, 1981). For the wider context of Kepler's work see also Robert S. Westman, *The Copernican Question: Prognostication, Skepticism, and Celestial Order* (Berkeley: University of California Press, 2011), 309–41.

9. *KGW*, vol. 19, 324–5; Kepler would go on to defend the usefulness and ingenuity of mechanical devices, *KGW*, vol. 8, 218–32.

10. *KGW*, vol. 13, 222–3; 225.

11. Nick Jardine, 'The Many Significances of Kepler's Contra Ursum', in F. Boockmann *et al.*, eds, *Miscellanea Kepleriana: Festschrift für Volker Bialas zum 65. Geburtstag* (Augsburg: Rauner, 2005), 135 and 138.

12. See also Adam Mosley, 'Objects of Knowledge: Mathematics and Models in Sixteenth-Century Cosmology and Astronomy', in Sachiko Kusukawa and Ian Maclean, eds, *Transmitting Knowledge: Words, Images, and Instruments in Early Modern Europe* (Oxford: Oxford University Press, 2006), 193–216.

13. Kepler uses the reference to the heavens as like a clockwork machine in this precise sense to Herwart, 10.2.1605, Caspar and von Dyck, *Kepler in seinen Briefen*, 219; *KGW*, vol. 15, 146.

14. Steven Shapin, *The Scientific Revolution* (Chicago: Chicago University Press, 1996), 35.

15. *KGW*, vol. 13, 222.

16. On the importance of biology for his thinking see Patrick Boner, *Kepler's Cosmological Synthesis: Astrology, Mechanism and the Soul* (Leiden: Brill, 2013), 12, quote 30, on the cleaning of the ether, 32; this explanation of how spirits are formed in a letter to Brengger, 5.4.1608, Caspar and von Dyck, *Kepler in seinen Briefen*, 309, *KGW*, vol. 16, 148.

17. *KGW*, vol. 15, 70, Br. 303; *KGW*, vol. 21.2.2., 537–43, 687; vol. 16, 434–6.

18. Horst Bredekamp, *Antikensehnsucht und Maschinenglauben. Die Geschichte der Kunstkammer und die Zukunft der Kunstgeschichte* (Berlin: Wagenbach, 2000), 41.

19. *KGW*, vol. 13, 225–6.

20. Regina Pörtner, *The Counter-Reformation in Central Europe: Styria 1580–1630* (Oxford: Oxford University Press, 2001), 112–14, 158–64; and on his mother's crucial influence see Katrin Keller, *Erzherzogin Maria von Innerösterreich (1551–1608): Zwischen Habsburg und Wittelsbach* (Cologne: Böhlau, 2012).

21. Keller, *Erzherzogin Maria*, 110.
22. Gabriele Praschl-Bichler, *Geheimnisse des Mittelalters und der Renaissance: Der Grazer Vergangenheit auf der Spur* (Graz: L. Stocker Verlag, 2005), 108–9.
23. *KGW* vol. 14, 45, Letter to Mästlin, 29.8.1599; Caspar and von Dyck, *Kepler in seinen Briefen*, 113.
24. *KGW*, vol. 19, 345, 7, 54; vol. 4, 431, 81–98; vol. 16, 239–40; for his request to send letters to Leonberg see *KGW*, vol. 14, 161; Caspar and von Dyck, *Kepler in seinen Briefen*, 151, to Mästlin, 8.2.1601.
25. *KGW*, vol. 14, 447; Caspar and von Dyck, *Kepler in seinen Briefen*, to Herwart, September 1603, 191.
26. Caspar and von Dyck, *Kepler in seinen Briefen*, to Sybilla, 19.3.1611, 380; *KGW*, vol. 16, 370–1.
27. *KGW*, vol. 16, 168–9, 9./19.3.1611; 371–2, same date; 464–5 on the consistory's response and 240–3 for Kepler's letter in 1609. These positions were reiterated over the following years in his exchanges with his former professor, Hafenreffer.
28. Adam Mosley, *Bearing the Heavens: Tycho Brahe and the Astronomical Community of the Late Sixteenth Century* (Cambridge: Cambridge University Press, 2007).
29. *KGW*, vol. 19, 344.
30. *KGW*, vol. 19, 325, 7, 23.
31. Caspar and von Dyck, *Kepler in seinen Briefen*, from Herwart, 9.11.1604, 205; *KGW*, vol. 15, 63.
32. See, for instance, *KGW*, vol. 17, 801, 20.10.1618.
33. *KGW*, vol. 4, 422–5.
34. Johannes Kepler, in his treatise on optics in 1604, Rolk Riekher, ed., *Schriften zur Optik 1604–1611* (Frankfurt am Main: Harri Deutsch, 2008), 76.
35. J. Cambers, see Keith Thomas, *Religion and the Decline of Magic* (Harmondsworth: Penguin, 1978), 426.
36. *KGW*, 7/66, vol. 19, 350–1.
37. Caspar, *Kepler*, 182, Melchior Schäfer; this triggered the physician Feselius's treatise to which Kepler responded in turn.
38. 'quests for manuscripts, strategies dictated by confessionality and tactics dictated by the search for publicity', Ian Maclean endorsing the quote by Martin Mulsow, in *Scholarship, Commerce, Religion: The Learned Book in*

the Age of Confessions, 1560–1630 (Cambridge, MA: Harvard University Press, 2012), 45–6.

39. For the most important analysis see Nicholas Jardine, *The Birth of History and Philosophy of Science: Kepler's A Defence of Tycho against Ursus with Essays on its Provenance and Significance* (Cambridge: Cambridge University Press, 1984). Kepler finally became exceptionally committed towards causal analysis and theoretical progress through systematically related bodies of consistent propositions rooted in practice, developing criteria to resolve theoretical disputes and a specific methodology for achieving progress.

40. James R. Voelckel, *The Composition of Kepler's Astronomia Nova* (Princeton: Princeton University Press, 2001), 250–2, and for the following his 'Conclusion'.

CHAPTER 5

1. StAL, *Inventar-und Theilungsbuch*, 1615–32.
2. WAL, Cod.hist.fol.562, *Heinrich Schickardt Inventarbuch* 1631, 147r–169r.
3. StAL, *Inventar-und Theilungsbuch*, 1615–32, 5.11.1631, Catherina Besserer; No.11 Bastian Beutelsbacher; for the interest in such artwork see Fleischhauer, *Renaissance*, 215–16.
4. Volker Trugenberger, *Zwischen Schloss und Vorstadt: Sozialgeschichte Leonbergs im 16. Jahrhundert* (Vaihingen: Melchior, 1984), Michel Schmid, Nr.295.
5. Trugenberger, *Zwischen Schloss*, Stoffel Bulling, Nr.54.
6. Trugenberger, *Zwischen Schloss*, Werner Brunnenfels, Nr.51.
7. Trugenberger, *Zwischen Schloss*, Mathis Plüderhäuser (1586–1613), Nr.256.
8. Frisch, *Opera*, 401.
9. Frisch, *Opera*, 367, HStASt, 29.11.1616.
10. Frisch, *Opera*, 367, HStASt, 2.12.1616.
11. *KGW*, vol. 17, report from Johannes Strauss to Kepler, 21.9.1616.
12. David W. Sabean, *Property, Production and Family in Neckarhausen, 1700–1870* (Cambridge: Cambridge University Press, 1990), 260–71, 344, 421–6.

13. He mentions this to his stepdaughter, *KGW*, vol. 19, 470.

14. See Hella Kothmann, 'Die Reisen des Johannes Kepler. Eine Chronologie—ein Itinerarium', in F. Boockmann et al., eds., *Miscellanea Kepleriana. Festschrift für Volker Bialas zum 65. Geburtstag* (Augsburg: Rauner, 2005), 229–46.

15. Thus, one Bavarian peasant in 1628 promised Mary a mass and a foot of wax after a heavily laden haycart had damaged her daughter's legs. By November, mother and daughter were able to hike up to the mountain shrine to give thanks. Renate Blickle, 'Peasant Protest and the Language of Women's Petitions: Christina Vend's Supplication of 1629', in Ulinka Rublack, ed., *Gender in Early Modern German History* (Cambridge: Cambridge University Press, 2002), 186.

16. Frisch, *Opera*, 388–9.

17. Werner Fleischhauer, *Die Renaissance im Herzogtum Württemberg* (Stuttgart: Kohlhammer, 1971), 258–9.

18. HStASt, G 60, Bü7, Verzaychnus: 'Christoff Käppler Khanttengiessern, wegen verfertigung deß Bäadlinß im Schloß geben 173fl 18kr'.

19. StAL, *Kauff-und Contractbuch* 1609–43, fol.75a–76a.

20. HStASt, Frisch, *Opera*, 367–71.

21. Frisch, *Opera*, 371, 7.1.1617.

22. Frisch, *Opera*, 371–2, n.day, January 1617.

23. For information see Pfeilsticker, *Dienerbuch*; J. A. Vann, *The Making of a State: Württemberg 1593–1793* (Ithaca: Cornell University Press, 1984), 60. Unfortunately, records for these meetings only survive from 1602–3, Vann, *The Making of a State*, 84.

24. *KGW*, vol. 17, 213–17; see also commentary on these advocates in *KGW* vol. 12, 329; Caspar and von Dyck, *Kepler in seinen Briefen*, vol. 2, 79–86.

25. Frisch, *Opera*, 372, January 1617.

26. Frisch, *Opera*, 373.

27. Frisch, *Opera*, 373, 9.3.1617.

28. Frisch, *Opera*, 373–4, 11.3.1617.

29. StAL, *Vogtrüggericht* 1619.

30. Frisch, *Opera*, 375, 27.3.1617.

31. Frisch, *Opera*, 375, 28.3.1617.

32. Caspar and von Dyck, *Kepler in seinen Briefen*, to Brengger, 30.11.1607, 305; *KGW*, vol. 16, 87.

33. *KGW*, vol. 19, 469–72.

34. *KGW*, vol. 19, 356–7. She died on 9 February 1618, see Kepler's account of the year 1617, also in Justus Schmid, *Johann Kepler: Sein Leben in Bildern und eigenen Berichten*, 2nd edn (Linz: Trauner, 1970), 251.

35. It is argued, for instance, that investigations always vindicated accusations made by children, although rumours and denunciations in general were not allowed to qualify for an arrest, Johannes Dillinger, *'Evil People': A Comparative Study of Witch Hunts in Swabian Austria and the Electorate of Trier*, trans. Laura Stokes (Virginia: University of Virginia Press, 2009), 121.

36. Lyndal Roper, *WitchCraze: Terror and Fantasy in Baroque Germany* (New Haven: Yale University Press, 2004), esp. ch. 7; Charles Zika, *Appearances of Witchcraft. Visual Culture and Print in Sixteenth-Century Europe* (London: Routledge, 2005); on old age see also Heide Wunder, *'He is the Sun, She is the Moon': Women in Early Modern Germany*, trans. T. Dunlap (Harvard: Harvard University Press, 1998), 16–84.

37. For a sixteenth-century diarist's struggle with old age through the prism of ancient literature, see Hermann Weinsberg, *Liber senectutis and decrepitudinus*, which are available online and discussed in Matthew Lundin, *Paper Memory: A Sixteenth-Century Townsman Writes His World* (Cambridge, MA: Harvard University Press, 2012). For a discussion of women, age, and witchcraft see Roper, *WitchCraze*, 161; Kaspar von Greyerz, *Passagen und Stationen. Lebensstufen zwischen Mittelalter und Moderne* (Göttingen: Vandenhoeck, 2010), 200.

38. Reinbold's brother, the doctor, as 'fortune teller', who had been consulted but had been taken over by the devil as instrument of evil in deciding that Katharina was the cause of his sister's illness. This is a difficult passage to interpret: 'Dabey aber der bösse Geist durch seine Instrumenta, die warsager, so man anderseitz zurath gezogen, das seinige auch gethan.'

39. Frisch, *Opera*, 381–3, 1.9.1617. This means that his siblings had received their share already, while Kepler would claim his part when the property was finally divided after Katharina's death.

40. Frisch, *Opera*, 384, Decretum 23.9.1617.

41. Frisch, *Opera*, 384, 8.11.1617.

42. Trugenberger, *Zwischen Schloss.*

43. *KGW*, vol. 17, 254; on Hebenstreit and Ulm, see Ruth Kastner, *Geistlicher Rauffhandel: Illustrierte Flugblätter zum Reformationsjubiläum 1617* (Bern: Lang, 1982), 56–63.
44. Frisch, *Opera*, 384–6, November 1617.
45. Frisch, *Opera*, 386, 22.11.1617.
46. Frisch, *Opera*, 388–9.

CHAPTER 6

1. *KGW*, 21, 2.2, 577.
2. *KGW*, 21, 2.2, 3 (Sebald), 11 (Heinrich), for grandmother and comments on Katharina (26); Schmid, *Johann Kepler*, 219.
3. *KGW*, vol. 13, 377–82.
4. Max Caspar's careful comments point in the same direction, but have often been overlooked subsequently, see his *Kepler* (New York: Dover, 1993), 34.
5. See Anthony Grafton, *Cardano's Cosmos: The Worlds and Work of a Renaissance Astrologer* (Cambridge, MA: Harvard University Press, 1999); and for Cardano's comments on his mother see his autobiography, *My Life*, trans. J. Stoner (New York: New York Review of Books, 2002), 9.
6. *KGW*, vol. 19, 7/30, 328–37; *Johannes Kepler, Selbstzeugnisse*, trans. Esther Hammer, ed. Franz Hammer (Stuttgart: Frommann Verlag, 1971), 16–30.
7. *KGW*, 21, 2.2, 573.
8. *KGW*, vol. 21, 2.2, 398, 1116.
9. *KGW*, vol. 21, 2.2, 573.
10. See, for instance, *KGW*, vol. 21, 2.2, 449; 459.
11. *KGW*, 21, 2.2, 440: 'Sag demnach auch ietzo, zu abhelffung viles ungemachs gehört mehrer leütte Hülff und naigung, ohne die geschicht nichts. Niemand stehet es zue, E(urer) M(ajes)t(ät) dero mühe zu entladen, dan dero selber.'
12. *KGW*, 21, 2.2, 441. On Kepler's earlier emphasis on Mars as lord of Rudolph's geniture see esp. H. Darrel Rutkin, 'Celestial Offerings: Astrological Motifs in the Dedicatory Letters of Kepler's Astronomia Nova and Galileo's Sidereus Nuncius', in W. R. Newman and A. Grafton, eds,

Secrets of Nature: Astrology and Alchemy in Early Modern Europe (Cambridge, MA: MIT Press, 2001), 133–72, 152.

13. See, for instance, *KGW*, vol. 4, 72.

14. *KGW*, vol. 4, 163; 179, 'beständige Wissenschaft'.

15. *KGW*, vol. 4, 204 below; a very important passage.

16. *KGW*, vol. 4, 209–10.

17. *KGW*, vol. 4, 225; 230.

18. *KGW*, vol. 4, 231.

19. *KGW*, vol. 4, 232–3.

20. *KGW*, vol. 4, 234.

21. Johannes Kepler, *Weltharmonik*, trans. and ed. Max Caspar (Oldenburg: Wissenschaftsverlag, 1983), 165.

22. Heinz Schott, 'Die Heilkunde des Paracelsus im Schnittpunkt von Naturphilosophie, Alchemie und Psychologie', in Peter Dilg and Hartmut Rudolph, eds, *Resultate und Desiderate der Paracelsus-Forschung* (Stuttgart: Steiner, 1993), 38.

23. *KGW*, vol. 14, 325; Caspar and von Dyck, *Kepler in seinen Briefen*, to Fabricius, 2.12.1602, 176.

24. Kepler, *Weltharmonik*, 165.

25. Kepler, *Weltharmonik*, 167.

26. Kepler, *Weltharmonik*, 181.

27. Johannes Kepler, *Schriften zur Optik 1604–1611*, ed. Rolf Riekher (Frankfurt am Main: Harri Deutsch, 2008) 81; the other dedication with a military analogy is in the *Astronomia Nova*.

28. Johannes Kepler, *Selbstzeugnisse*, ed. Franz Hammer (Stuttgart: Frommann, 1971), 48.

29. See, for instance, *KGW*, vol. 4, 114, with Kepler's comments.

30. Kepler, *Selbstzeugnisse*, 48.

31. Kepler, *Selbstzeugnisse*, 52.

32. Kepler, *Selbstzeugnisse*, 55.

33. Kepler, *Selbstzeugnisse*, 55.

34. On his dislike of washing see Caspar and von Dyck, *Kepler in seinen Briefen*, to Fabricius, 11.10.1605, 258; *KGW*; vol. 15, 247; and his self-characterization in Kepler, *Selbstzeugnisse*, 42.

35. Kepler, *Selbstzeugnisse*, 46. See also Gadi Algazi, 'Johannes Keplers Apologie: Wissenproduktion, Selbstdarstellung und die Geschlechterordnung' in B. Reich, F. Rexroth, and M. Roick, eds, *Wissen, maßgeschneidert:*

Experten und Expertenkulturen im Europa der Vormoderne (Munich: Oldenbourg, 2012), 215–249; Elizabeth Harding, *Der Gelehrte im Haus: Ehe, Familie und Haushalt in der Standeskultur der frühneuzeitlichen Universität Helmstedt* (Wiesbaden: Harrassowitz, 2014).

36. Caspar and von Dyck, *Kepler in seinen Briefen*, vol. 1, 154–6.
37. See his discussion of this as prolapsarian in *KGW*, vol. 4, 158–9.
38. Kepler, *Weltharmonik*, 257.
39. The Guldenmanns hardly featured, even though it needs to be noted that peasants of previous generations were not in the habit yet of writing down or remembering their day and hour of birth.
40. Kepler, *Weltharmonik*, 32.
41. Kepler, *Weltharmonik*, 195.
42. Johannes Kepler, *The Harmony of the World*, trans. and ed. E. J. Aiton, A. M. Duncan, and J. V. Field (American Philosophical Society, 1997), 2.
43. Kepler, *Weltharmonik*, 260–1; Kepler, *Harmony*, 364–5.
44. *KGW*; Caspar, mistaken translation in English edition, emphasis added.
45. Kepler also introduced the figure of protective spirits or angels into his reflections. Bad luck could be explained through a person's immoral behaviour which had driven them away, *Weltharmonik*, 273. On the consistory see *KGW*, vol. 16, 464.
46. *KGW*, vol. 17, 184 and 479; 355, 25.4.1619; 359, 10./20.7.1619; see also 191 about the delay, 21.1.1616.

CHAPTER 7

1. Frisch, *Opera*, 390–4.
2. Frisch, *Opera*, 405.
3. Frisch, *Opera*, 407. See also Michael Stolberg, *Homo Patiens. Krankheits- und Körpererfahrung in der Frühen Neuzeit* (Weimar: Böhlau, 2003), 50–1.
4. Stolberg, *Homo Patiens*, 73–5.
5. *KGW*, vol. 21, 2.2, 17.
6. KGW, vol. 21, 2.2, 17; Caspar, *Kepler*, repr. (New York: Dover 2003), 35.
7. *KGW*, vol. 13, 6.
8. *KGW*, vol. 13, 153–4. This letter in the end was not sent, 394; Kepler also reflected on his brother in his autobiographical sketch in Graz.
9. *KGW*, vol. 17, 74–5, 134–5, 472.
10. Frisch, *Opera*, 404.
11. Frisch, *Opera*, 403, Gertrute Osswaldt Zahnen Hausbecken Hausfrau.

12. Frisch, *Opera*, 404.

13. Frisch, *Opera*, 404.

14. Frisch, *Opera*, 408.

15. Frisch, *Opera*, 411.

16. Frisch, *Opera*, 409–10, Barbara Stahl.

17. Frisch, *Opera*, 412–14, Bastian Würth.

18. Frisch, *Opera*, 412.

19. For the Württemberg situation in the eighteenth century see Sabine Sander, *Handwerkschirurgen: Sozialgeschichte einer verdrängten Berufsgruppe* (Göttingen: Vandenhoeck, 1989).

20. Frisch, *Opera*, 417.

21. *KGW*, vol. 4, 179, 245, 247.

22. William Eamon, 'Markets, Piazzas and Villages', in L. Daston and K. Park, eds, *Cambridge History of Science* (Cambridge: Cambridge University Press, 2008), 218–19, with further examples; on Boyle see Harold Cooke, *Matters of Exchange: Commerce, Medicine and Science in the Dutch Golden Age* (New Haven: Yale University Press, 2007), 414.

23. Bruce T. Moran, *The Alchemical World of the German Court: Occult Philosophy and Chemical Medicine in the Circle of Moritz of Hessen (1572–1632)* (Stuttgart: Steiner, 1991), 45.

24. She allegedly had used such a fire-stone with one woman: see Frisch, *Opera*, 410, Barbara Stahl.

25. See also Stolberg, *Homo Patiens*, 36.

26. Frisch, *Opera*, 403, Oswald Zahn's wife.

27. Frisch, *Opera*, 405.

28. E. Fucikova, ed., *Rudolf II and Prague: The Court and the City* (London: Thames & Hudson, 1997), 601.

29. Mauritzhuis Den Haag, 1630, 39,5 × 56 cm.

30. Alexandra Walsham, *The Reformation of the Landscape: Religion, Identity, and Memory in Early Modern Britain and Ireland* (Oxford: Oxford University Press, 2012), 555–7.

31. On Maria and Sybille's ingredients HStASt, G 60, Bü.8, 96r; on Tancke see Moran, *Alchemical World*, 137–8.

32. Moran, *Alchemical World*, 64.

33. For countless examples from Rudolf's possessions see Fucikova, ed., *Rudolf II and Prague*.

34. See James R. Palmitessa, *Material Culture & Daily Life in the New City of Prague in the Age of Rudolph II* (Krems: Medium Aevum Quotidianum, 1997), 111.
35. Frisch, *Opera*, 11.8.1620, and 470.
36. HStaSt, A 209, Bü.371, Bietigheim, 1.2.1619.
37. Frisch, *Opera*, 409.
38. Frisch, *Opera*, 411.
39. Frisch, *Opera*, 412.
40. Frisch, *Opera*, 420, 3.7.1620.
41. Frisch, *Opera*, 419, 20.3.1620.

CHAPTER 8

1. Joachim Whaley, *Germany and the Holy Roman Empire* vol. 1 (Oxford: Oxford University Press, 2012), 496.
2. On Schaller see Whaley, *Holy Roman Empire*, 543; on Kepler's writing on the 1618 comet see Marion Gindhart, *Das Kometenjahr 1618: Antike und zeitgenössisches Wissen in der frühneuzeitlichen Kometenliteratur des deutschsprachigen Raumes* (Wiesbaden: Harrasowitz, 2006), 180.
3. A. E. Adam, ed., *Württembergische Landtagsakten: Unter Herzog Johann Friedrich 1608–1620* (Stuttgart: Kohlhammer, 1910), 738.
4. Axel Gotthard, *Konfession und Staatsräson: Die Außenpolitik Württembergs unter Herzog Johann Friedrich (1608–1628)* (Stuttgart: Kohlhammer, 1992), 273–6, 280–1.
5. Sauer, *Herzog Friedrich I von Württemberg*, 141–2.
6. HStASt, *Blutbücher*, 19.1.1620, n.p.
7. HStASt, A 209, Bü.149, Christina Dürr, 12.4.1617. Her sentence remains unclear, but it is very unlikely that she would have been executed.
8. See, for instance, in the testimony provided in the Frisch case on 14.12.1619, Barbara Beutelsbacher.
9. HStASt, A 309, Bü.56, 14.12.1619.
10. HStASt, A 309, Bü.289, 18. January 1620, on his title see Trugenberger, *Zwischen Schloss*, 157.
11. HStASt, A 309, Bü. 235.
12. HstASt, A 309, Bü.235, 29.1.1620.
13. HStASt, *Blutbücher*, 23.2.1621.
14. StAL, *Armenkastenrechnung 1620*.

15. StAL, *Gerichtsprotokoll,* 1619/20, 24.4.1619.
16. StAL, *Testamente,* 1556–1616.
17. StAL, *Gerichtsprotokoll,* 1619/20, 17.10.1619.
18. StAL, *Vogtgerichtsakten* late 1619 to 1620.
19. StAL, *Gerichtsprotokoll,* 1619/20, 30.10.1619. The record then went on merely to state that the parties had made peace.

CHAPTER 9

1. StAL, *Vogt-und Rügerrichtsprotokolle,* 24.8.1620.
2. StAL, *Kaufbuch* 1609–43, fol.751–76a, entered only in 1.2.1619.
3. Joachim Whaley, *Germany and the Holy Roman Empire,* vol. 1 (Oxford: Oxford University Press, 2012), 496.
4. A. E. Adam, ed., *Württembergische Landtagsakten. Unter Herzog Johann Friedrich 1608–1620* (Stuttgart: Kohlhammer, 1910), 738–65, quote 746.
5. StAL, *Vogt-und Rügerrichtsprotokolle,* 18.5.1620.
6. StAL, *Vogt-und Rüggerichtsprotokolle* 1619/20; *Armenkastenprotokolle.*
7. Axel Gotthard, *Konfession und Staatsräson: Die Außenpolitik Württembergs unter Herzog Johann Friedrich (1608–1628)* (Stuttgart: Kohlhammer, 1993), 319–20.
8. Frisch, *Opera,* 435, 25, and 26.8.1620; reply 26.8.1620.
9. Frisch, *Opera,* 15.8.1620.
10. *KGW,* vol. 18, 39.
11. Frisch, *Opera,* 24.7.1620.

12.   *Heiss mir Gott willkommen*
     Sonn und Sonnentag.
     Kompst daher geritten,
     Da stehet ein Mensch, lass dich bitten,
     Gott, Vatter, Sohn und Hailiger Gaist
     Und die hailige Dreyfaltigkhait,
     Geb diesem Menschen bluet und flaisch
     Auch guete gesundhaitt.

13. Frisch, *Opera,* 11.8.1620.
14. Frisch, *Opera,* 434, 18.8.1620.
15. Frisch, *Opera,* 26.8.1620. He remained in charge until 1634, Pfeilsticker, *Dienerbuch.*

16. Frisch, *Opera*, 436, 27.8.1620.
17. Frisch, *Opera*, 436–7, 30.8.1620.

CHAPTER 10

1. Frisch, *Opera*, 421–4.
2. Frisch, *Opera*, mid-August 1620, 437–8.
3. Frisch, *Opera*, 438–9.
4. Frisch, *Opera*, 4.10.1620, 439. In respect of the legal documentation, Kepler was entitled to receive copies of any missing documents he wished to see.
5. Frisch, *Opera*, 439–41.
6. Frisch, *Opera*, 442, 14.11.1620.
7. Frisch, *Opera*, 442, 453, 24.11.1620.
8. Frisch, *Opera*, 441, 28.10.1620 and 30.10.1620. The chancellery asked him to wait, as the files were presently with Dr Matthäus Hiller as advocate who had acted previously.
9. Frisch, *Opera*, 443–4, 4.7.1620.
10. Frisch, *Opera*, 444–7, 4.10.1620.
11. Frisch, *Opera*, 447, 18.10.1620, Johann Kraus.
12. Frisch, *Opera*, 453, late November 1620.
13. HStASt, A 209, Bü.1053.
14. UAT, 84/3, 266.
15. Sauer, *Herzog Friedrich I von Württemberg*, 190.
16. HStASt, A 209, Bü.1057.
17. Frisch, *Opera*, 457, 17.12.1620.
18. Frisch, *Opera*, 468.
19. Frisch, *Opera*, 479, Hanss Josenhanss.
20. Frisch, *Opera*, 477.
21. Charlotte Methuen, *Kepler's Tübingen: Stimulus to a Theological Mathematics* (Farnham: Ashgate, 1998), 112.
22. Alfred Hartmann, ed., *Thomas Platter, Lebensbeschreibung*, 2nd edn (Basel: Schwabe, 1999), 58.
23. Frisch, *Opera*, 481.

CHAPTER 11

1. *KGW*, vol. 18, 43; on Matthäus Bernegger (1582–1640) see in particular Wilhelm Kühlmann, *Gelehrtenrepublik und Fürstenstaat: Entwicklung und Kritik des deutschen Späthumanismus in der Literatur des Barockzeitalters* (Tübingen: Niemeyer, 1982).
2. On Kepler's notion of natural cheerfulness see his preface to the *Dissertatio cum Nuncio Sidereo*, 3.5.1610, Caspar and von Dyck, *Kepler in seinen Briefen*, 343; *KGW*, vol. 18, 42.
3. Sir Henry Wotton, *Reliquiae Wottonianae, or, A collection of the lives, letters and poems* (London: Roycroft, 1672), 291.
4. *KGW*, vol. 118, 50.
5. *KGW*, vol. 18, 68–70; 479.
6. Steven Shapin, 'The Man of Science', in L. Daston and K. Park, *Cambridge History of Science: Early Modern Science* (Cambridge: Cambridge University Press, 2006), 184.
7. *KGW*, vol. 12, S.302–3; vol. 17, 367–71. He supported a Calvinist understanding which celebrated communion as a meal of remembering Christ's last supper before the crucifixion instead of the Lutheran belief that Jesus's body and blood were materially present in the host and wine.
8. His great-grandfather Sebald had a daughter who married a governor of the Breitschwert family, and their own daughter had married Besold's son, Gerd Wunder, 'Die Ahnen und Verwandten von Johannes Kepler', in *Geneaolgisches Jahrbuch*, vol. 19/1 (1979), 125.
9. Sabine Holtz, *Bildung und Herrschaft: Zur Verwissenschaftlichung politischer Führungsschichten im 17. Jahrhundert* (Leinfelden-Echterdingen 2002), 67 on qualifications of officials, 114–16 on Varnbühler.
10. *KGW*, vol. 12, 250–2; 413–15.
11. Ulinka Rublack, 'Frühneuzeitliche Staatlichkeit und lokale Herrschaftspraxis in Württemberg', in *Zeitschrift für historische Forschung*, 24 (1997), 347–76.
12. Axel Gotthard, *Konfession und Staatsräson: Die Aussenpolitik Württembergs unter Herzog Johann Friedrich (1608–28)* (Stuttgart: Kohlhammer, 1993), 320–1.
13. Sauer, *Herzog Friedrich I von Württemberg*, 106.
14. *KGW*, vol. 18, 56.

15. *KGW*, vol. 18, 63; 274.
16. *KGW*, vol. 18, 480.
17. Charlotte Methuen, *Kepler's Tübingen: Stimulus to a Theological Mathematics* (Farnham: Ashgate, 1998), 135 and 155–6.
18. Jakob Heerbrand (1521–1600); Matthias Hafenreffer (1561–1619); Stephan Gerlach (1546–1612); Johannes Georg Sigwart (1554–1618); on the comments passed on to the duke see the addition to Kepler's letter to Johann Frederick of Württemberg in May 1609, Caspar and von Dyck, *Kepler in seinen Briefen*, 331; *KGW*, vol. 16, 239.
19. *KGW*, vol. 18, 68.
20. *KGW*, vol. 18, 71; 480.
21. Frisch, *Opera*, 489–90, read by the chancellery on 25.5.1621.
22. Frisch, *Opera*, 488, 23.6.1621.
23. *KGW*, vol. 18, 82, December 1621, HStASt, A 256, B.107, 350r.
24. Caspar, *Kepler*, 297–8; on the illustrations see Isabelle Pantin, 'Kepler's Epitome: New Images for an Innovative Book', in Sachiko Kusukawa and Ian Maclean, eds, *Transmitting Knowledge: Words, Images, and Instruments in Early Modern Europe* (Oxford: Oxford University Press, 2006), 217–38.
25. Nicholas Jardine, *The Birth of History and Philosophy of Science: Kepler's Defence of Tycho against Ursus, with Essays on its Provenance and Significance* (Cambridge: Cambridge University Press, 1984), 178.
26. WLB, Cod.math.qt.43, *Kometenbeschreibung*, 1619, with a prologue describing the encouragement by Ursula, which has not been noted in the literature; Wilhelm Schickard, *Briefwechsel*, ed. Friedrich Seck, 2 vols (Stuttgart: Frommann-holzboog, 2002), 124; Benigna von Krusenstjern, 'Gelehrtenexistenz im Dreißigjährigen Krieg. Wilhelm Schickard in seinen Briefen', in Alf Lüdtke and Reiner Prass, eds, *Gelehrtenleben. Wissenspraxis in der Neuzeit* (Colgone: Böhlau, 2008), 33–46; Horst Mauder, 'Die Kometenschriften von Schickard und Kepler', in F. Seck, ed., *Zum 400. Geburtstag von Wilhelm Schickard* (Stuttgart: Steiner, 1995), 151–66.
27. Schickard first wrote to Kepler on 30.12.1617; quote Schickard, *Briefwechsel*, 1/48, 139.
28. For this pioneering argument see Robert von Friedeburg, 'The Juridification of Natural Law: Christoph Besold's Claim for a Natural Right to Believe What One Wants', *Historical Journal*, 53/1 (2010), 1–19.

29. *KGW*, vol. 17, 3.11.1618, 283; for Besold's work see, for instance, *Christoph Besold—Synopse der Politik*, trans. Cajetan Cosmann, ed. Laetitia Boehm (Frankfurt am Main: Insel, 2000), 300–2, 310–16.

30. Martin Brecht, 'Christoph Besold: Versuche und Ansätze einer Deutung', *Pietismus und Neuzeit*, 26/2000, 11–28, the title of Besold's penultimate lecture as chancellor in 1614 was *De periculis nostri saeculi*, 18; Besold, *Synopse der Politik*, 2000; Martin Brecht, *Johann Valentin Andreae 1586–1654: eine Biographie* (Göttingen: Vandenhoeck & Ruprecht, 2008), 46–50, 170–3; Ann-Charlott Trepp, *Von der Glückseligkeit alles zu wissen: Die Erforschung der Natur als religiöse Praxis in der Frühen Neuzeit (1550–1750)* (Frankfurt am Main: Campus, 2009), 71–3; Ulrich Bubenheimer, 'Wilhelm Schickard im Kontext einer religiösen Subkultur', in Friedrich Seck, ed., *Zum 400. Geburtstag von Wilhem Schickard* (Sigmaringen: Thorbecke, 1995), 67–92.

31. See Brecht, *Andreae*, and on Maria as widow see Carl Philipp Conz, *Kleinere prosaische Schriften*, vol.1 (Tübingen: H. Laupp, 1821), 86–106.

32. Johann Valentin Andreae, *Rosenkreuzerschriften*, ed. Roland Edighoffer (Stuttgart: Frommann-holzboog, 2010), 143, 201.

33. Claus Bernet, *'Gebaute Apokalypse': Die Utopie des Himmlischen Jerusalem in der Frühen Neuzeit* (Mainz: Philipp von Zabern, 2007), 174, and below, 181.

34. Johann Valentin Andreae, *Christianopolis*, ed. and trans. E. H. Thompson (Dordrecht: Kluwer, 1999), 168–9 and on plants 213 and 273–4.

35. Brecht, *Andreae*, 144–51.

36. Andreae, *Christianopolis*, 273 and 275.

37. Brecht, *Andreae*, 158–60.

38. 'Als diesem Orden auf meine und die Veranlassung Christoph Besolds hin schon Wilhelm Schickard in Tübingen, Matthias Bernegger in Straßburg, Johannes Kepler in Linz, Daniel Schwenter in Altdorf und andere beigetreten waren und Wense seine Bekannten von überall her dafür einzunehmen begonnen hatte, brach das Unglück über Deutschland herein und vereitelte all diese, wie ich glaube, nicht unrühmlichen Bestrebungen', Johann Valentin Andreae, *Gesammelte Werke: Nachrufe*, 'Jonathan Wensius' (Stuttgart: Frommann-Holzboog, 1995), 754; *KGW*, 17, 853; In 1619, Georg Christoph von Schallenberg wanted to borrow the *Fama Fraternitatis* from Kepler (which had been published in Kassel in 1614), 389, 484.

39. The best detailed reconstruction of facts is *KGW*, vol. 12, 329–31.

40. On Greek notions of musical harmony see Vincenzo Galilei, *Dialogue on Ancient and Modern Music*, ed. Claude V. Palisca (New Haven: Yale University Press, 2003), 263.

41. Trans. and adapted from Kepler's *Harmony* for the American Philosophical Society, 1997, 276, in relation to Max Caspar's translation of the *Weltharmonik*. For the argument that this reflected a neo-Tacitan approach see Aviva Tova Rothman's important discussion in her Princeton DPhil thesis *Far From every Strife: Kepler's Search for Harmony in an Age of Discord*, January 2012, esp. 281–92, available at, <http://dataspace. princeton.edu/jspui/handle/88435/dsp018623hx767>.

42. Trans. and adapted from Kepler, *Harmony*, 276.

43. Kepler, *Hamony*, 276.

44. Bodin's 1580 treatise *De la démonomanie des sorciers* was translated into German six years later and of particular influence on German magistrates. For this and the following see the magisterial discussion by Stuart Clark, *Thinking with Demons*, final chapter, 668–82, as well as Jean Bodin, *La démonomanie des sorciers*, 4th edn (Lyon: Antoine de Harsy, 1598); Claudia Opitz-Belakhal, *Das Universum des Jean Bodin: Staatsbildung, Macht und Geschlecht im 16. Jahrhundert* (Frankfurt am Main: Campus, 2006); Ann Blair, *The Theatre of Nature: Jean Bodin and Renaissance Science* (Princeton: Princeton University Press, 2010, 12.

45. Kepler, *Harmony*, 266.

46. Kepler, *Harmony*, 279.

47. *KGW*, vol. 12, 251; 415.

CHAPTER 12

1. For this characterization see Clark, *Thinking with Demons*, 519.

2. Clark, *Thinking with Demons*, 519; Johann Georg Gödelmann, *Tractatus de magis, veneficis et lamiis* (Frankfurt am Main: N. Bassaei, 1591), 58–60.

3. Clark, *Thinking with Demons*, 118, 519.

4. A complete edition of Rio's book had been published two years earlier and claimed that, like all heretics, Lutherans were inhabited by the devil and infected others with demonism, Clark, *Thinking with Demons*, 535; *KGW*, vol. 16, 2.11.1610, 598; Martin Del Rio, *Investigations into Magic*, ed. and trans. P. G. Maxwell-Stuart (Manchester: Manchester University Press, 2000), 252; for the letter to James I see Caspar and von Dyck, *Kepler*

in seinen Briefen, October 1607, 297; *KGW*, vol. 16, 103–4; James I, *Daemonologie* (Edinburgh 1597, reprint Amsterdam 1969: Da Capo), 43–4, 81.

5. Wolfgang Behringer, *Witchcraft Persecutions in Bavaria: Popular Magic, Religious Zealotry and Reason of State in Early Modern Europe* (Cambridge: Cambridge University Press, 1997), 181, fn.252; 241; 245.

6. Behringer, *Witchcraft*, 248.

7. Behringer, *Witchcraft*, 268–9.

8. For an authoritative exploration of this wider theme see Richard Serjeantson, 'Proof and Persuasion', in L. Daston and K. Park, eds, *Cambridge History of Science*, 132–75.

9. Caspar and von Dyck, *Kepler in seinen Briefen*, preface to Dioptrik, spring 1611, 368.

10. A. Grafton, *Defenders of the Text: The Traditions of Scholarship in an Age of Science, 1450–1800* (Cambridge, MA: Harvard University Press, 1994), 203.

11. Frisch, *Opera*, 494.

12. Frisch, *Opera*, 496.

13. Marktplatz. 11, Bühler, *Leonberg*, 61.

14. Frisch, *Opera*, 496–7.

15. Frisch, *Opera*, 497.

16. Frisch, *Opera*, 498.

17. Frisch, *Opera*, 501.

18. Frisch, *Opera*, 504.

19. Frisch, *Opera*, 506.

20. Frisch, *Opera*, 502.

21. Rankin, *Panaceia's Daughters*.

22. Frisch, *Opera*, 505.

23. Frisch, *Opera*, 505–7.

24. Frisch, *Opera*, 508–9.

25. Frisch, *Opera*, 509.

26. Frisch, *Opera*, 509.

27. Frisch, *Opera*, 510–17.

28. Kepler had also added to the Litis contestatio in his own hand. For the defence-writing, the first hand wrote fol.1r–21v, 44r–49v; hand two 22r–43v; hand three 50r–64r, *KGW*, vol. 12, 330–1.

29. Frisch, *Opera*, 522; 527.

30. Frisch, *Opera*, 535.
31. Frisch, *Opera*, 535.
32. Frisch, *Opera*, 537.
33. Frisch, *Opera*, 543. For such gendered languages in strategies of defence see Laura Kounine, 'The Gendering of Witchcraft: Defence Strategies of Men and Women in German Witchcraft Trials', *German History*, 31, 3 (2013), 295–317.
34. Frisch, *Opera*, 538; *KGW*, vol. 12, 332; Oswalt Gabelkhover, *The boock of physicke*...(Dorte: Isaak Caen, 1599).
35. Frisch, *Opera*, 538.
36. Johann Zanger, *Tractatus de quaestionibus seu torturis reorum* (Wittenberg: Lehmann, 1593), 9.
37. Frisch, *Opera*, 489, 23.8.1621. This request was not granted.
38. Sabine Holtz, *Bildung und Herrschaft. Zur Verwissenschaftlichung politischer Führungsschichten im 17. Jahrhundert* (Leinfelden: Schriften zur süddeutschen Landeskunde, 2002), 227–9 on the literature, 237 on the case load, 439 on witchcraft percentage.
39. Marianne Sauter, *Hexenprozess und Folter: Die strafrechtliche Spruchpraxis der Juristenfakultät im 17. und beginnenden 18. Jahrhundert* (Stuttgart: Verlag für Regionalgeschichte, 2010), 230.
40. Sauter, *Spruchpraxis*, 241–50.
41. Sauter, *Spruchpraxis*, 256–9.
42. Frisch, *Opera*, 548–9; UAT 84/5, 462v–463v.

CHAPTER 13

1. See, for instance, HStASt A 209, Bü.661, Anna Gentner, 27.8.1618.
2. Joel F. Harrington, *The Faithful Executioner: Life and Death, Honour and Shame in the Turbulent Sixteenth Century* (New York: Farrar, Straus and Giroux, 2013), 57.
3. HStASt, A 209, Bü.660.
4. HStASt, A 209, Bü. 581, 1618/9, no date on this specific document.
5. Frisch, *Opera*, 550.
6. Frisch, *Opera*, 553.
7. Frisch, *Opera*, 555. They never arrived, so that one assumption has been whether Einhorn simply suppressed the file, even though of course

the copies in the ducal chancellery survive and were never passed on either.

8. Many of the documents in *KGW* vol. 19 record these practices, which of course were entirely normal for the period; for particular insights into his management of finances during his first marriage see 454–5.

9. *KGW*, vol. 19, 369, 1622; A minute from the Linz estates in 1621 still implied that Kepler would receive his salary despite his absence, 19.4.1621, *KGW*, vol. 19, 141.

10. For the negotiations in 1621 see StAL *Kauf- und Contractbuch* 1609–43, 220–3, 10.3.1621.

11. StAL, *Rechnungen* 1623 and *Wachtzedell* 1628.

12. *KGW*, vol. 19, 371, 10.12.1622.

13. Frisch, *Opera*, 559, 10.5.1624.

14. Caspar and von Dyck, *Kepler in seinen Briefen*, vol. 2, 19.4.1620, to Schickhart.

15. Gotthard, *Konfession*, 473.

16. *KGW*, vol. 18, 83.

17. *KGW*, vol. 18, 80–1.

18. All these letters are printed in *KGW*, vol. 18.

19. *KGW*, to Crüger.

20. Ian MacLean, *Scholarship, Commerce, Religion: The Learned Book in the Age of Confessions, 1560–1630* (Cambridge, MA: Harvard University Press, 2012), 222–3.

21. Fernand Hallyn, *The Poetic Structure of the World: Copernicus and Kepler* (New York: Zone, 1990), 279.

22. Kepler's *Somnium: The Dream, or Posthumous Work on Lunar Astronomy*, ed. and trans. Edward Rosen (Madison: University of Wisconsin Press, 1967).

23. Kepler, *Somnium*, 40–1; for the earlier identification of Volkersdorf see 40, n.42.

24. On biographical data see *KGW*, vol. 12, 336, note 70.32.

25. Cit. in Aviva Rothman, *Far From Every Strife: Kepler's Search for Harmony in an Age of Discord*, Princeton PhD, 2012, 229, fn.90; *KGW* 7.359, 17.

26. See Chapter 4, this volume.

27. *KGW*, vol. 17, No.643; and the letter he wrote about her full of praise to Tobias Scultetus, 13.4.1612; in April 1599 to Herwart he had still written

about Barbara's fate as informed by an astrological constellation which made her virtuous but too simple-minded, corpulent, and less than cheerful.

28. Trugenberger, *Zwischen Schloss*, Reinbolt family, Nr. 469.
29. Kepler, *Somnium*, 43, fn.58.
30. On Loew see R. J. W. Evans, *Rudolph II and His World: A Study in Intellectual History 1576–1612* (London: Thames & Hudson, 1997), 238–42, and André Neher, *Jewish Thought and the Scientific Revolution of the Sixteenth Century: David Gans (1541–1613) and his Times* (Oxford: Oxford University Press, 1986), 247.
31. Kepler, *Somnium*, 53.
32. *KGW*, vol. 16, 158; Caspar and von Dyck, *Kepler in seinen Briefen*, to Tanckius, 12.5.1608, 312.
33. Kepler, *Somnium*, 14.
34. Kepler, *Somnium*, 58–60.
35. Kepler, *Somnium*, 63.
36. Kepler, *Somnium*, 49.
37. Kepler, *Somnium*, 50 and fn.78
38. Nicholas Jardine, 'God's "Ideal Reader": Kepler and his Serious Jokes', in R. L. Kremer and J. Wlodarczyk, eds, *Johannes Kepler: From Tübingen to Zagan* (Warsaw: Studia Copernica, 2009), 41–51. The Compendium is by Otto Melander.
39. Kepler, *Somnium*, 65.
40. Kepler, *Somnium*, 49.
41. Kepler, *Somnium*, 72, fn.72 (Oh how magical!).
42. Anthony Grafton, 'Kepler as a Reader', *Journal of the History of Ideas*, 53, 1992, 561–72.
43. Kepler, *Somnium*, 85.
44. Johannes Kepler, *Schriften zur Optik 1604–1611*, ed. Rolf Riekher (Frankfurt am Main: Harri Deutsch, 2008), 399.
45. Timothy Reiss, *The Discourse of Modernism* (Ithaca: Cornell University Press, 1982), 150.
46. Grafton, *Reader*, 570.
47. For other readings of *The Dream* see, in particular, Elizabeth Spiller, *Science, Reading, and Renaissance Literature: The Art of Making Knowledge, 1580–1670* (Cambridge: Cambridge University Press, 2004), 101–36;

Reiss, *The Discourse of Modernism*, 140–67; Mary Baine Campbell, *Wonder & Science: Imagining Worlds in Early Modern Europe* (Ithaca: Cornell University Press, 1999), 133–43.

48. On Kepler's religious position see Jürgen Hübner, *Die Theologie Johannes Keplers zwischen Orthodoxie und Naturwissenschaft* (Tübingen: Mohr, 1975); and, in English, Charlotte Methuen, 'Kepler, Religion and Natural Philosophy: A Theological Biography' (forthcoming); as well as the argument about him as a man of individual faith who moved beyond confessions advanced by Maximilian Lanzinner, 'Johannes Kepler: A Man without Confession in the Age of Confessionalization?', *Central European History*, 36, 2003, 531–45.

49. I have consulted the 1634 copy extant in the British Library, London.

50. Volker Trugenberger, *Zwischen Schloss und Vorstadt: Sozialgeschichte der Stadt Leonberg im 16. Jahrhundert* (Vaihingen: Melchior, 1984), 469.

51. In 1628, Christoph was also put in charge of overseeing the care-home for the sick and elderly; Kirchenregisteramt: Information kindly supplied by Bernadette Gramm, Stadtarchiv Leonberg.

52. Mechthild Lemcke, *Johannes Kepler* (Hamburg: Rowohlt, 1995), 138.

53. Stadtarchiv Fellbach, she signs this 'aged 59', even though she should have been sixty-five by then.

54. See Thomas A. Brady Jr, *German Histories in the Age of Reformations, 1400–1650* (Cambridge: Cambridge University Press, 2009), 347; 402. Among all confessions, it seems that Lutheranism continued a particularly marked pluralization of its faith, see Thomas Kaufmann, *Dreißigjähriger Krieg und Westfälischer Friede* (Tübingen: Mohr Siebeck, 1998), 142–5.

EPILOGUE

1. He next became mayor of Leonberg from 1948 to his death in 1953. The Eltingen street was named after him in 1954.

2. He intimated that the monument, made by a Swabian professor of sculptural art informed by the 'great German masters', had only been made possible by private sponsorship. The artist, Jakob Wilhelm Fehrle, in fact had received his formative education in Paris and was most influenced by the French sculptor Maillol. A dictionary entry claims that his work was marginalized as un-German during the Third Reich.

3. *Leonberger Tagblatt*, 25. Oktober 1937, 'Eltingen einst und jetzt'. Even the local music society 'Lyra', which performed the overture 'Stradella' by Flotow to celebrate the occasion, still exists.

4. The Catholic church and its supporters held against all this that witch persecution had been a deplorable Germanic tradition which Christianization had been unable to root out. The details of all these positions and their main protagonists are brilliantly discussed in Wolfgang Behringer, 'Geschichte der Hexenforschung', in Sönke Lorenz and Jürgen Michael Schmidt, eds, *Wider alle Hexerei und Teufelswerk. Die europäische Hexenverfolgung und ihre Auswirkung auf Südwestdeutschland* (Ostfildern: Jan Thorbecke Verlag, 2004), 559–69.

5. J. L. C. Breitschwert, *Johann Keppler's Leben und Wirken, nach neuerlich aufgefundenen Manuscripten* (Stuttgart: Löflund, 1831); Berthold Sutter, *Der Hexenprozeß gegen Katharina Kepler* (Weil der Stadt: Heimatverein, 1979); Eberhard Walz, *Johannes Kepler Leomontanus, gehorsamer Unterthan vnd Burgerssohn von Löwenberg* (Leonberg: Stadtarchiv, 1994); Anita Raith, 'Das Hexenbrennen in Leonberg', in Renate Dürr, ed., *Nonne, Magd oder Ratsfrau* (Leonberg: Stadtarchiv, 1998), 53–73, 269–72.

6. For the notion of her as difficult and mentally unstable see James A. Connor, *Kepler's Witch: An Astronomer's Discovery of Cosmic Order Amid Religious War, Political Intrigue, and the Heresy Trial of His Mother* (New York: Harper Collins, 2004), for a novel which develops the idea that she was a strong heroic healing woman, see Katja Doubek, *Katharina Kepler. Die Hexenjagd auf die Mutter des großen Astronomen* (Munich: Piper, 2004).

7. Arthur Koestler, *The Sleepwalkers: A History of Man's Changing Vision of the Universe* (Harmondsworth: Penguin, 1989), 232.

8. Kitty Ferguson, *The Nobleman and His Housedog: Tycho Brahe and Johannes Kepler—The Strange Partnership that Revolutionised Science* (London: Headline Review, 2002), 93.

9. The Weil craze took off around 1625, see Wolfgang Schütz, '"Nemmet ihr mir schon umb unschuldt mein Leben, könnet ihr mir doch die Seel nehmen": Die Hexenverfolgung in der Reichsstadt Weil 1560–1629', *Heimatverein Weil der Stadt: Berichte und Mitteilungen*, 51/2005/2006, esp. 7.

10. *KGW*, 12, 327–8: 'In der Tat ist jene Fiolxhilde das Urbild der Mutter Keplers. Katharinas ungestüme, hartherzig anmutende Art mag in jenem Vorfall zum Ausdruck kommen, der Fiolxhilde veranlasst, ihren Sohn Duracotus zu verstoßen'.

11. John Banville, *Kepler* (London: Picador, 1999), esp. 89–108, 169–73.

12. Johannes Kepler, *Schriften zur Optik 1604–1611*, ed. Rolf Riekher (Frankfurt am Main: Harri Deutsch, 2008), 370–1.

13. Max Caspar was born in 1880 and completed his landmark biography of Kepler in 1948; for his characterization of Kepler as 'unpolitical one' in a time 'fraught with disaster' see Max Caspar, *Kepler* (New York: Dover, 1993), 17, 27.

14. J. L. Heilbron, *Galileo* (Oxford: Oxford University Press, 2012), 2–3; 104–5; 153–4; Dava Sobel, *Galileo's Daughter: A Drama of Science, Faith and Love* (London: Fourth Estate, 1999), 94; David Wootton, *Galileo: Watcher of the Skies* (New Haven: Yale, 2010), 95.

15. My thoughts have been inspired in particular by Carol Gilligan, *Joining the Resistance* (Cambridge: Polity, 2011), and Lyndal Roper, *Witch-Craze: Terror and Fantasy in Baroque Germany* (New Haven: Yale University Press, 2004), as well as her *The Witch in the Western Imagination* (Charlottesville: University of Virginia Press, 2012).

16. Carlo Ginzburg, *The Cheese and the Worms: The Cosmos of a Sixteenth-Century Miller*, was first published in 1976; Natalie Zemon Davis, *The Return of Martin Guerre* was first published in 1983.

17. J. H. Elliott, *History in the Making* (New Haven: Yale University Press, 2012), 162.

Further Reading and Viewing

———— ∞∞∞ ————

Leonberg and Eltingen have preserved much of their character, and a short excellent video of Leonberg can be found if you look up 'Luftportrait Leonberg' on YouTube. This provides a particularly good sense of Duchess Sibylle's reconstructed garden towards the end of the clip. Leonberg and Eltingen are easily reached from Stuttgart by public transport.

For further reading on witchcraft I recommend Malcolm Gaskill, *Witchcraft: A Very Short Introduction* (Oxford: Oxford University Press, 2010), which mentions the Kepler case, as well as Wolfgang Behringer, *Witches and Witch-Hunts: A Global History* (Cambridge: Polity, 2004), and for more specialized reading on the early modern see Robin Briggs, *Witches and Neighbours: The Social and Cultural Context of European Witchcraft* (Harmondsworth: Penguin, 1998), and Lyndal Roper, *Witch-Craze: Terror and Fantasy in Baroque Germany* (New Haven: Yale University Press, 2004). Alison Rowlands has edited a collection of essays which draws attention to the fact of men's involvement in trials, *Witchcraft and Masculinities in Early Modern Europe* (Basingstoke: Palgrave Macmillan, 2009). On the natural philosophy of the time a general reader might first turn to Lawrence M. Principe, *The Scientific Introduction: A Very Short Introduction* (Oxford: Oxford University Press, 2011), and then to the excellent *Cambridge History of Science*, vol. 3, edited by Lorraine Daston and Katherine Park in 2006. Books on Kepler's work tend to be highly specialized, but Max Caspar's biography *Kepler* (New York: Dover, 1993) conveys much detail of Kepler's science in an accessible way that will interest readers. As reading on gender and women in early modern

Germany I recommend Heide Wunder, *'He is the Sun, She is the Moon':* *Women in Early Modern Germany* (Cambridge, MA: Harvard University Press, 1998), as well as Alisha Rankin's recent *Panaceia's Daughters: Noble-women as Healers in Early Modern Germany* (Chicago: Chicago University Press, 2013), which explores the links of women to medicine and natural philosophy. Those looking for a new general history of the German lands must turn to Joachim Whaley, *Germany and the Holy Roman Empire,* vol. 1: *Maximilian to the Peace of Westphalia 1493–1648* (Oxford: Oxford University Press, 2012). A recent micro-history of witchcraft in the German Lutheran lands is Thomas Robisheaux, *The Last Witch of Langenburg: Murder in a German Village* (New York: Norton, 2009), while Joel Harrington's *The Faithful Executioner: Life, Death, Honour and Shame in the Turbulent Sixteenth Century* (New York: Farrar, Straus and Giroux, 2013) reconstructs the life of an executioner in a Lutheran city during the late sixteenth and early seventeenth centuries.

After its publication in 2015, *The Astronomer and the Witch* provided inspiration for an opera. For more information on the making of the opera and related resources, including a translation of Kepler's defence of his mother, visit http://keplers-trial.com/

Acknowledgements

⌐∞∞∞⌐

This is a book that I have wanted to write for twenty years, and it is a great pleasure to acknowledge the support and enthusiasm of those who shared in its making. I could not have undertaken it without the support of Bernadette Gramm, the Leonberg archivist who helped me in every possible way, took me on a tour of the town during her lunch break, brought every file I requested and discussed all my questions with me as they arose. Renate Dürr hosted me at home during my stays and, as editor of a book on women in Leonberg, was an expert long before I became one. She read the whole manuscript and discussed many of its aspects. Thanks also go to all those who encouraged me early on, especially Kathryn Hughes, and to many of my colleagues at St John's College, Cambridge, who once more provided an ideal community alongside Chris Dobson, our Master. Sue Mansfield supported me in printing out various versions of manuscripts, and Kathryn McKee greatly helped by taking photographs in the College's collection of rare books. Christian Staufenbiel and David Lowe were wonderful in providing access to books at the University Library when I needed them—real books, not e-books. Special thanks also go to Anna Becker, Sachiko Kusukawa, Regine Maritz, Charlotte Methuen, Andrew Morrall, Heike Talkenberger, and Laura Tisdale, who all provided invaluable help through hints or help with photographs. I have particularly treasured conversations with Carol Gilligan and Natalie Zemon Davis, who both read a proposal and early introduction and gave me much inspiration through their own work and comments. Juliet Mitchell made me far more aware of the importance of sibling relations for families.

Jacqueline Rose supported me throughout the final editing process and discussed Kepler's *Dream* with me. Joel Harrington kindly read the whole manuscript and gave crucial advice for rewriting it, while Laura Kounine proof-read and discussed the manuscript with great skill. Her forthcoming work on gender in the Württemberg witchcraft trials is pioneering. I am particularly grateful to Catherine Clarke, my agent, for her interest in reading the book with immense sensitivity and for her cheerful support. Marion Kant and Jonathan Steinberg, as always, were enthusiastic from the beginning, while Marion closely worked through the manuscript and gave crucial advice. Christopher Clark, Bridget Orr, and Ruth Scurr commented on and helped me to revise earlier drafts of the introduction, and, as friends and colleagues, shared in formulating a vision of the book. Simon Schaffer memorably discussed the chapter on Kepler's *Dream* with me, and Nick Jardine did so much to support me when he told me early on that he would be happy to read the manuscript. I heard Nick talk about Kepler's jokes as I started my research; and some of his insights underpinned my work all along. Above all, Lyndal Roper's path-breaking work on witchcraft and gender has been a great inspiration for many years. She read *The Astronomer and the Witch* with extraordinary intensity and a precise sense of where and how it might be improved: thank you, Lyndal! At Oxford University Press I once more wish to thank Matthew Cotton for his cheerful responses which promptly arrive with complete reliability. Luciana O'Flaherty repeatedly worked through the manuscript to improve the clarity of my writing, and I am very grateful for what she and my copy-editor Elizabeth Stone alongside my exemplary production editor Emily Brand and proof-reader Kathleen Gill have achieved. Three reviews of the manuscript provided helpful advice. My family, finally, shared these years with unflagging interest in what I do—my brother, Christoph Rublack, travelled to Leonberg to photograph buildings, my mother, Ursula Nelle, kept asking about *Frau* Kepler, and so did my sister, Susanne Rublack, and my maturing children, João and Sophie. Francisco Bethencourt, my husband, began his career by working on witches in Portuguese archives—he knows how disorienting it feels to emerge from a day's work on these trials. Francisco brought pleasure, warmth, and wider worlds into every day of my life and otherwise was always available to read a draft or critically discuss an idea. This book is dedicated to him with all my love.

Index

Drawings and pictures are given in italics.